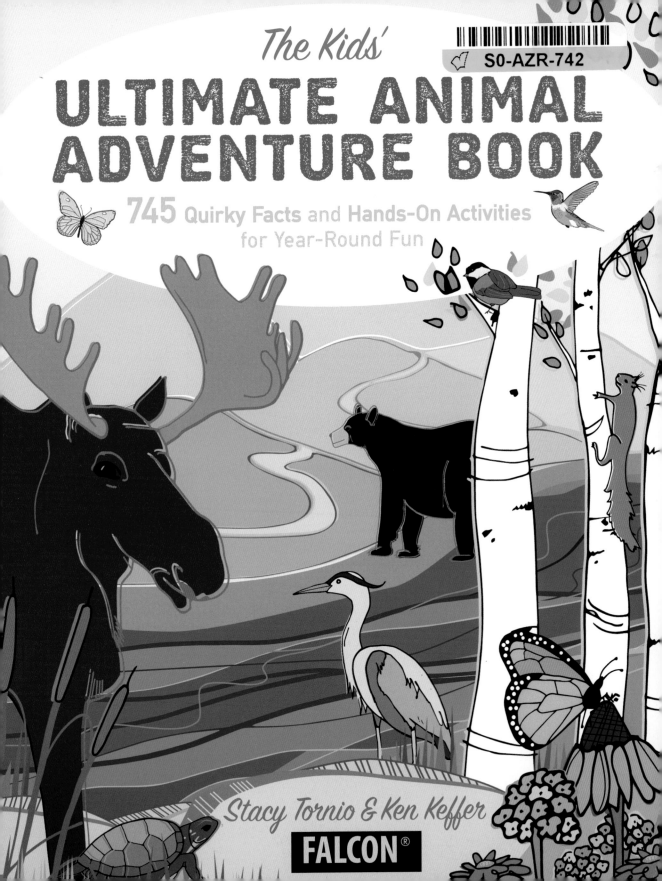

The Kids'

ULTIMATE ANIMAL ADVENTURE BOOK

745 Quirky Facts and Hands-On Activities
for Year-Round Fun

Stacy Tornio & Ken Keffer

FALCON®

An imprint of Globe Pequot
Falcon and FalconGuides are registered trademarks and Make Adventure Your Story is a trademark of Rowman & Littlefield.

Distributed by NATIONAL BOOK NETWORK
Copyright © 2017 by Stacy Tornio and Ken Keffer

Cover Illustration by Corissa Nelson
Illustrations by Rachel Riordan © Rowman & Littlefield

British Library Cataloguing in Publication Information available
Library of Congress Cataloging-in-Publication Data available

ISBN 978-1-4930-2972-3 (paperback)
ISBN 978-1-4930-2973-0 (e-book)

♾™ The paper used in this publication meets the minimum requirements of American National Standard for Information Sciences—Permanence of Paper for Printed Library Materials, ANSI/NISO Z39.48-1992.

Printed in the United States of America

CONTENTS

SEE

Learn some cool and little-known facts about North America's most common animals.

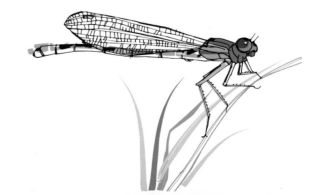

LEARN

Take a look at common animal myths and bust them once and for all!

DO

Go outside and learn about animals with these hands-on activities.

BONUS: PROJECTS, GAMES, AND MORE

Have fun, get project ideas, and more with this hands-on section.

INTRODUCTION

Nature is filled with animals. Whether you go exploring in your own backyard or like to climb mountaintops, you're sure to encounter birds, insects, reptiles, amphibians, fish, and all kinds of amazing mammals along the way.

As a family who likes nature and enjoys being outside, you probably already know about a lot of the cool creatures you can find in the great outdoors. Yet when it comes to animals, you always want to see, learn, and do more. Now you can!

Inspired by the popular FalconGuides series from Stacy Tornio and Ken Keffer, this book takes all the great animal tips and information from their three books—*The Kids' Outdoor Adventure Book, The Truth About Nature,* and *The Secret Lives of Animals*—and combines it into one.

Going outside is never going to be the same because this book will make you see and understand animals and their habitats in a whole new way. From learning fascinating facts and looking for animal signs to exploring on your own, you'll definitely gain a whole new appreciation for all of North America's great creatures. Get out there and explore!

HOW THIS BOOK WORKS

SEE

In this first section you'll discover some of the coolest and most common animals found in North America, including invertebrates, fish, mammals, and more. For each animal, you will read all kinds of little-known facts. These will help you learn to recognize the animals when you're out in the wild and notice signs of them all around you.

LEARN

With so much different and even conflicting information out there about animals, how do you know what you should believe? In this section you'll learn about some of the most common myths about animals in North America. From basic myths to more challenging ones, you'll learn the truth for each one. This way you can pass along the right information to others once and for all.

Psst! Keep an eye out for the "Myth Scale" listed in this section. With Level 3, the myths are completely false, Level 2 the myths are mostly false, and Level 1 the myths might have a tiny bit of truth to them.

DO

Now that you know cool facts and the truth about North America's most popular animals, it's time to start checking out the great outdoors with your family! Think of this section as your adventure checklist of activities that all kids should do before they grow up. You'll find stuff for beginners, more advanced explorers, and even challenging items for those who consider themselves nature pros! Ready? Get outside to learn about animals as you go!

Psst! Look for the "Adventure Scale" listed on the activities, which gives you an idea of difficulty level—1 is the lowest and 5 is the highest.

BONUS

Don't forget to check out this bonus section of games, projects, and more. This hands-on area will offer hours of fun. Plus, look for unique ideas on how to put an animal twist on these activities! Learn some cool and little-known facts about North America's most common animals.

SEE

SECTION 1:
THE INVERTEBRATES

Don't be fooled by their size. Learn why these animals are definitely worth looking for when you're out and about in the great outdoors.

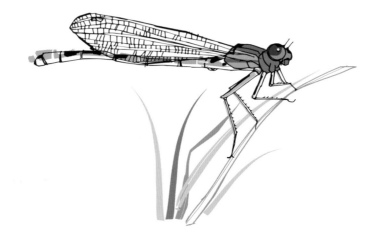

DRAGONFLY

It might be tempting to lump all dragonflies together. After all, they do look similar, zipping up, down, and all around water. But it's worth taking a closer look when you see these fliers because there are many, many species. They seem to come in every color imaginable too. So the next time you see a big-eyed dragonfly flying your way, try to notice its size, the color of its body and wings, and more. Then get out an insect book and challenge yourself to identify (ID) it.

LITTLE-KNOWN FACTS

1. Many people think girl dragonflies are called damselflies, but that's not true. Damselflies are just one kind of dragonfly. Damselflies rest with their wings folded behind their bodies, while dragonflies rest with theirs

held out to the side.

2. Dragonflies date back more than 300 million years. In fact, fossils show us that they were once quite big. Some records show dragonflies with wingspans of 2 feet. Imagine seeing that flying around!

3. The larval stage of dragonflies can last up to two years. They live underwater, and you might not recognize them as dragonflies.

4. Dragonflies are amazing fliers and hunters. In fact, they combine the two really well as they do all of their hunting while flying.

5. The lifespan of an adult dragonfly can range from just a couple of weeks to about a year.

6. Dragonflies can eat one hundred or more mosquitoes a day.

7. Dragonflies have amazing vision. Their two compound eyes can see practically 360 degrees.

8. A few dragonflies, like green darners, will migrate each year.

Types: Thousands of species around the world
Size: Most have a wingspan of 2 to 4 inches and have bodies similar in size.
Eats: Plants, tadpoles, bugs, young fish
Eats them: Birds, frogs, and other bug-eating animals
Range: Worldwide

GO OUTSIDE

You can find dozens of different dragonfly species right in your own neighborhood. So head outside and challenge yourself to find at least three different dragonflies. You might want to take your binoculars along for a closer look. And get ready because they sure do move fast! Some of the largest dragonflies can give you a little pinch, so be careful—for their sake as well as yours—if you are handling them.

WORM

"Worm." What do you think of when you see this word? Maybe you think of a wiggling worm that makes great fishing bait. Or perhaps you think of the worms you uncover while digging in the garden. They might be small and overlooked, but crawlers can be extremely useful. They're pretty darn cute too. Go ahead. Try to hold a wiggling worm without breaking into a huge grin!

LITTLE-KNOWN FACTS

1. Worm poop, also called castings, is valued by gardeners as nutrient-rich soil. In fact, there's a whole garden movement called vermicomposting that involves planning your garden with worms in mind.

2. Segmented worms are made up of many little segments, so they look like a bunch of rings pushed together. They are also related to leeches and polychaetes.

3. Earthworms have numerous body segments. The head end can sometimes survive if the tail end is damaged, but the tail end won't regenerate. (Flatworms have more regeneration abilities, but they are different altogether.)

4. The longest worms in North America are about a foot long, but some species in other regions can be many feet long.

5. Worms can burrow several feet underground. They like it down there where it's moist and cool.

6. Worms survive the winter by digging some more. They just move down below the frost line.

7. Worms lack lungs, so they use other tactics to breathe. For instance, their mucus helps them transfer oxygen through their skin.

8. Even though they don't have eyes, worms can still distinguish light from dark.

9. Tiny bristlelike appendages, called setae, help worms crawl along. So

imagine these teeny tiny brushes (that you can't even really see) helping them move.

10. Here's a funny word related to worms: clitellum. This is the thick band on earthworms, and it's where they put their eggs.

11. The very popular and well-known night crawlers aren't native to North America. They were introduced here and are quite abundant today.

12. Don't mistake caterpillars for worms. Yes, it's easy to think that all crawlers are a type of worm, but this isn't the case. Caterpillars have a job to do, and that is to turn into beautiful butterflies or moths. Go ahead and try to trick your friends with this one.

Types: Up to 200 species in the United States; many more worldwide
Size: Most species are several inches long.
Eats: Vegetation and soil matter
Eats them: Birds, small mammals, reptiles, amphibians
Range: Widespread throughout the world

GO OUTSIDE

Earthworms are the most popular worms to dig for, but there could be other inverts crawling around in there too. Take your time when you dig, and search for other critters as well. You're like a scientist, searching for the unknown. Just make sure you're not digging in someone's garden!

SCIENCE Q&A: How Do Animals Interact with One Another?

Animals often interact with other animals, both individuals of the same species and of other species. Sometimes these exchanges can be short and sweet. Other times they are complex. Let's explore some of the different types of relationships between different species of animals.

Why not get the most negative one out of the way first? Parasitism happens when one species benefits but the other is harmed from their interactions. Some animals (parasites) depend on other animals for survival. They get all their nutrients from another species (known as the host). The goal of the parasite isn't to kill the host, but sometimes the parasite will make the host weaker or sick. Many parasites are invertebrates. Think of fleas and ticks—they eat the blood of other animals. They aren't like mosquitoes though, which dart in and out for a quick meal. Fleas and ticks can live on the host animal for an extended period.

Mutualism is when both species benefit from their interactions. The cowbirds of North America, like the oxpeckers of Africa, can be examples of mutualism. They'll eat the ticks off large mammals like bison or wildebeest. The mammals benefit because the birds remove parasites from them, and the birds benefit by scoring a meal. Pollination is sometimes thought of as mutualism too. Hummingbirds, bees, and others help pollinate plants while they gain nutrients.

Commensalism can be a little trickier to understand. It is when one species benefits from the relationship, but the other one isn't really affected one way or the other. It doesn't gain a benefit, but it isn't harmed either. If the birds from our earlier example are eating the bugs from the ground that the mammals have stirred up by walking by, that can be considered commensalism. Barnacles living on whales is another example. The barnacles aren't parasites on the whales; they are simply permanent hitchhikers.

Biologists have a fancy term for when things live in close association with each other. It's called symbiosis. These interactions can sometimes be positive, but they aren't always. These interactions are what make nature so neat to learn about.

BEETLE

Beetles are abundant and diverse. They are the most abundant type of critter around, and there could be as many as 25,000 different species of beetles in the United States alone. The term "could be" is important to note. Because there are so many, scientists are sure there are more species that haven't even been discovered. The ones that have been discovered are as unique and different as ladybugs, weevils, dung beetles, Hercules beetles, and longhorn beetles. There are even aquatic beetle species. With all these species to choose from, how can you possibly pick a favorite?

LITTLE-KNOWN FACTS

1. Most beetles have specially modified forewings called elytra, which form a hard, protective outer shell.
2. Beetles use their hind wings for flight.
3. Beetles use their strong mandibles to chew, which is a pretty rare characteristic for insects.
4. There are estimates of more than 350,000 known beetle species, but some researchers estimate there could be as many as three million species total. This means there's a lot left to discover!
5. A single ladybug beetle can eat more than 2,500 aphids in its lifetime.
6. Many species of beetles use chemical repellents to keep them safe from potential predators. Two extreme examples of this are the bombardier and blister beetles, which can cause a lot of pain to human skin.
7. Beetles have been around for more than 230 million years.
8. You might say that beetles are big fans of poop. Some species of dung beetle eat poop. Others lay their eggs in it.

9. Mealworms, which are popular as birdfeed, are the larval stage of a beetle.
10. Some species of beetles are considered pests because of the damage they do to crops and trees. Many of these are not native to North America and have been introduced (often accidentally) from other areas.

Types: More than 25,000 species in the United States
Size: Most are less than 1 inch, though some can be larger.
Eats: Most eat plant materials; some eat insects, meat, or fungi.
Eats them: Birds, small mammals, insects, fish
Range: Worldwide

GO OUTSIDE

Count the spots on a ladybug. Some people say this helps tell their age, but this isn't actually true. However, it can help you find out what type of ladybug you're looking at. For instance, one with seven spots is likely the seven-spotted ladybug. So count those spots, find a good field guide or ID book, and see what you can find out.

FIREFLY

Of all the species of beetles out there, fireflies are some of the most celebrated, so they deserve their own entry. (Yes, fireflies are a type of beetle.) These little fliers, best known as lightning bugs for giving off a soft glow on warm summer nights, bring lots of fun to backyards across the country. The next time you go out looking for fireflies at dusk, keep some of the following odd and interesting facts in mind. Then share them with your friends to teach them a thing or two.

LITTLE-KNOWN FACTS
1. Not all firefly species have the ability to glow. But this fancy glow also has a fancy name. It is called bioluminescence.

2. The light that fireflies give off is their way of communicating with one another. Often this glow is used to attract another firefly.
3. Fireflies will eat one another. In fact, some fireflies will glow just to lure in another one. Then they will eat it. Now that's really a sneak attack!
4. You can help scientists learn more about fireflies by signing up online for the firefly watch. This is a cool way to get involved in citizen science. Sign up through the Museum of Science at mos.org.
5. While fireflies do exist in most parts of the world, it's hard to find them in parts of the West. Coauthor Ken Keffer did not grow up with fireflies in Wyoming, but coauthor Stacy Tornio did grow up with them in Oklahoma.

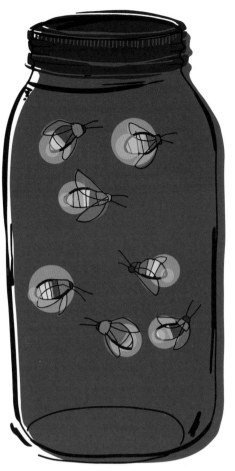

Types: More than 2,000 species
Size: Around an inch or less
Eats: Pollen, plants, other insects
Eats them: Many bug-eating predators, such as birds, frogs, lizards
Range: Worldwide in warm environments

GO OUTSIDE

If you've never spent an evening catching fireflies, then now is the time. The classic method is to get a clear jar and punch holes in the top. You can also take a mesh bag (like a laundry bag) and turn it upside down as a way of capturing them. Try to collect ten to twelve, and then watch how they light up your container. Do you notice their different flashing patterns? Be sure to release them after a short while.

SCORPION

Many venomous critters get a bad rap, and scorpions are no exception. Even the name sounds a bit menacing, doesn't it? Scorpions are nocturnal creatures for the most part, meaning they move around at night. People in the Southwest know to watch out for scorpions. In fact, they'll often check their shoes in case any scorpions came along to find a place to rest during the night. While most species aren't dangerous to people, getting stung by a scorpion wouldn't be fun. This is one insect where you should err on the side of safety.

LITTLE-KNOWN FACTS

1. When there's not a lot of food around, scorpions can slow their metabolism to conserve their energy, which helps them survive better. No wonder they're so resilient.

2. While scorpions are tough survivors, there is one thing they really can't live without: soil. Scorpions need soil because they burrow down into it.

3. Scientists can't exactly explain why, but if you put scorpions under an ultraviolet light, they look fluorescent. What a cool trick!

4. Scorpions can have as many as six to twelve eyes, but their eyesight is pretty poor overall. Their poor eyesight and overall sensitivity to light are major reasons they mostly come out at night.

5. When they are really little, young scorpions will often ride on their mothers' backs.

6. Antarctica is the only continent where you won't find scorpions.

7. Even though most scorpions won't harm you, there is one species in the United States that could potentially kill a person, especially if that person is sensitive to the venom. It's the Arizona bark scorpion. This is one of the reasons you should definitely take them seriously!

Types: 1,500 species around the world
Size: Just a few inches to more than 8 inches
Eats: Insects, spiders, lizards, other scorpions
Eats them: Rodents, snakes, lizards
Range: Found worldwide

BUTTERFLY

It seems like everyone loves butterflies, and rightfully so. They are amazing and beautiful, often sporting bright colors and patterns. The monarch butterfly is perhaps the most recognized and popular butterfly, but there are many more species in the United States. You should learn about butterflies beyond the monarch because they truly are fascinating creatures. Some people like to keep track of all the different species they've ever seen. They call it a life list, and it's similar to the way people keep track of the number of birds they see. How many species can you say you've seen? Time to get out the butterfly book!

LITTLE-KNOWN FACTS

1. Many people think that butterflies emerge from cocoons, but this is not true. Moths come from cocoons. Butterflies emerge from the same type of thing, but it's called a chrysalis. Go ahead and trick your friends with this one!
2. Butterflies use their feet to taste things. Now that is being resourceful!
3. Butterflies have a really cool tongue. It's called a proboscis. It stays curled up until they uncurl it and use it like a straw to sip up nectar.
4. Yes, butterflies eat nectar, but that's not all. They'll engage in an activity called puddling. It's where they gather at mud puddles and soak up nutrients from the mud and other materials (sometimes even pee and poop).
5. Butterflies absolutely love hot weather. In fact, if it's cold, they're often

not able to fly. Their body temperature has to be 86°F in order to fly. You know how you wake up early with the birds? Well, then you stay up for the butterflies, because they are most active by midmorning.

6. The largest butterfly is the Queen Alexandra birdwing butterfly, with a wingspan of a foot wide. It lives in New Guinea, and it's worth noting that the female is bigger than the male.

7. Monarchs migrate for winter, but this is a unique behavior for butterflies. When they travel south, they gather up in large groups in late summer and fall. Then they roost by the thousands at night. This is quite a phenomenon if you ever get the chance to see it.

8. Here's a good trick for telling the difference between a male and female monarch: Males have a little added dot along the lower part of their wings. You can see this on both sides, especially when they have their wings out. Females lack this little spot.

9. Most butterfly adults only live for two to four weeks total.

10. Many butterflies are brightly colored as a defense mechanism. Bright colors are often a warning sign in the wild, so this helps deter predators.

11. Many butterflies have host plants, so they lay their eggs on a specific type of plant. Monarchs only lay their eggs on milkweed. It's important to plant host plants in your backyard to support all butterfly populations.

12. After butterflies lay their eggs, little caterpillars (also called larvae) hatch. They are caterpillars before they create a chrysalis. If you find a caterpillar in your area, take a picture and try to figure out what kind of butterfly or moth it eventually will be.

Types: 700-plus species in the United States alone
Size: Several species can be less than an inch, though monarchs and swallow-tails are several inches.
Eats: Nectar, plants while they are caterpillars
Eats them: Many insect-eaters, including frogs, birds, lizards
Range: Tons of butterfly species in every part of the world

GO OUTSIDE

Every summer there are events held to count butterflies. This helps scientists learn about the butterfly populations and how they are doing. Get involved in a counting event near you—or just count on your own. You can learn more through the North American Butterfly Association website at naba.org.

MOTH

Moths are sometimes the overlooked cousins of butterflies. Moths and butterflies look similar at first glance, but there are some key differences. No, it's not that butterflies are bright and moths are not, because in reality there are brown butterflies and also brightly colored moths. After you learn these cool facts, you're going to want to be on the lookout for moths just as much as you are for butterflies. Don't worry: There are easy ways to attract them. For starters, you can try leaving your porch light on at night.

LITTLE-KNOWN FACTS

1. One of the biggest differences between moths and butterflies is that moths have straight or feathery antennae, while butterflies' antennae have a knob at the end.

2. While most people think of moths as being night fliers (yes, many truly are), this isn't always the case. Sphinx moths are active during the day.

3. Here's another trick to telling the difference between moths and butterflies. Most moths hold their wings flat against their body (or straight out) when they rest, while butterflies

generally hold their wings out behind them.

4. Many moths don't eat at all. Some don't even have mouthparts.
5. Most adult moths only live for a week or two.
6. People in other countries eat caterpillars regularly, including moth caterpillars. This is because they provide good nutrition.
7. The largest moth in the world is the Atlas moth of Taiwan, with a wingspan of more than a foot.
8. Moths are so popular that they actually have a week dedicated to them. Look for National Moth Week, which takes place every year in July.

Types: More than 10,000 species in the United States alone
Size: Mostly range from less than 1/2 inch to several inches
Eats: Nectar, plants, sometimes nothing at all
Eats them: Birds, frogs, spiders, other animals that eat insects
Range: Thousands of species in all parts of the world

GO OUTSIDE

Want to attract moths? Besides leaving your porch light on, you can also use a special bait to attract them. Make a paste of mashed banana and brown sugar or molasses, then just smear it on a tree and wait for them to come. Black lights can also be used to attract night fliers.

SPIDER

Don't you dare call a spider an insect! The often-feared but ever-so-cool spider is classified as an arachnid. It's their eight legs that give them away as not being insects (since most insects have a mere six legs). Most people associate spiders with webs. And while it's true that they are known for making webs to catch food, this isn't true for all spiders. So what else is different about the arachnids that you thought you knew? Here are some more fascinating facts.

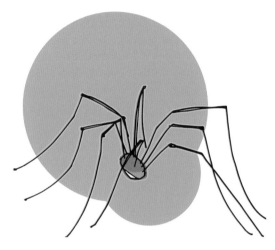

LITTLE-KNOWN FACTS

1. The thing that makes spiders different from other arachnids (like scorpions) is their ability to produce silk. While silk is used to make webs, spiders also use it for other purposes, like lowering themselves through the air or protecting their eggs.
2. Spiders share another habit with scorpions. They inject venom into their prey to kill them. All spiders except one family use venom.
3. Even though most spiders have eight eyes, most spiders can't see very well with them. Some spider species (like the cave-dwelling spiders) don't even have eyes at all.
4. Tarantulas are well-known spiders, and yes, they do exist in North America—mostly in southwestern areas. Most of the tarantulas in North America are brown or black, but those in other parts of the world can have bright colors.
5. The classic spiderweb—rounded and getting smaller as you move more

into the center—is usually woven by orb weaver spiders.

6. Not all spiders have webs. For instance, wolf spiders don't spin webs. Jumping spiders don't either. They just jump on their prey.

7. Some female spiders can lay a few hundred eggs at a time.

8. While spiders are venomous, most are pretty harmless. Plus they eat many bugs, so go ahead and support most spider populations. They aren't anything to shriek over.

9. Some reports say that as many as 50 percent of people are afraid of spiders. This fear is called arachnophobia.

Types: More than 40,000 species around the world
Size: They can be a few inches long, but most are less than an inch.
Eats: Small insects like flies
Eats them: Birds, wasps, reptiles
Range: Many types of spiders throughout the world

GO OUTSIDE

Grab your magnifying glass and head outside to look for a spiderweb. Once you find one, use your magnifying glass to carefully study the web pattern. Notice how it's woven very close together, which helps it trap spiders' prey. Be careful, and make sure you don't break the web.

BEE

Next time you see a bee buzzing about, be sure to thank it. Much of the food you eat is a direct result of bees. How is that possible? Here's why: Pollination is essential for plants to develop, grow, and produce. This makes bees essential to people. Having bees around ensures we have food. The bee populations have been declining over the past several years, so it's important to do what you can to help them thrive and survive.

LITTLE-KNOWN FACTS

1. Bee colonies, or hives, are led by female leaders called queen bees.
2. Bees have two compound eyes. This means they are made up of thousands of tiny lenses. They also have three more eyes on top of the compound ones.
3. In a single lifetime a honeybee produces about one-tenth of a teaspoon of honey. Imagine how many bees and how much work it takes to produce a single jar.
4. Queen bees can lay one thousand eggs a day and more than one million in a lifetime!
5. Bees in a hive all have different jobs. Some worker bees make the honeycomb, while others go out to gather the nectar and pollen. When they have a job, they usually have it for life.
6. In a bee colony the queen and all the worker bees are females. Male bees (called drones) are only around in spring; at other times it's the girls that do all the work.
7. Worker bees might only live three or four weeks before the next generation comes along to work in the hive. The queen bee lives three or four years.
8. Only certain species of bees make honey. Many more bee species aren't honey makers at all.
9. At its peak a bee colony could contain as many as 40,000 to 60,000 bees.

10. Here's an exhausting fact: Bees don't really sleep. They are active 24 hours a day, always working.

Types: More than 1,000 honeybees and related species worldwide
Size: Around 1/8 inch to 1 inch
Eats: Nectar and pollen from flowers
Eats them: Some birds; animals like foxes and skunks will attack beehives.
Range: Worldwide

GO OUTSIDE

Many people are afraid of bees, but there's no reason to be in most cases. (Of course, if you're allergic to bee stings, you definitely have a reason.) In fact, the bee population needs our help to survive. During spring or summer plant some flowers just for the bees. You can research good flowers for bees (bee balm is a good one) or ask someone at the garden center for a recommendation.

SCIENCE Q&A: Do People Eat Invertebrates?

Have you ever been riding your bike when suddenly a bug hits you right in the face? Maybe you swallowed it down before you even realized what happened. Have you ever wondered if people eat insects on purpose?

Sure, lots of people really enjoy eating invertebrates, like shrimp, crab, lobster, and oysters. But what about insects? The answer is yes. In many parts of the world, insects are a regular part of the diet. Nearly 2,000 invertebrate species have been consumed around the globe. Beetles, mealworms, caterpillars, scorpions, spiders, grasshoppers, cicadas, and crickets are some of the most widespread.

Insects as food are growing in popularity in the United States too. And not just joke foods like chocolate-covered grasshoppers either. One of the easiest ways to incorporate insects into the human diet is in the form of cricket flour. Cricket flour is nutrient packed, easy to use, and—perhaps the best part—doesn't have any eyes or legs to get caught between your teeth.

Some people like to snack on ants too. They can have a refreshing burst of citrus lemon flavor. Be careful if you try this yourself though. They tend to bite you before you can bite them. Fire ants should probably be avoided.

Insects can be easily raised, and they don't require much food, water, or space. Many are responsible for pollinating the food we eat. But others can also be the food we eat. Don't expect them to completely take over the menu though. Hamburgers and chicken nuggets are probably here to stay.

GRASSHOPPER

Take a summer walk in the prairie, and the grasshoppers will likely scatter like popping popcorn in all directions. You can hardly watch where one lands before another one takes off and distracts you. Grasshopper watching (and catching) is a great activity for any age. Sneaking up on a grasshopper and trying to catch it is an entertaining, and often challenging, way to spend an afternoon.

LITTLE-KNOWN FACTS

1. Female grasshoppers are larger than the males in most cases.
2. Unlike crickets (closely related), which use their wings to make sound, grasshoppers make sound by rubbing their legs or other body parts together.
3. Do you know where grasshoppers have their ears? They're on their bellies!
4. Most people think of grasshoppers as being great hoppers, and they are. But they have wings and can fly as well.
5. Locusts and grasshoppers are the same thing in many cases. Here's an easy way to remember it: All locusts are grasshoppers, but not all grasshoppers are locusts.
6. When grasshoppers get together, they can do a lot of harm. Called locusts, large grasshopper groups can destroy farm crops.

7. Have you ever had a grasshopper "spit" at you? They produce this brown liquid material, which is a type of self-defense. It might seem like they are spitting at you, but it won't hurt you at all.

8. Some species of lubber grasshoppers have stubby wings and are not able to fly.

Types: 10,000 species around the world
Size: Range from ⅜ inch to more than 3 inches
Eats: Plant material
Eats them: Frogs, birds, reptiles, other bug-eaters
Range: Worldwide

GO OUTSIDE

Gather up some family or friends and try out the grasshopper challenge. The rules are simple: Just set a time limit (like 15 or 30 minutes), and see how many grasshoppers you can catch during that time. You can split up into teams or have everyone be on his or her own.

SNAIL

Wouldn't it be handy to just haul your home around with you everywhere you go? This is what a snail does. It hauls around a shell, which it also relies on for protection. You can find snails in just about any damp area in the world. They will burrow in the mud if it gets too hot, and they'll hibernate in winter.

LITTLE-KNOWN FACTS

1. Most snails in North America are only a few inches long, but the giant African land snail can be more than a foot long.
2. Snails can't hear, but they can see.
3. Fossil snails have been found from over 600 million years ago.
4. You can't tell the difference between male and female snails because they are all both genders. This is called a hermaphrodite.
5. Snails have what is called a radula. This is a tongue covered with lots of sharp little "teeth."
6. Some of the most common snails in the United States are garden snails. Look for them in your garden.

Types: Thousands of species
Size: Most are just a few inches long.
Eats: Algae, limestone, sometimes each other
Eats them: Birds, frogs, other small animals
Range: In damp areas worldwide

GO OUTSIDE

Here's something you can do with snails or slugs: Find snail or slug "slime," which they leave behind when they move, and take a closer look at it. Don't worry, it's not going to hurt you. Some people even think it can be used as a medicine for certain things. If you don't want to touch it, at least get a closer look.

JELLYFISH

Jellyfish can vary quite a bit in behavior from one species to the next. Some move around a lot, while others do not. Some are strong hunters; others mostly wait for the food to come to them. No matter what, these squishy-bodied sea creatures are pretty cool. Many people think they are dangerous, but it's time to get the facts straight.

LITTLE-KNOWN FACTS

1. Jellyfish aren't fish.
2. Jellyfish do not have brains.
3. Jellyfish that sting (not all do) have tentacles that contain venom. This is how they catch their prey—they capture and shock them.
4. Where is a jellyfish's mouth? It's not where you might think it is. It's really hard to see because it's directly under its dome-shaped body.
5. You can actually help scientists monitor jellyfish. Whether you live near jellyfish areas or you're just visiting, help out with this citizen science project by observing the jellyfish in the area. Then go and record your sightings at jellywatch.org.
6. When jellyfish gather in large groups (sometimes there will be thousands), it's called a bloom. Jellyfish blooms are very cool phenomena.

Types: More than 200 species
Size: Bodies of a few inches to several feet
Eats: Eggs, smaller fish, larvae
Eats them: Sea turtles, some fish
Range: A variety of species worldwide

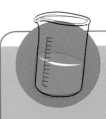

SCIENCE Q&A:
What Is the Intertidal Zone?

The intertidal zone is a unique place. It can be home to lots of cool aquatic invertebrates, among other things. But before we get into the intertidal zone, we need to talk about tides.

Tides are the changes in the ocean level caused by the gravitational pull of the sun and the moon coupled with the rotation of the Earth. The water in the oceans shifts around based on this. Some places experience one high and one low tide per day. Others have two of each. The area that is underwater at high tide but not underwater at low tide is known as the intertidal zone. The plants and animals that live here are very specialized. They constantly experience extreme changes in their environment.

The things living at the higher end of the intertidal zone are out of the ocean water the most. The things living at the lower end of the intertidal zone are underwater much of the time, but not always. Mussels, clams, and barnacles all live in the intertidal zone. Their shells help seal them up so they don't dry out when the water is at low tide. Then they open up to feed as water covers them.

Sometimes jellyfish, horseshoe crabs, and other sea critters get stranded on the beach as the tide goes down. Be extra careful; you might need an adult to help you, but you can return these creatures back to sea when this happens.

Have you ever heard of tide pools? Maybe not if you live far from the ocean. These are small, rocky depressions that water remains trapped in as the tide goes out. They are some of the neatest places to explore. Be careful not to slip on the wet rocks, but everyone should get to take a peek inside tide pools before they grow up. Look for sea anemones with their tentacles shifting in the waves. Do you see any sea stars? Can you spot some crabs, or perhaps a fish, in the tide pool?

Don't just sit there on the beach. The intertidal zone is a favorite place in nature for people. Explore the plants and animals that call this dynamic landscape, and waterscape, home.

DESTINATIONS: Public Beaches

Ah, the beach. It's one of the most sought-after destinations in the world. Nothing seems to make people happier than sitting with their toes in the sand, staring out at blue-green water. So what are you waiting for? Get out there and hit the beach this season!

WHO? You can be any age to enjoy the beach because you can pretty much do anything while you're there. Young kids will just like sitting in the sand with a shovel and some toys while older kids will definitely want to hit the water. Best of all, you can set up your chairs or umbrella anywhere and be close to all the action.

WHAT? Don't think the beach is just about sitting around. There are lots of activities to take part in—from swimming and building sand castles to playing volleyball and Frisbee. You can also bring a picnic lunch, rent equipment from area vendors, or take your bike or in-line skates for a beachfront ride. This doesn't even include some of the classic beach to-dos, like waiting for the tide to come in, burying your feet in the sand, or looking for seashells.

WHEN? Many people think of the beach as a summertime activity, but spring is actually ideal in a lot of locations. If you're in the South, a beach trip can be the perfect springtime weekend getaway before it gets too hot and crowded. Be sure to check out the beach in all seasons too. People often overlook beaches when it's not warm and sunny out, but these are ideal days to go. It's less crowded overall, and you can appreciate the natural, simple beauty of the area instead.

WHERE? You can find great beaches all over the country. While the East, West, and Gulf Coasts are great places to start, don't be limited by those alone. You can also find great beaches along the shores of the Great Lakes—or any lakes for that matter. Scope out some beaches near you—and pay them a visit this spring. Even if they're not in full swing until summer, it's a great time to become familiar with them and check out the wildlife nearby.

WHY? The beach is filled with sea and water life that you might not otherwise come into contact with. Don't forget about this precious resource, and share it with a friend. You're bound to discover something new with each and every visit.

While it's great to go to the beach on a hot, busy day, it's even better to go when there aren't a lot of people around. If this means checking it out on a cloudy day or early in the morning, go for it. During these times you'll gain a better understanding and appreciation for the nature life in that area.

CRAB

Here's another animal that you're likely familiar with. At least it seems like you're familiar with it, right? This is probably because you see it on the menu of so many seafood restaurants. True, millions of crabs are consumed each year (people especially love crab legs), but there are many, many more species out there that never see a dinner plate. And all the different types make up a pretty fascinating bunch.

LITTLE-KNOWN FACTS

1. Crabs have five pairs of legs, so ten legs total. The most famous two are the top ones. They are considered the pincers.
2. The horseshoe crab is not a crab at all. Instead, it is a closer relative to arachnids. Horseshoe crabs are still pretty amazing though. You can check them out along the Gulf and Atlantic coasts, especially when they come ashore in spring to lay their green eggs.
3. Have you ever heard that a crab walks sideways? It's true. Just take a look for yourself sometime. They actually swim sideways too!
4. Here's a fun fact: Want to know what a group of crabs is called? A cast!
5. A male crab is called a Jimmy. A female is called either a Sally if it's young or a Sook if it's an adult. Look at the shape of the apron on the underside of a crab. If it's long and skinny, the crab's a Jimmy. If it's shaped like a

triangle, the crab's a Sally. And if the apron has a bell shape, it's a Sook.

Types: Thousands of species
Size: A few inches to several feet
Eats: Algae, worms, other crustaceans
Eats them: Octopuses, fish, rays, turtles
Range: Worldwide

GO OUTSIDE

It's time to try your hand at crabbing! Even if you don't want to save the crabs to eat, catching them is still a fun experience. You'll want to go with an experienced person who can show you the ropes. Some people even use chicken necks as bait.

OCTOPUS

With its eight massive and impressive tentacles, the octopus is a well-known marine animal. You're not likely to see one, though, unless you visit an aquarium. Why is this? Just take a moment to check out how an octopus lurks in the dark and rarely moves around. This is how octopuses behave in the ocean as well. They don't often come out in the open. Study that cool octopus at the aquarium; you'll definitely gain a whole new appreciation for this animal.

LITTLE-KNOWN FACTS

1. You might think birds are the only animals that have beaks, but octopuses do too. They need the strong beak to break open the hard shells of the prey they eat.
2. The eight tentacles of octopuses also have strong suction discs on them. This really helps them grab hold of their prey so it can't escape.
3. Octopuses have a unique defense mechanism. If attacked, they can release a type of dark ink from an ink sac. This looks similar to smoke in the water. It will distract predators so they can get away.
4. Octopuses have a unique siphon to help them move. This helps them

propel (usually backward) through the water, much like a jet engine or an outboard motor. So if an octopus isn't crawling along the bottom of the ocean floor, it's jetting across with its cool propeller!

5. The largest octopus species is the Giant Pacific. It grows to more than 9 feet, weighs more than 600 pounds, and can be found off the west coast of the United States.

6. Baby octopuses spend the first few months of their lives up on top of the sea. They are really vulnerable during this time, so they really have to watch out for predators. They eventually settle down at the ocean floor.

7. Octopuses have large and powerful eyes, similar to human eyes, which they use to spot prey.

Types: More than 250 types; the common octopus, the most prevalent, is found throughout the world.
Size: Most range from 1 to 3 feet.
Eats: Fish, shellfish
Eats them: Sharks, large fish
Range: Worldwide

CRAYFISH

You can think of crayfish (often called crawfish in the South) as the lobster's little freshwater cousin. These water critters also go by names like crawdads, mud-bugs, and freshwater lobsters. Take one look at them and you'll see that they are similar in appearance to lobsters, with large claws at the front of their bodies. They are also popular pets, so look for crayfish in the next fish tank you see. You'll have the chance to observe them up close.

LITTLE-KNOWN FACTS

1. You can find crayfish in every state in the United States, in Mexico, and in Canada. With hundreds of species, it's fun to see how many different

types you can discover. Remember to look for differences, like claw shape, size, and color.

2. Nearly all crayfish burrow in the mud or silt along riverbanks and other bodies of water. This is good if you like to catch them. Lift up a rock, and you just might see a crayfish scurry out from under it.

3. Crayfish are very popular among people who like to fish. They will catch dozens of crayfish to eat.

4. You might think of antennae as something just for bugs, but crayfish have them too. They use their antennae to taste the water around them and to help find food.

5. Crayfish have special internal gills, though they can survive out of the water for an extended amount of time.

6. Crayfish build amazing tunnels, and the tops are called chimneys. Made of mud, they stick up out of the ground. The impressive tunnels can go several feet into the ground.

Types: Hundreds of species
Size: Usually a few inches, though some species are much bigger.
Eats: Plants, shrimp, dead fish
Eats them: Raccoons, opossums, muskrats, many others
Range: Worldwide

GO OUTSIDE

Go on a crawfish hunt. This is a pretty common activity in the South, and you should experience it at least once. Some people use a pole to catch crawfish, while others use buckets or nets. Just remember to keep your fingers away from their pinchers.

LOBSTER

Lobsters are a popular seafood item all over the world. In fact, they are considered a really special treat for most people. The lobster-fishing business is a huge one. It's a multimillion-dollar industry. With their large, iconic claws, lobsters probably draw up a very specific image in your mind. This is a great start, but it is just the beginning.

1. To grow, lobsters shed their shells. They usually do this two or three times during their life.
2. You probably think of lobsters as being red, but they're not. Most of them are actually an olive-green color in the wild, but they turn red when they get heated up.
3. Here's a question you can trick your friends with: How many legs do lobsters have? They have ten.
4. Lobsters can and will attack (and eat) one another with their strong and powerful claws.
5. Most of the lobsters that are fished (more than 200,000 tons a year) are a cold-water species known as the American or European clawed lobster. However, there are dozens of other species, including both clawed and clawless species.

Types: Dozens of species worldwide
Size: From less than a foot to more than 3 feet
Eats: Fish, mollusks, some algae, plant life
Eats them: Large fish
Range: Worldwide

STARFISH

Is the name starfish or sea star? Both are acceptable names of this well-known ocean animal. What do you think makes them so popular? Maybe it's their shape, or maybe it's the way they attach themselves to things. You can often spot sea stars in tide pools and along shorelines, so be sure to keep your eye out if you're planning a trip to the seashore.

LITTLE-KNOWN FACTS

1. Many people think starfish are a type of fish, but they aren't. They don't have gills, scales, or fins. So don't make the mistake of putting them in the fish family.
2. Starfish can regrow parts of their body! For instance, if they lose an arm, they can regrow it over time.
3. Starfish don't swim like fish do. Instead, they move with the little tubes on their underside. These tubes act like little suction cups, and a single sea star can have hundreds of them.
4. Starfish have a small mouth on their underside, but this doesn't

stop them from eating larger prey. They can actually push their stomach through their mouth to eat something bigger—and then pull it back.

5. You might think all sea stars have a classic star shape with five arms, but this isn't always the case. Sometimes they have several more arms. In fact, some have as many as forty!

6. If you look closely at a sea star, you'll see that it is very well protected. It has little spines on the top of its body, almost like protective armor, that keep it safe from predators.

Types: More than 2,000 species
Size: Can range from a few inches to more than 3 feet
Eats: Mollusks, including clams, oysters, and mussels
Eats them: Sharks, rays, crabs
Range: Worldwide

GO OUTSIDE

Tide pools are a great place to explore. You can find all kinds of critters, including sea urchins and starfish if you're lucky. Remember, these star-shaped animals will use their little suction cups to grab onto the side of rocks, reefs, and more, so make sure you look closely.

SECTION 2: THE FISH, HERPTILES, AND BIRDS

EEL

Some people think eels are pretty odd-looking fish with long, snakelike bodies. You have to look past that though. While these fish are mostly found deep in the ocean, they are still pretty fascinating. Most eels are known for ambushing their prey—this means they lurk behind rocks and in the dark before they dash out to kill it.

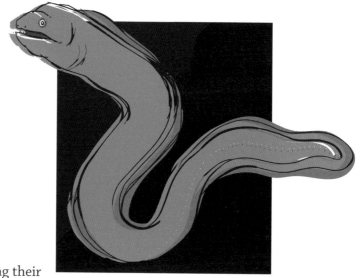

LITTLE-KNOWN FACTS

1. The pelican eel has an expanding stomach, so it can eat fish almost as big as its body!
2. Both pelican and gulper eels have a cool trick to attract prey: They have luminescent organs at the tips of their tails. This lures in curious fish so the eels can catch and eat them.
3. The avocet snipe eel is mostly found in semitropical areas of the eastern half of the United States. It has a unique look because its jaw can't shut

all the way—so it looks like it's always open a bit. If you think about it, this can make the eel look kind of evil.

4. Eels can have more than one hundred vertebrae.
5. In general, scientists don't know a lot about eels. They are mostly deep-sea fish, so they don't get caught and studied a lot.
6. Lots of water snakes get mistaken for eels. People tend to call anything with a long body an eel, but don't make the same mistake.
7. Have you ever heard of the deadly electric eel that can deliver a shock strong enough to kill people? While this is a real animal, it's not actually an eel at all. It's more closely related to a catfish.

Types: A number of species off the coast of North America (mostly on the East Coast), including the avocet snipe, gulper, and pelican eel
Size: Ranges a great deal. The pelican and avocet eels are both around 3 feet long; the gulper eel can be 5 to 6 feet long.
Eats: Small fish, crustaceans
Eats them: Larger fish
Range: Most eels are found off the eastern coast of the United States; the pelican eel is also found along the West Coast.

SCIENCE Q&A:
What Is a Taxonomy?

In biology the naming and classifying of organisms is called taxonomy. Taxonomists don't just name new species though. They also figure out how the different species are related to one another. Scientists look at the DNA of the organisms. Sometimes species can look almost identical, and DNA helps tell them apart. Other times organisms can look similar, but they aren't closely related at all.

Carolus Linnaeus and other scientists first started naming and ordering species in the 1700s. Taxonomists still use a similar order to classify a species. It goes from broad categories down to each individual species. One way to remember the order is "King Phillip Came Over for Good Spaghetti." Or you can come up with your own mnemonic. Like "Ken's Pants Caught On Fire, Get Sprayer."

Kingdom
Phylum
Class
Order
Family
Genus
Species

Sometimes you'll see organisms referred to by their scientific names. (These scientific names are the genus and species names. They are always written in italics; the genus is capitalized and the species isn't.) Rainbow trout (*Oncorhynchus mykiss*) are the same genus, *Oncorhynchus*, as cutthroat trout (*Oncorhynchus clarkii*), but they are different species.

Taxonomists have named almost two million different species of organisms, but there could be as many as thirty million species, so there are plenty more to discover and describe. It is important to know the differences between the species and how they all relate to one another.

SHARK

Sharks are some of the most well-known and popular swimmers in the ocean. They are both celebrated and misunderstood. The popularity of sharks on television does show that people are curious about these fascinating creatures. But at the same time, many people consider sharks scary and dangerous, which usually just isn't the case. It's time to turn things around. Share these cool facts with people, and tell them not to be so scared of sharks!

LITTLE-KNOWN FACTS

1. Sharks lose teeth frequently, but there are replacements waiting. In fact, sharks can go through as many as 20,000 to 30,000 teeth during their lifetime.

2. Sharks don't have any bones. Even the legendary fin that people think of when they think of sharks is made up of cartilage.

3. While sharks have a bad reputation for attacking humans, this is actually rare. For instance, you have a better chance of being struck by lightning than getting attacked by a shark. In contrast, humans kill millions of sharks each year.

4. The whale shark is the largest shark (and fish) in the world. It can reach nearly 40 feet! This giant shark feeds mostly on plankton.

5. Three of the most dangerous sharks in the world include the great white, hammerhead, and tiger. All of these species are found in parts of North America.

6. While most sharks are pretty independent, some do form schools. The hammerhead species is one of these species.

7. You might not think of sharks as having a great sense of hearing, but they do. Through sound, they can detect prey thousands of feet away.

8. Scientists have evidence that sharks have been around for millions of years—they were around when dinosaurs roamed the earth.

9. There's a myth that says sharks must constantly swim to stay alive. While it is true that many sharks need to swim to force water over their gills as a way to breathe, they can take swimming breaks without dying.
10. A few of the sharks found in North American waters are the great white, sand tiger, bull, and leopard sharks.

Types: More than 500 species around the world
Size: Ranges a great deal, from a few feet to 40 feet or more
Eats: Mostly fish, but some will go after marine animals too
Eats them: Not many predators other than people and killer whales
Range: Throughout the world, often near coasts

BASS

Bass are some of the most popular fish in the world. People who like fishing love to catch species like smallmouth, large-mouth, and striped bass. There are all kinds of tournaments and records that people go after with bass. Luckily, it's not so hard to find them if you do like to fish. They are adaptable and survive in lakes, ponds, and streams.

LITTLE-KNOWN FACTS
1. Bass are in the sunfish family.
   They can be really beautiful too. So if you catch one or get the chance to see one up close, notice their colors or patterns.
2. Male bass have a strong role in the nesting process. The males build a nest for the females to lay eggs. Then the males protect the eggs until

they hatch.

3. Bass are most active when it's warm. When it's colder, their metabolism slows down and they eat a lot less.
4. Bass do not have eyelids. Take a close look and see if you can verify this for yourself.
5. "Otolith" is a weird word, right? Otoliths are the ear bones of fish. These help fish detect other fish and prey to eat.

Types: Around twelve species in North America
Size: Most are 16 to 24 inches.
Eats: Aquatic insects, crayfish, frogs, smaller fish
Eats them: People, fish-eating animals like bears, eagles, raccoons
Range: Found in freshwater throughout North America

GO OUTSIDE

Challenge yourself to catch both a large- and smallmouth bass. First you'll want to know the difference between the two. If the mouth extends behind the eye, it's a largemouth. If it only goes as far back as the middle of the eye, then it is a smallmouth. Then see if you can catch both types. This is a fun challenge!

SEAHORSE

This creature might have a good chance of winning a sea popularity contest. With their long-snouted head, seahorses are fascinating-looking creatures. Because of their head and the bold shape of their belly, they do resemble a horse. They truly are some of the most unusual animals in the sea.

LITTLE-KNOWN FACTS

1. Most seahorse pairs are together for life. Male and females get together and then stick together for a long time. This is very unusual in the fish world.

2. Male seahorses have a pouch in the front of their belly where the females place the eggs. Then he carries them around until they hatch. That's right, the males are carrying those babies!

3. Seahorses are constantly eating. They might consume more than 3,000 shrimp in a single day.

4. There's a reason seahorses are constantly eating: They don't have teeth or

a stomach, so food goes through them very quickly.

5. Some seahorses are endangered because of habitat loss and overharvesting. Many other countries use seahorses as an ingredient in medicines.

6. Types: Around thirty-five different species in the world

Size: From 1/2 inch to 12 to 14 inches
Eats: Plankton, tiny shrimp, algae
Eats them: Crabs, stingrays, tuna
Range: In shallow, tropical waters throughout the world

CATFISH

These popular fish are like the cats of the fish world. Catfish have cool whiskers, which give them their name. Catfish are also a popular fish for eating. They can get really big, so people are always searching for those big catfish. There are actually many fish within the catfish family, but the channel, flathead, and blue catfish are some of the most well-known species in the United States.

LITTLE-KNOWN FACTS

1. Some catfish have sharp spines on their fins, so you have to be careful not to get poked if you ever catch one.
2. Some catfish are really big, but most average much smaller.
3. Most catfish have a head that is flattened. They also have whisker-like body parts outside their mouth that they use for touch and taste.
4. Catfish are known for hanging out along the bottom of waters and in dark or murky areas.

5. While some catfish feed on other water animals, many are actually filter feeders. This means they filter out food like plants from the water.
6. Channel catfish generally reach 5 to 10 pounds, but they can get to be more than 40 or 50 pounds. These are the ones that anglers are after the most. (Psst! "Angler" is just a fancy word for someone who likes to fish.)
7. After a female channel catfish lays her eggs, she leaves, and the male guards the nest.
8. Noodling is a common hobby in the South where people fish for catfish with their bare hands.
9. Some catfish are called bullheads.

Types: More than 3,000 species of catfish and their relatives
Size: Mere inches to several feet
Eats: Insects, clams, crayfish, worms, amphibians, other fish
Eats them: Other fish, alligators, raccoons, bears, other fish-eating animals, people
Range: Worldwide

GO OUTSIDE

The whiskers on a catfish are really cool, and they're worth taking a really close look at! The best way to do this is by catching one, though make sure you don't keep it out of the water too long. Study how long the whiskers are, and try to count them.

SALMON

People love to eat salmon so much that there are salmon farms throughout the country. They are really good fish, and they are good for you too. This fish has more to it than just being tasty though. They are important to ecosystems too. Lots of other animals depend on wild salmon for their own survival.

LITTLE-KNOWN FACTS
1. Salmon go into lakes and streams (freshwater) to lay their eggs. This is called spawning. Then after they hatch, they migrate to salt water. This makes salmon anadromous animals, living both in freshwater and salt water.
2. Salmon have very strong tails, which allow them to leap up waterfalls and get through other tricky areas to reach their spawning area.
3. The Atlantic salmon has a darker color in freshwater. When they enter salt water, they lighten and develop a silvery sheen.

4. Most salmon weigh less than 50 pounds, but the largest chinook (also called king) salmon can reach more than 100 pounds.
5. Sockeye salmon are known as red salmon because of the cool transformation they go through. Before they spawn, they have blue heads and backs. After, they have bright-red bodies.
6. Here's another cool fact about salmon: They return to the place they were born, usually about four years later. They return to lay their eggs before they die.
7. Bears, eagles, and lots of other critters take advantage of the salmon, making meals of them as they move to their spawning waters.

Types: A handful of species around North America, including the Atlantic and five species along the Pacific coast
Size: 3 to 5 feet
Eats: Plankton, smaller fish, water insects
Eats them: Larger fish, fish-eating animals, people
Range: Mostly in northern, colder areas

GO OUTSIDE

Everyone should watch salmon spawning at least once. It's a pretty amazing natural occurrence, with hundreds of salmon swimming upstream at the same time. Find out if there are salmon in your area, then head to the river to see this for yourself.

TROUT

Trout are related to salmon and char. They are cold-water fish found mostly in freshwater. The most widespread native trout include rainbow trout, native to the western United States; cutthroats in the intermountain West; and brook trout in the Great Lakes and the East. They are also very popular among anglers. You can read all kinds of tips and tricks about the best way to catch trout.

LITTLE-KNOWN FACTS

1. Trout have teeth on the roof of their mouth; salmon don't.
2. Brown trout are native to Europe, but like other trout, they have been widely released to many nonnative habitats around the globe.
3. Rainbow trout that spend time in the ocean before returning to freshwater streams to breed are known as steelhead.
4. Cutthroat trout are named for the orange-colored slash marks under their jaws.
5. Rainbow trout have reddish or pinkish stripes along their sides.

6. The brook trout is the state fish of nine states: Michigan, New Hampshire, New Jersey, New York, North Carolina, Pennsylvania, Vermont, Virginia, and West Virginia.

7. Lake trout were historically a northern species. They are now causing problems in Yellowstone National Park because they were introduced there illegally. Now they outcompete the native cutthroats.

8. Darker backs and lighter bellies can create a camouflage effect for many species of trout.

9. The eyes on trout allow them to see above them, helping them avoid predators.

10. Fly fishers often try to mimic invertebrates and other trout food, while others prefer to do their fishing with worms or other bait.

Types: Dozens of species and numerous subspecies
Size: From a few inches to a few feet long
Eats: Fish, invertebrates, small mammals, aquatic vegetation
Eats them: Fish, birds, mammals
Range: Throughout the United States

GO OUTSIDE

Trout species can vary a great deal from one area to the next. Do a little research to find out which trout are common in your state or region. Then put your family and friends to the test. How many different species did they know about?

WALLEYE

Walleyes (and the closely related sauger) are easily recognizable by their unique eyes. Their large eyes have special adaptations for gathering light, and they can look almost shiny. Walleyes are popular with the sportfishing crowd. They can be fun to catch and yummy to eat. There is also a large commercial fishery for walleyes, especially in the Canadian Great Lakes. In the wild they can live to be more than 20 years old, but 10 to 12 is more common. Still, this is pretty long for a fish.

LITTLE-KNOWN FACTS

1. The walleye is the state fish of Minnesota.
2. Port Clinton, Ohio, celebrates New Year's Eve with the annual walleye drop. It's kind of like in Times Square, only with a 20-foot-long, 600-pound fiberglass walleye being dropped instead of a ball.
3. Walleyes can live in lakes or in rivers. They often feed in the shallow areas at night and move to deeper water during the daytime.
4. The way to tell a walleye from a sauger is that walleyes don't have black spots on their dorsal fin (that's the spiky one on the back) and saugers do.
5. Walleyes and saugers sometimes mate with each other, and these hybrids are called saugeyes.
6. Walleyes were historically native to the midwestern United States and Canada, but now they are found throughout North America.

Types: One species in the world
Size: Most are about 2 feet, though the largest can be well over 3 feet and weigh more than 20 pounds.
Eats: Smaller fish, frogs, invertebrates, small mammals
Eats them: Bass, pike, muskie
Range: North America

TURTLE

Turtles have been around for millions and millions of years. From small turtles you can find around your backyard to those several feet long that live in or closer to the sea, they are some pretty fascinating creatures. Turtles have hard protective shells that also serve as a home. With many species throughout North America, you won't have trouble spotting turtles. Instead, challenge yourself with how many different species you can see.

LITTLE-KNOWN FACTS

1. Nearly all turtles lay twenty or more eggs at a time. They lay them in mud or sand, so when the babies hatch, they have to dig themselves out.

2. You want to be careful around a snapping turtle—it can shoot its neck out about half the length of its body and curve it around too. It will bite you if it feels threatened.

3. Snapping turtles tend to give all turtles a bad reputation, but you shouldn't be afraid. Like most animals, if you leave them alone, they'll leave you alone.

4. If you've never heard of the alligator snapping turtle, you should look it up. It's the largest freshwater turtle in the world—reaching more than 200 pounds! It has a jagged shell that looks like a coat of armor.

5. Have you ever seen turtles lined up on a log, sunning themselves? Chances are those were painted turtles. Look for the yellow stripes along their necks.

6. Most turtles live along the water, but wood turtles will wander a bit,

often heading into woods and crossing roads.

7. Turtles are very active after it rains. So use this as an excuse to go for an exploratory nature hike.
8. Turtles are in the reptile family—just like snakes.
9. The top of a turtle shell is called a carapace, and the underside is called a plastron.
10. You can find saltwater turtles along the coasts of North America. Look for the leatherback turtle, which can reach up to 6 feet, or the green sea turtle, found in the South and East.

Types: Many species in North America; most common include spotted, painted, box, and common snapping turtle.
Size: Can range a great deal, from a 4- to 5-inch spotted turtle to an 18-inch snapping turtle
Eats: Most turtles are herbivores, constantly foraging for plants; snapping turtles will eat small mammals, birds, fish, and plants, which makes them omnivores.
Eats them: Birds, fish, raccoons, and other small mammals
Range: Snapping turtles are found in the eastern half of the United States, as are spotted, box, and painted turtles. Painted turtles are one of the only turtles whose range extends to areas of the West.

GO OUTSIDE

You can often find turtles lined up on a log near the water, sunning themselves. Head out on a bright, sunny day and see how many turtles you can count. There could be a dozen or more! Then make sure you take a closer look, because you might see more than one species.

SCIENCE Q&A:

What Is Metamorphosis?

Amphibians and insects are the classics when it comes to metamorphosis, but there are a few other animals that also experience it. Metamorphosis is a great change. Sure, you will change as you grow up, but not like animals that go through metamorphosis. You pretty much look like your parents and all other humans. Human babies are born with all the same parts that adults have. What about insects and amphibians though?

Let's start by examining frogs. As amphibians, frogs usually lay eggs in or around water. These jellylike egg masses can include hundreds or even thousands of eggs. Not all these eggs will survive to become frogs though. These eggs can be stuck to underwater vegetation or, in some species, just floating on the water's surface.

What hatches out of these frog eggs? No, it's not frogs—it's tadpoles. Tadpoles look more like minnows than frogs. They have a plump body, a tail, and no legs. For most species, the tadpoles live in the water for a few weeks; but some, like bullfrogs and green frogs, can remain as tadpoles for up to a year. Tadpoles swim around nibbling on algae and plant matter. They don't even have tongues yet. But they will.

Metamorphosis is a big change, and going from a tadpole to a frog certainly describes this. This change happens quickly too; it usually takes only about 24 hours. The tadpole tail is absorbed for nutrients, and frog legs grow. Tadpoles breathe through gills, while lungs develop for frogs to breathe with. Frogs tend to keep close to water, but they are no longer able to survive underwater like tadpoles do.

This is only one example. Butterflies, moths, and plenty of other insects go through a complete metamorphosis (other insects have what's called a simple metamorphosis). Butterflies and moths start off as eggs. Each species of butterfly or moth lays its eggs on certain species of host plants. Caterpillars hatch out of the eggs. This is the larval stage. After growing bigger and bigger, the caterpillars form a chrysalis (for butterflies) or a cocoon (for moths). This is the pupae stage of life. Adults will emerge from their casings, and they look nothing like the caterpillars they started out as.

Isn't metamorphosis amazing? Can you imagine changing from a tadpole to a frog? Or going into a chrysalis as a caterpillar and coming out as a butterfly?

TORTOISE

Tortoises are like land turtles. They have dome-shaped shells that offer them protection from predators. Stout legs are built for walking along on the land and for digging out burrows. Tortoises mostly live in hot environments, so they often seek shelter underground. In fact, they can spend up to 95 percent of their life underground. All three species found in the United States have experienced population declines, so you might have a hard time finding these awesome animals. Spring can be the best time to see them as they are on the move looking for mates.

LITTLE-KNOWN FACTS

1. The desert tortoise is California's state reptile. (Not all states have a state reptile, but it's worth checking out to see if your state does.)
2. Desert tortoises can dig tunnels more than 30 feet in length. Gopher tortoises dig even longer tunnels, up to 50 feet long.

3. Desert tortoises sometimes spend the winter burrowed together in small groups.
4. Tortoise burrows can also serve as homes for more than 350 other animal species, including small mammals, snakes, toads, invertebrates, and even burrowing owls.
5. Like turtles, tortoises lay eggs. The female might dig for several hours before she is finally ready to lay her eggs.
6. Tortoise shells are made up of between fifty-nine and sixty-one bones covered in scutes (plates) made of keratin, similar to our fingernails.
7. Tortoises can live to be many decades old.
8. The average speed of a desert tortoise is 0.2 mile per hour.
9. Male tortoises will sometimes push each other around like sumo wrestlers.
10. Tortoises can store water in their bladders. It's a survival method. This way they can survive long periods without water.

Types: Three species in the United States, around forty worldwide
Size: Most are 8 to 12 inches.
Eats: Vegetation, including grasses, flowering plants, and even cactus
Eats them: Coyotes, bobcats, ravens
Range: The southern half of the United States, from South Carolina to Southern California.

SNAKE

Snakes are some of the most misunderstood animal species out there. Don't write them off though. They are cool. In total, there are about 3,000 different species worldwide. However, there are similarities among all of them. For instance, they all have long, slender bodies. Also, their scaled bodies aren't slimy like you might think. Instead, they are smooth and feel dry. Look for snakes sunning themselves along the road or trail.

LITTLE-KNOWN FACTS

1. Most snakes lay leathery eggs. However, in some species the eggs hatch inside the female snake. Then she gives birth to live babies.
2. Snakes don't have eyelids. This is one reason they can look intimidating. They don't blink at all.
3. Snakes' forked tongue helps them detect pheromones (chemical signals), so snakes are really smelling with their tongues! Isn't that fun? Go ahead and try it. Stick out your tongue and see what you can smell.
4. The shortest snake in the United States is the blind snake (also called the worm snake), and they can be just 5 inches long. The longest snake in the United States is the indigo snake, which can reach nearly 9 feet.
5. Snakes grow throughout their lives, but the rate slows down after they reach maturity. As they grow, they shed their skin.
6. Snakes can unhinge their jaws, which allows them to swallow large prey whole.
7. There are seventeen species of venomous snakes in the United States, but if you leave them alone, they'll usually leave you alone. Don't be afraid of snakes, because snakebites are actually quite rare.
8. Some people think you can tell how old a rattlesnake is by counting the number of rattles, but this is a myth.
9. Snakes are popular pets, but

you should never release a pet into the wild. Places like the Everglades in Florida have become home to numerous pythons and boas, and these nonnative species can damage the local ecosystems and animals that live there.

10. There are native boas in the United States. The rosy and rubber boas are two examples.

Types: 115 species in the United States
Size: From a few inches to many feet, though most around a couple of feet long
Eats: From small invertebrates to medium-size mammals
Eats them: Birds, mammals, other snakes
Range: All continents except Antarctica

GO OUTSIDE

It's such a cool experience to find a snake's skin out in the wild. The skins can be fragile, so it isn't always an easy task to find one still intact. To increase your chance of success, look along rocks or crevices that snakes would crawl over while trying to shed their skin.

LIZARD

Lizards are the most diverse group of reptiles, with almost 5,000 species in the world. They have dry, scaled skin, external ear openings, and eyelids. Some lizards can shed their tail—a handy trick if you are trying to avoid getting eaten by a predator. It can even grow back in some instances. Depending on where you live, lizards can be common in your backyard. They can be hard to spot, though, so maybe you've never seen one. It's worth it to seek one out to watch. Lizards can be quite fascinating.

LITTLE-KNOWN FACTS

1. Most lizards lay eggs, but a few species give birth to live young.
2. Not all lizards have legs. Legless and glass lizards don't.
3. Oklahoma was the first state with an official state reptile. Adopted in 1969, it is the common collared lizard. Other states with lizards as the official state reptile include New Mexico (whiptail lizard), Texas, and Wyoming (horned lizard for both).
4. The largest lizard in the world is the Komodo dragon, weighing a whopping 180 pounds and stretching to 10 feet long.
5. The largest lizard in the United States is the Gila monster, a mere 2 feet and 5 pounds. It's pretty small compared to that Komodo dragon!
6. Skinks are a kind of lizard that have extra-smooth scales.

7. Some lizards perform an action that looks like push-ups. This is a way to display themselves to another lizard (especially during mating season) or a way to defend their territory.

Types: About 5,000 species worldwide
Size: Most are between 5 and 18 inches.
Eats: Varies among species, but can include crickets, caterpillars, and other bugs
Eats them: Birds, mammals, other reptiles
Range: Throughout North America and the world, except in extremely cold places

GO OUTSIDE

Lizards can be hard to spot because they're often camouflaged against the background. They also are great about holding still, so you don't see them until they start to move. Make it a goal to go out and find a lizard before it moves.

ALLIGATOR AND CROCODILE

If you want to sound like a true scientist, you can call crocs and alligators by this name: crocodilians. This is their collective name, and it represents the amazing twenty-plus species that have been around since the age of the dinosaurs. They tend to have a bad reputation to many, but they are magnificent large reptiles.

LITTLE-KNOWN FACTS

1. Crocodilians can close a flap of skin at the back of their throat. This allows them to capture prey with their jaws without water seeping down their throat.

2. Baby crocodilians often ride in their mother's mouth to get around. They also stay with their mom for several months or up to a year before they go out on their own.

3. In the 1950s the American alligator (found in the Southeast) was quickly becoming endangered because many hunted it for its skin. Conservation efforts have helped this species rebound though, and it's doing much better today.

4. During incubation the eggs of alligators are determined to be male or female by the temperature! If it's below 86°F, the hatchlings will be female. If it's above 91°F, they will be males.

5. For the most part, alligators are found in North, Central, and South America, while crocodiles are mostly found in Asia, Africa, and Australia, with a few species in Central and South America and even occasionally in south Florida.

6. Most crocodilians are freshwater animals (one exception is the saltwater crocodile in Asia and Australia, which can grow to more than 20 feet). If you want to see one in the United States, go to places like Texas, Florida, and Louisiana.

7. You mostly think of crocodilians in the water, but they can also climb.

They might climb a tree to get a better view of the area.

8. The crocodilian bite is famous for being powerful and deadly, and it's easy to understand why. They have more than sixty teeth, and they bite down with a force of thousands of pounds.

9. Even though crocodilians can bite down with a huge force, they can't open with the same power. In fact, a crocodilian's mouth can be held shut with a rubber band.

10. Another tooth fact: These large animals go through a lot of teeth. They lose and replace teeth often. They could go through thousands of teeth in a lifetime.

11. Crocs and gators are excellent swimmers and spend a lot of time in the water. They can also hold their breath for an hour.

12. They have excellent hearing. When the young start to hatch from their eggs, the mothers hear this and go to check on them.

Types: More than twenty species throughout the world
Size: 5 to 20 feet
Eats: Fish, birds, small mammals
Eats them: Anacondas, pythons, jaguars, leopards
Range: Worldwide

FROG AND TOAD

Frogs and toads are a common and welcome animal in backyards and alongside ponds and streams. It's just not summer unless you find a frog or a toad. They're fun to catch, examine, and then release to go hopping along their way. Check out some of these amazing facts about the thousands of species of frogs and toads in the world.

LITTLE-KNOWN FACTS

1. Unlike most amphibians, frogs and toads have no tail. They lose their tail while they are transforming from their larval (tadpole) stage to adults.
2. While frog and toad feet can vary based on needs, they all have four toes on the front and five on the back. Those toes can vary from being webbed (for good swimming) to long, fingerlike structures for climbing and gripping.
3. Have you ever heard frogs and toads call? It's definitely not just a ribbit, ribbit. Their calls are so varied and so cool! They are able to do this with vocal sacs. The sacs fill up with air, producing the sound.
4. Some frogs and toads have this amazing ability to freeze during the winter—for instance, the wood frog of North America. They slow down their metabolism and even form ice crystals inside their bodies. But the high levels of glucose in their bodies keep their organs from freezing completely.
5. Some of the deadliest animals in the entire world can be frogs. While you don't have to worry about poisonous frogs in the United States, they are out there. They're mostly found in tropical areas, like the brightly colored poison dart frogs of Central and South America.
6. This fact is both cool and gross: Most frogs shed their skin often—they'll even eat it!
7. A group of frogs has a really awesome name. They are called an army!
8. Frogs don't chew their food. They have to swallow it whole.
9. Frog and toad eggs vary a great deal— they can be distributed in the water, in large groups, or even sit on the back of a

frog. In fact, a toad in Europe called the midwife toad has the male carry the eggs on his back.

10. We want to set the record straight about something. There's a myth that says you can get warts by just touching a toad. This is not true. You can't get warts by touching toads or frogs.

11. Many people define toads as being more common on land, with rougher skin, while frogs spend more time around the water and have smoother skin. This isn't entirely the case, but it's a good rule of thumb.

12. Frogs don't need to drink water—they can just absorb it through their skin.

Types: More than 5,000 species worldwide
Size: Varies, mostly from 2 to 8 inches
Eats: Mice, birds, snakes, insects
Eats them: Many predators, including birds and otters
Range: Lots of frogs and toads worldwide

GO OUTSIDE

It's fairly easy to catch a toad or a frog, so put your skills to the test in a different way. Catch a tadpole instead. You will probably need a little net to help you out. After all, they are tiny, and they move fast! Once you do capture one, take a closer look and imagine that thing turning into a frog.

SALAMANDER

Salamanders are grouped in with newts in the amphibian world. While they might look like a lizard at first glance, they are actually more closely related to frogs and toads. The range varies quite a bit, but you can find at least one type of salamander in much of the United States, so be on the lookout for these cool critters.

LITTLE-KNOWN FACTS

1. Some salamanders have an impressive ability to regrow parts of their body, including toes and tails. Sometimes they can do this in as little as two weeks!
2. Yes, salamanders look like lizards, but unlike lizards, they actually have smooth and glossy skin. They have to stay moist.
3. A salamander has a very long tongue for catching its prey. Some salamanders have tongues longer than their bodies!
4. Most salamanders have both gills and lungs, but there is a family of salamanders that doesn't have lungs at all. They breathe through their skin instead.
5. The mudpuppy is a type of salamander found in North America. They have feathery outer gills that are bright red and look like they are bleeding.
6. The largest salamander in the world is the Chinese giant salamander. It can reach more than 6 feet long!
7. The tiger salamander is one of the most widespread in the United States. It's one of the most colorful salamanders too, with yellow stripes and blotches across its body. Females can lay up to 7,000 eggs in a single season.

Types: Hundreds of species worldwide; more than a dozen in North America
Size: From a few inches to more than 40 inches
Eats: Frogs, leeches, insects, eggs, worms
Eats them: Fish, reptiles, larger amphibians
Range: Small ranges, though species found throughout North America

SCIENCE Q&A:
What Are Ephemeral Ponds?

"Ephemeral" is a fancy term for something that only lasts for a short while. So ephemeral ponds are only ponds for part of the year, and then they dry up. They aren't just puddles of water though. Ephemeral ponds (sometimes called vernal pools) are essential habitats for numerous plants and animals that depend on these unique areas. These are really cool spots to explore.

Ephemeral ponds are usually low areas that collect melting snow or rainwater. They can be surprisingly deep, and the water might remain in them for many months. The water slowly soaks into the ground; some of it also evaporates. You might think that nothing could live in a pond that isn't a pond all year long. But there are many species that are adapted to survive these annual wet and dry cycles.

Ephemeral ponds can be especially important to amphibians. Major movements of amphibians can occur in spring as the adults head to these ponds for breeding. They can lay their eggs in the ponds. These hatch out, and the larvae survive in the water. The larvae then go through metamorphosis and reach the adult stage. They then can breathe air and no longer need to live underwater, so it doesn't matter that their pond is drying up. Fish can be major predators of amphibian eggs and larvae, so one major advantage of ephemeral ponds for amphibians is that fish can't survive in them.

Amphibians aren't the only things that call ephemeral ponds home though. So do lots of invertebrates, which the amphibians can feast on.

Spring is often the best time for exploring ephemeral ponds. It might be your only chance during the year to spot some salamanders or frog tadpoles. So put on some rubber boots, get out there, and explore.

HUMMINGBIRD

Nicknamed "flying jewels" by many people, these tiny creatures are true wonders of the bird world. They are mostly known for showing up in summer, and there are oodles of fascinating facts about them. If you don't already love these teeny-tiny fliers, you will soon. You'll be putting out a sugar-water feeder to attract them.

LITTLE-KNOWN FACTS

1. Hummingbirds are the only birds that can fly backward.
2. A hummingbird's egg is about the size of a jellybean!
3. Though the hummingbird species in North America are limited, there are more than 300 species around the world.
4. The average hummingbird weighs about as much as a nickel.
5. A hummingbird's heart beats at a rate of more than 1,000 times per minute, which is nearly ten times the rate of most people! At rest, these birds also take about 250 breaths per minute.
6. In most species the male hummingbird is the one with the bright, flashy colors. They are the ones with the colorful red, purple, and blue throats and heads. Female hummingbirds are mostly green all over.
7. Hummingbirds have a long tongue, which they use to lap up nectar.
8. A hummingbird's nest is about the size of a golf ball. Hummingbirds lay an average of two eggs.
9. When it's cold hummingbirds can conserve their energy by going into a state of torpor. This means they lower their metabolism and body temperature.
10. When flying, hummingbirds can reach speeds of about 30 miles per hour. When diving, that speed can be as high as 60 miles per hour.
11. The bee hummingbird (though not found in North America) is the

smallest bird in the entire world. It's only a couple of inches long!

12. Hummingbirds are found only in the Western Hemisphere, so they aren't worldwide. This means you're not going to see a hummingbird in a huge part of the world, including Asia.

Types: More than a dozen species in North America
Size: Very small, most only 3 to 4 inches
Eats: Lots of insects, nectar from flowers, and sugar water from backyard feeders
Eats them: Larger birds, small mammals, even praying mantids
Range: The ruby-throated hummingbird is found in the eastern half of the United States. Other hummingbird species are concentrated in the West, especially the Southwest.

GO OUTSIDE

You can attract hummingbirds by mixing up four parts water to one part sugar. Make sure the sugar completely dissolves, and then put it in a sugar-water feeder. Don't add red food coloring to the water. It's not necessary, and it could even harm the birds. Late spring is the perfect time to attract hummingbirds.

DESTINATIONS: Nature Centers

Nature centers can be great places to explore during the spring. Reptiles and amphibians are reemerging from their winter stupor. Migratory birds return in waves. And tree buds start to pop, so there's something to see wherever you go.

WHO? Nature centers can be good for a short visit, or they can offer a place to explore day after day all year long. They'll have activities and learning opportunities for all ages. Nature tot programs are growing in popularity for the youngest of explorers. Or ask about starting up a family nature club or a young-birders club at your local nature center. Nature centers often offer programs for schools, scouts, and civic groups. Some even host birthday parties!

WHAT? A nature center can be a grand place to explore on your own or with a professional naturalist guide. Many will have interpretive trails to help you understand what you see around you. Be sure to check out the inside of the center for a chance to explore touch tables, see displays, and learn about upcoming events. Get up close to nature while exploring the bird-feeding stations or butterfly gardens.

WHEN? Take advantage of the longer days and the warmer temperatures to explore outside. Some nature centers will have shorter trails while others will have an extensive network of trails suitable for all-day excursions. Many are open sunrise to sunset, and some will offer special night-hike events and owl prowls.

WHERE? Nature centers can be operated by any number of organizations, but the one thing they all have in common is they are outstanding places to go for nature adventures. Many are free, while some require a small entrance fee, trail fee, or program fees. Family memberships can often get you year-round access to these wonderful facilities.

WHY? Nature centers are perfect because they highlight the local plants and animals that you'll be able to find in your own backyard. They'll have tons of hands-on learning experiences for everyone.

TIPS AND TRICKS: Bird observatories are similar to nature centers, but they have an added focus on researching birds. Many bird observatories offer educational programs and bird-banding demonstrations, and some host International Migratory Bird Day celebrations each May. If you have a special interest in birds, look into this great resource. You can also consider volunteering. They'll have something you can do to help out.

DUCK

Lots of birds get lumped into the duck family, but you might want to be careful about lumping all water birds as ducks. For instance, grebes, loons, coots, and auks all look duck-like, but they are different bird families altogether. Ducks are often underappreciated too. It's easy to see ducks swimming on a lake or river, but you probably don't really pay them much attention. It's time to show ducks some respect!

LITTLE-KNOWN FACTS

1. Ducks are divided into dabblers and divers. The dabblers stay mostly on top of the water and just dip their heads in the water for food. But the divers actually dive down for food.
2. Ducks are another bird with males that are usually more brightly colored. For instance, the male mallard has a bright-green head, while the female is brown overall.
3. You often see or hear about people who have pet ducks. These are usually domestic ducks, and they often look a bit different from wild

ducks. Every once in a while, a domestic duck will escape, and you might mistakenly think you've discovered a new species.

4. Male ducks have a grand name. They are called drakes. Doesn't that sound like royalty?
5. Most ducklings take off and swim to the water almost immediately after hatching. They can be swimming within a few hours.
6. You know the duck's quack sound? Well, not all ducks quack. Plus, it's often the female that is doing that familiar quacking. Most male ducks make a few sounds, but they're not the traditional quack we think of.
7. Ducks can keep one eye open when they sleep as a way to watch out for danger.

Types: More than thirty species in North America
Size: Many ducks are around 20 inches, but the size can vary.
Eats: Algae, plants, and insects; some ducks eat small water creatures, including some fish.
Eats them: Birds of prey, snakes, turtles; people during duck-hunting season
Range: Many duck species throughout the United States; most migrate, so they'll head to coasts in winter.

GO OUTSIDE

You're almost guaranteed to find ducklings if you visit local ponds in spring. See how many different duck species you can see, and count the ducklings.

SCIENCE Q&A:
What Is Migration?

What do birds do in winter? They fly south, don't they? Or do they? Lots of birds migrate south for the winter, but plenty of others stay in the same location all year long.

Migration is a seasonal movement between areas. Some species fly a few hundred miles south, but others move to the tropics, thousands of miles away, for the winter. All the species that migrate need to have places to stop and rest along the way. They'll refuel with food and water. They might stick around for a few weeks, or they might just make a short pit stop. Then they continue on their journey.

Hummingbirds fly nonstop across the Gulf of Mexico on their migration, and blackpoll warblers fly for three days straight over the Atlantic Ocean on their way to South America. Migration can be dangerous and really hard on birds, so why do they do it? It often has to do with food, which is a pretty essential requirement. Birds fly to find the food they need to survive.

The arctic tern has the most epic migration. It flies from the Arctic to near Antarctica and back every year. These elegant fliers can cover more than 25,000 miles each year. They basically follow summer around the globe. Much of this migration happens out over the ocean, but you can sometimes see them from the coasts or near other bodies of water.

Birds aren't the only animals that migrate. Some mammals also migrate. The caribou herds of Alaska and northern Canada make long migrations each year between their calving and wintering grounds. Some species of bats migrate south for the winter. Another flier, the monarch butterfly, is a champion migrator. Most head to Mexico or California for winter.

Some people mark the arrival of spring on their wall calendar. But people who like nature often define spring as the moment their favorite migrating bird returns from its southern wintering range.

EAGLE

This next bird is one of the most well known and respected in the country. The bald eagle is our national symbol, often associated with freedom and patriotism. All eagles are graceful, magnificent birds that never fail to impress when you see them in the wild. They always look grand, whether they're just perched or flying high in the sky. There are plenty of reasons to be impressed by these stunning birds.

LITTLE-KNOWN FACTS

1. Bald eagles return to the same nest year after year. Eventually the nest can weigh hundreds of pounds! So if you can find where a bald eagle nest is, you can see young bald eagles every year.
2. Eagles were in serious trouble in the 1950s because of a chemical called DDT, which really hurt these birds by affecting their eggshells. Today they are thriving once again, a true conservation success story.
3. Bald eagles have that classic white head, but it actually takes them a few years to get it. When they are young, they are all brown, and they can often be mistaken for golden eagles.
4. All eagles can live a really long time. In the wild they might live twenty or thirty years.
5. When they dive eagles can reach a speed of nearly 100 miles per hour.
6. While most young birds leave the nest a couple of weeks after hatching, eagles stay for about three months. Even when they do leave, they stick around the area, begging their parents to keep feeding them for a few more weeks.
7. Eagles are fierce hunters, but they'll also take a free meal. You might see them scavenging for dead animals.

Types: Two eagle species in North America—the bald eagle and the golden eagle

Size: Both sit around 30 inches tall and have a wingspan of 80 inches.

Eats: Eagles feed on a wide range of both large and small mammals as well as reptiles, amphibians, and other birds.

Eats them: Eagles are at the top of the food chain, and they don't have many predators as adults. Mammals will prey on the eggs or young.

Range: Look for bald eagles throughout North America; golden eagles have a smaller range, mostly in the West, but they will migrate to areas of the East.

GO OUTSIDE

Eagle nests can be a challenge to find, but once you do find one, you can usually find it again, year after year. Make this the year you find an eagle's nest, usually in the tops of trees. If you need help, reach out to your local bird club or Audubon organization to see if they know where one is in the area.

OWL

Owls fascinate people all over the world. They have gained a lot of popularity in the past several years, maybe in part because of Harry Potter. Actually, there have been lots of owl characters in movies and literature over the years. No matter how you think of owls, they are interesting creatures. They have reputations for being wise and mysterious. While this may or may not be true, they do have some pretty amazing abilities.

LITTLE-KNOWN FACTS

1. While owls mostly stick to themselves, a group of owls is called a parliament.
2. It might seem that owls can turn their heads all the way around, but that's not really the case. They can turn their heads about 270 degrees but not a full 360 degrees.
3. Some owls often have to survive in the cold because their range goes well into northern areas. One thing that allows them to do this is having feathers that go all the way down on their feet too.
4. Owls don't create (or excavate) their own nests out of trees. Instead they find nests that have been created by other birds.
5. They are one of the earliest nesters around. Many owl species will seek out a nest and lay eggs when it's still winter.
6. The eyes of owls are unique. They don't really have eyeballs like we do. Think of them as having long eye tubes instead that go way back into their heads.
7. Owls are fantastic hunters, and a big reason is because of their amazing hearing. They can detect prey animals from a great distance and then swoop in to kill them.

8. Owls have amazing feathers. They not only keep the bird extremely warm with great insulation but also help it be stealthy. You can barely hear owls fly. This helps them be great hunters.

9. All owls hoot, right? Not true. Some owls barely make sounds of more than a squeak.

10. Some owls nest in tree cavities. Owls in the Southwest will nest in cacti.

11. Owls don't chew their food. They swallow it bones and all. Later on, they cough up something called an owl pellet. This looks almost like a piece of poop, and it contains things the birds aren't able to digest, like teeth or claws!

12. Most owls are farsighted, so they see much better far away than right in front of them.

Types: Nearly twenty species in North America

Size: Varies a great deal, from the small elf owl (only 5 inches) to the great gray owl (27 to 30 inches)

Eats: Also at the top of the food chain, owls feed on a wide variety of small mammals, birds, snakes, reptiles, and more.

Eats them: Few things eat owls, but other large raptors will, and mammals will try to eat their eggs or young.

Range: Owls are common throughout the country. The great horned owl is most common, found almost everywhere in North America year-round.

GO OUTSIDE

If not all owls hoot, what do they do? Go online and look up these three owls—great horned owl, screech owl, and snowy owl. You'll quickly see that owls don't sound alike at all. Now learn these sounds, especially of the great horned and screech owls. These are the two you're most likely to hear around your backyard.

HAWK

Hawks are smaller than eagles, and you can find lots of them in your area, flying alongside highways and even showing up in backyards. Hawks can be both challenging and fun to try to identify. First test your skills when hawks are perched. Then if you want a challenge, test them out when hawks are flying. They are powerful, just like eagles and owls, and they definitely deserve your respect.

LITTLE-KNOWN FACTS

1. If you think eagles are fast, you'll really be impressed by hawks. Some species can reach speeds of 150 miles per hour when diving.
2. For many animals, the males are bigger. But this isn't the case with hawks. Females are larger than the males.
3. Hawks have hooked bills, which are very strong. They use these bills to tear flesh from their prey.
4. During mating seasons hawks perform a mating ritual of acrobatic flight. This can last several minutes as the males try to impress the females.
5. Hawks have impressive eyesight. They can see prey (like a rabbit) more than a mile away.
6. If you have bird feeders in your backyard, you'll likely see a hawk stalking it sometime, waiting for an unwary songbird. Chances are you're seeing a Cooper's hawk or a sharp-shinned hawk. They are the most common backyard bird hunters.
7. If hawks have a big meal, they can go many days without needing to eat again.

Types: Around twenty different hawks in North America
Size: Most hawks range between 17 and 20 inches, with wingspans between 30 and 50 inches.
Eats: Small mammals and birds, reptiles, amphibians
Eats them: Like other birds of prey, few things eat hawks, but they have to watch out for large mammals, especially when they are young.
Range: Hawks are found across the country, with the red-tailed being the most widespread, but be sure to look for other species in your specific area.

WOODPECKER

Several woodpecker species are common in the backyard, and they'll come to feeders to eat suet, peanuts, peanut butter, and seed. Go ahead and get to know your backyard woodpeckers. You might be surprised at how many different species you can attract. Beyond the backyard, though, you can find many other types of woodpeckers throughout the country. All the birds in this family have similar features and abilities.

LITTLE-KNOWN FACTS

1. Why do woodpeckers peck wood? It's usually either to dig out a hole for nesting or to search for bugs to eat. The drumming sound can also help establish territory and attract mates.
2. The tongue of a woodpecker can be two or three times the size of its head. Woodpeckers use this extremely long tongue to help them reach into trees to catch insects.
3. The name "woodpecker" is pretty literal—it means that the birds peck

wood. They can peck up to twenty times per second.

4. The woodpecker's skull is unique because it has special air pockets. This allows their brain to be safe and protected from all of that pounding.

5. Most woodpeckers have zygodactyl feet, which means they have two toes in the front and two in the back. Of course there can be exceptions, like the three-toed woodpecker. This structure helps them grip onto trees and other surfaces.

6. You can see woodpeckers on every continent except Australia. Worldwide, there are about 200 species.

7. Woodpeckers have many different nesting habits. They nest in trees and birdhouses, and those in the Southwest also use cacti.

8. With many woodpecker species, the males have red on their heads while the females do not. Get a good field guide to see what you're looking for.

9. A couple of now-extinct woodpeckers were huge. The imperial woodpecker, for example, was nearly 2 feet long!

10. Sapsuckers are a type of woodpecker that drill in trees, looking for sap. You can find signs of their drilling by looking for several holes in a row on a tree.

Types: Nearly twenty species in North America; some of the most common include hairy, downy, and red-bellied woodpeckers.

Size: Woodpeckers range in size from the downy woodpecker at 6 inches to the pileated woodpecker at 17 inches.

Eats: Insects, nuts, berries; backyard feeders for suet and seeds

Eats them: Larger birds and mammals that eat birds

Range: You can find a few different woodpecker species anywhere in North America, so find out which woodpeckers to look for in your area.

GO OUTSIDE

Woodpecker holes are all over backyards, parks, and woods. If you don't know what the holes look like, do a little research online first. Then go on a hike to see how many different woodpecker holes you can find. You could even make it a game and challenge your friends!

CARDINAL

Though the popular northern cardinal is found only in the eastern half of the United States, it's still one of the most well-known birds in North America. You can easily spot cardinals year-round because the male birds are so flashy with their vibrant red feathers. The females' red hues are more subtle, but they are still easy to recognize. When you see a male, there's a good chance a female is nearby.

LITTLE-KNOWN FACTS

1. The northern cardinal is the state bird of seven states: Illinois, Indiana, Kentucky, North Carolina, Ohio, Virginia, and West Virginia.
2. Female cardinals sing. This is uncommon in the bird world, because males usually do the singing.
3. Cardinals can raise multiple clutches of babies each summer.
4. Young cardinals have dark beaks that turn bright red-orange by fall.
5. The massive bill helps crack open seeds and nuts. In addition to black oil sunflower seeds, some people attract cardinals to their feeders with safflower seeds.
6. Northern cardinals and pyrrhuloxias (desert cardinals) are closely related to the vermilion cardinal of South America. They are more distantly related to some bunting and grosbeak species.
7. Male cardinals can be quite territorial during breeding season and are sometimes seen pecking at their own reflections on windows.

Types: The northern cardinal is in the eastern United States; the pyrrhuloxia, or desert cardinal, is found in the Southwest.
Size: 9 inches
Eats: Insects, seeds
Eats them: Larger birds, small mammals
Range: Northern cardinals are mostly eastern birds, so they aren't found in places like California or Montana; the pyrrhuloxia has a very small North American range in Texas, Arizona, and New Mexico.

PELICAN

When you think of a pelican, the first thing you probably imagine is a bird with a huge bill, right? Well, this is true, but this isn't the only thing that makes these birds ultra-cool. Look for pelicans around water, often near the ocean but sometimes far inland.

LITTLE-KNOWN FACTS

1. Although the average lifespan is much less, the oldest brown pelican lived to be 43 years old and the oldest American white pelican was more than 23 years old.
2. It might be tempting to think so, but pelicans don't actually store fish in their large bill pouches.
3. Flying brown pelicans feed by making a plunge-dive into the water.
4. American white pelicans feed a little differently. They scoop up fish while swimming along.
5. Brown pelican populations have rebounded since the United States implemented pesticide restrictions.
6. Pelicans will sometimes flap their throats and pouches. This is called a gular flutter, and it helps keep the birds cool.
7. Pelicans can incubate their eggs with their feet.
8. There are only about sixty total breeding colonies of American white pelicans. One of the largest is on Yellowstone Lake in Yellowstone National Park.
9. Pelican species are found on every continent except Antarctica.

Types: Two species in North America—the American white pelican and the brown pelican
Size: White pelicans are roughly 60 inches, with a wingspan of 108 inches; brown pelicans are smaller, 50 inches and a wingspan of 84 inches.
Eats: Fish
Eats them: Because they're bigger birds, they don't have a lot of predators, but an alligator or coyote would eat one if it could catch it.
Range: American white pelicans are found along the Gulf Coast, Florida, and California. They'll also go inland in specific areas of North America in summer and during migration. Brown pelicans mostly stick to the southern coasts of the United States.

SCIENCE Q&A:
What Does Habitat Mean for Animals?

Animals all need the same basic things to survive: food, water, shelter, and space. Together these are termed "habitat." Different species depend on different habitats though. For instance, a mallard duck needs different food than a red-headed woodpecker. A screech owl finds shelter in a tree cavity, while a roadrunner might seek shelter under a cactus.

You can help animals out by making sure they have protected habitats to live in. Animals might not get everything they need in your backyard, so this is where it's important to support conservation efforts. However, you can do a small part by adding valuable habitat right in your own backyard.

How? For starters, you can put up a bird feeder. Black oil sunflower seeds will attract the most birds. You can also add some suet and some thistle feeders. Before long you'll have a whole buffet for the birds.

Birdbaths can be a nice addition to a backyard habitat too. They aren't just for birds though. Plenty of squirrels, chipmunks, maybe even a raccoon after dark, will take a drink from the bath.

Shelter can take many forms for birds and other animals in your backyard. A simple brush pile can give animals a place to avoid predators and keep out of the rain or the snow. You can also put out homes for animals. Toad abodes can give shelter to toads. Nest boxes are popular for some bird species, including chickadees and wrens.

Space is a little trickier. Only so many animals can live in a certain area. Don't forget to support conservation efforts to preserve space so that future birds and animals have a place to live.

CHICKADEE

If you had a popularity contest for birds, the chickadee would make a run for the title. Sure, it might look like a plain, black-and-white bird at first, but these little guys are common all across North America. They are also often described as being friendly. No matter what type of chickadee you have in your area, these are pretty adorable birds that will surely go on your most-loved-birds list. That is if they're not on there already.

1. If it seems like chickadees are always coming to your feeder, it might be because they're taking the seeds off to hide them. They will hide (cache) seeds for later.
2. Many people have trained chickadees to eat from their hand.
3. Chickadees make a whistling call that sounds like Cheeeeeeeese-Bur-Ger. Listen for this sound when you're out and about.
4. Most chickadees travel in groups. So if you see one, there are usually more around.
5. Alaska has several chickadee species that the rest of North America doesn't see. Chestnut-backed, boreal, and gray-headed are all chickadees that you can only see in the far north.
6. If you head to the East, look for the Carolina chickadee. If you go to southern Arizona, look for the Mexican chickadee. There really are different chickadees in every part of the country!

Types: Seven different chickadee species in North America
Size: Most are right around 5 inches.
Eats: Seeds, berries, insects
Eats them: Larger birds and bird predators
Range: The black-capped chickadee is the most common and widespread in North America. Others chickadees, like the Carolina, boreal, mountain, and chestnut-backed, have more limited ranges.

SECTION 3: THE MAMMALS

BEAR

There are three different bear species in North America. You have the wide-spread black bear, found from the swamps of Florida all the way to Alaska. You have the polar bears of the Alaskan and Canadian Arctic. Then there's the brown bear in Alaska, Canada, and other small areas of the Northwest. No matter what species you're talking about, all bears are remarkable creatures. They are strong, powerful, and great survivors.

LITTLE-KNOWN FACTS

1. Did you think we were missing a bear because we didn't talk about grizzlies? They are actually the same species as brown bears.
2. Black bears aren't always black. They can be brown, cinnamon, or even blonde.
3. Black bear and grizzly bear cubs can stay with their mothers for up to eighteen months. Polar bears can stay together for nearly two and a half years!
4. Black bears and grizzly bears are omnivorous, meaning they eat both plant and animal matter. Polar bears have a more carnivorous diet, heavy in meat.
5. Ants and moth larvae can provide critical calories for bears, especially when other food is scarce. Grizzly bears will also dig up ground squirrels and plant roots with their long claws.

6. In preparation for hibernation grizzly bears can gain up to 3 pounds of body weight per day.
7. Not all bears actually hibernate. In warmer southern climates black bears do not. They stay active, looking for food; they'll also climb trees.
8. Polar bears can travel more than 20 miles in a single day.
9. If necessary, polar bears can go for months without eating, surviving on their stored body fat.
10. Polar bear babies are about a foot long and weigh just a pound or so when they are born in the winter. They nurse on their mother's milk for many months before emerging from the snow den.
11. Polar bears will sit at a breathing hole, waiting for seals to pop up from under the ice.
12. Underneath all that gorgeous white fur, polar bears have black skin.

Types: Three species in North America—black, brown, and polar
Size: Most are 4 to 9 feet; they can weigh from 100 to 2,000 pounds.
Eats: Highly variable, including both plant and animal matter
Eats them: Very few predators; they're most vulnerable when young, so mothers are very protective.
Range: Black bears are scattered throughout North America, brown bears are found in parts of the West up to Alaska, and polar bears are found throughout the Arctic.

GO OUTSIDE

Since it might be difficult to see several bear species all in one place in the wild, it's time to head to the zoo. Look for the different bears, and notice their similarities and differences. Also pay close attention to their behavior. How are they the same? How are they different? Can you find any bears at the zoo that aren't native to North America?

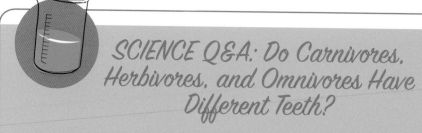

SCIENCE Q&A: Do Carnivores, Herbivores, and Omnivores Have Different Teeth?

Lots of animals have teeth, but mammal teeth are some of the most impressive and specialized. For example, the teeth of mammals are deep-rooted and covered with a hard enamel surface. While mammal teeth are similar in structure, there are many different types of teeth. Give yourself a big toothy smile next time you look in a mirror. Look at those back teeth too. Do they look the same as your front teeth? What about dogs and cats? Do their teeth look the same as yours?

Depending on what animals eat, the shape of the teeth can be very different. Carnivores are mostly meat-eaters. They have sharp teeth for shredding and cutting. Herbivores eat mostly plant materials. Their teeth are suited for grinding up plant matter. Omnivores eat a little bit of everything, so they have teeth that are able to chew both meats and vegetation. Nature centers often have skulls on display. Look for a herbivore skull (maybe a deer), a carnivore skull (perhaps a coyote), and an omnivore skull (like a black bear). What looks the same? What looks different?

Incisors are the front teeth. They are used to nip, cut, and bite. The first bite you take out of an apple is with your incisors. It's the same for animals. They'll bite off grass, a twig, or a chunk of meat. Rodents like mice and beavers have incisors that grow. The gnawing they are known for helps wear their teeth down and keeps them sharp and chiseled. Canine teeth are the long pointy teeth behind the incisors. Humans have them too. Human canines aren't that impressive, but carnivores can have major canine teeth. The upper and lower canine teeth can overlap when animals bite. This makes these teeth great for tearing off meat to eat. Some herbivores lack canine teeth, while others have stubby little canine teeth that aren't very useful. Walrus tusks are specialized canine teeth.

The premolars and molars are the back teeth. In herbivores these are broad and flat. This helps them grind and chew on plants. In carnivores the back teeth are sharp and pointy. They are like little meat tenderizers breaking down the meat. Omnivore premolars and molars are shaped a little bit in between the teeth of herbivores and carnivores. This makes sense because they eat both plants and meat.

You can learn a lot about an animal just by looking at its skull and teeth. Scientists can tell different species based on their teeth. Sometimes they can tell how old individuals are too. So look for skulls to examine next time you're on a nature hike, or hit that local nature center and ask questions.

SEA LION

You might just think of one type of sea lion when you think of this animal, but there are actually six species in North America, which includes both sea lions and fur seals. They're counted in the same group because they are both eared seals, which means they have external ears. While you do have to live near the ocean if you want to see these animals regularly, they're worth a trip to the shore to see if you can spot them in the wild. The Pacific coast is home to North America's eared seals, including the Steller's and California sea lions and the northern and Guadalupe fur seals. Otherwise, study these animals at the aquarium. These highly social animals can be fascinating to watch.

LITTLE-KNOWN FACTS

1. Populations of sea lions and fur seals are in serious danger, perhaps due to historic overhunting, declines in food sources, and shifting climates. We need to do our part to help conservation efforts for these wonderful animals.

2. They spend much of their lives at sea, diving deep to feed.
3. California sea lions can spend up to 20 minutes underwater.
4. Sea lion males have shaggy hair around the head and neck, similar but less obvious than a lion's mane. Males can also be four times larger than the females.
5. Sea lions can rotate their back flippers around, allowing them to walk on land. Well, "walk" might be a generous term, but you get the picture.
6. Sea lion males will vigorously defend the rocky coasts and protect multiple females during the breeding season.
7. Large gatherings of sea lions during breeding season are called rookeries. These can be really loud, with lots of grunting, roaring, and barking. Sea lions also have a loud, trumpeting alarm call when there is danger.
8. California sea lion males move north along the coast in the fall and winter.
9. Steller's sea lions are the largest species; they can weigh well over 1,000 pounds.
10. Sea lions' underfur can be up to fifty times thicker than land mammal hair. This, and a superthick layer of blubber, help keep the animals warm.
11. Some sea lions live in tropical areas like the Galapagos; others live in Australia and New Zealand.
12. Sea lions can swim up to 25 miles per hour.

Types: Six species
Size: 4 to 10 feet, 100 to 1,000 pounds
Eats: Fish, squid, octopuses, crabs, clams
Eats them: Sharks, orcas
Range: Pacific coast and Pacific Ocean

WALRUS

Even though very few people ever get to see them in the wild, the walrus is one of the most easily recognized species. Both the males and females have the iconic tusks. They are a North American animal, though you'll only find them in the extreme north. If you want to see one up close, your best bet is to hit your local aquarium or zoo.

LITTLE-KNOWN FACTS

1. Along with seals and sea lions, walruses are classified as pinnipeds. This means they are fin-footed.
2. As with other pinnipeds, the whiskers of the walrus are highly sensitive hairs called vibrissae. They have important functions, one of which is to help detect vibrations in the water.
3. The tusks of a walrus are a type of long canine teeth. They use their tusks to help pull their bodies out of the water and to chop breathing holes in the ice.
4. Males also use their tusks to display and attract females. Every once in a while, they will fight each other with them.
5. There are two subspecies of walrus, the Pacific and the Atlantic. As you've

probably guessed, one is found along the Pacific coast while the other is along the Atlantic.

6. Walrus pups sometimes "hitchhike" and get a ride on the backs of their mother.

7. The scientific name for walrus, Odobenus rosmarus, actually means "tooth-walking sea horse."

8. Walruses need thick skin to survive incredibly cold conditions. Their skin can actually be 4 inches thick.

9. Can walruses get sunburned? This might not be the right word for it, but their skin can change color. It's usually a grayish brown, but it turns rose-red if they bask in the sun.

10. Male walruses weigh about twice as much as females.

Types: One species (two subspecies), which can be found in extreme northern areas in North America and across the world
Size: 8 to 11 feet and up to 4,000 pounds
Eats: Mollusks, especially clams, shrimp, and crabs
Eats them: Polar bears, orcas
Range: Northern Pacific, Atlantic, and Arctic Oceans

SCIENCE Q&A:
Can People Really
Identify Animals by Their Scat?

The short answer is yes. But first, do you know what scat is? "Scat" is a fancy word for animal poop. You might think that all poop looks alike, but that's not true.

Many people can just look at a pile of poop and tell you exactly what animal it came from. That's right, this is a science, just like identifying animal tracks. And, yes, there are books on scat—size, shape, type—as well.

It's easy just to say that large scat is from large animals and small scat is from small animals, but it's not as simple as that. So it's time to start practicing. What are you looking for? Notice the size—is it big or small? Next, notice the shape—is it all in a big pile or is it long and skinny? Maybe it's in pellet form, which is probably one of the most common scats in backyards around the country. (This is likely rabbit scat.)

If you're brave enough, grab a stick and poke around in the scat you find. Based on what you find inside, you might be able to tell what the animal has been eating. For example, if you find hair and bones in the scat, it's definitely from a meat-eater.

You probably never thought you'd be looking at and analyzing scat so much, but it's a pretty fascinating area of science once you start looking. If you can increase your ability to recognize animal tracks and scat, you'll definitely know what animals are in your area. This is a great skill to have, because chances are there are many more animals in your area than you think. You might not ever get the chance to see them in person, but it's satisfying to know that you can recognize their other signs.

DEER

Deer are high on the list of wildlife that are somewhat easy to see. So if you're trying to increase your list of animals seen in the wild, try spotting a few different deer types. They are most active in the morning and at dusk, especially during the fall. Most deer populations are very strong. It's true that deer are popular among hunters, but here are a few things you might not know.

LITTLE-KNOWN FACTS

1. Does the white-tailed deer really have a white tail? It does, but it's mostly the underside of the tail that is white.
2. Male deer are called bucks; females are called does.
3. Mule deer sometimes hop along on all four legs like a pogo stick. This bounding is called stotting.
4. Breeding season for deer is called rutting. During this time two bucks might face off, bellowing and behaving aggressively. If things escalate, the two deer will lock antlers to fight.
5. Deer shed their antlers in winter, usually by February. In spring they start to grow a whole new set.
6. Even though deer grow new antlers every year, they can still be a sign of age. Larger, more developed antlers can mean a deer is older. The antlers of really old animals, and those that aren't healthy, won't grow as big.
7. Moose, elk, and caribou are actually part of the deer family.
8. Baby deer (called fawns) are born with spots on their backs. They lose those spots when they're around 5 months old.
9. A "buck rub" is when bucks rub their antlers on trees or shrubs to mark their territory. When you're out on a hike, you can look for buck rubs a few feet off the ground.

Types: Two species in North America—white-tailed and mule
Size: Most around 5 to 7 feet
Eats: Plants, fruit, acorns and other nuts
Eats them: Wolves, coyotes, big cats, people
Range: White-tailed deer throughout most of North America, mule deer in the West

GO OUTSIDE

Make it a goal to see a baby deer (called a fawn). It's really cool to see fawns in the wild, especially when they're really little and still have their spots, which will eventually fade. Sometimes the mother deer will hide her fawn in tall grass. If you come across one, you'll definitely want to keep your distance. Don't touch them or approach too closely.

CARIBOU

Caribou are great migrators of the North. Some populations make one of the longest mammal migrations in the world and can travel more than 3,000 miles each year over the tundra. Others remain in the same forest all year long. They are popular though. After all, Canadians put the caribou on the back of their quarter. Now that's a real tribute!

1. You want to know another name for caribou? Reindeer! Yep, they really are the same species.
2. Caribou are the only deer species in which both males and females grow antlers. Males shed their antlers in late fall, while females don't shed theirs until well into the winter.
3. Baby caribou (called calves) can stand shortly after they are born, and they can keep up with their mothers just days later.
4. Caribou calves lack the spots that most babies in the deer family have.
5. The forests of northern Idaho and eastern Washington once had a sizable population of caribou, but today they are extremely rare there.
6. Caribou feet are extra-large. This keeps the animals from sinking too deep in wet conditions, and the feet act as snowshoes in winter.
7. Their hollow hair helps insulate caribou. They also have adaptations in their noses that helps them breathe in cold air. This is because their nose hairs are short so they don't get frozen.
8. You might not think of these animals as being great swimmers, but they do just fine in the water.

Types: Numerous subspecies throughout northern North America
Size: Around 4 to 5 feet and about 250 to 600 pounds
Eats: Grasses, forbs, lichen
Eats them: Wolves, bears, golden eagles
Range: Throughout northern North America

GO OUTSIDE

You don't have to travel to the cold and snow to see reindeer. These animals have become popular pets. They have even been domesticated in some areas. Look in your area to see if there is an animal farm or somewhere else where you can visit reindeer and see them up close.

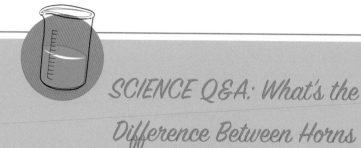

SCIENCE Q&A: What's the Difference Between Horns and Antlers?

Many people substitute the terms "horn" and "antler" with each other, but did you know they are really two very different things? If you see an animal sporting some headgear, how can you tell if they are horns or antlers?

To start with, horns are features found on cows, sheep, goats, and their relatives. In these species, both males and females can have horns, and they can be short or long. They can grow straight out like on mountain goats, or they can curl around like on bighorn sheep. They don't have forks, branches, or tines, though. They are a single beam. Animals that have horns keep them for their entire lives. They grow and grow. In some species you can see grooves that represent each year of growth, but this isn't always the case. Horns are made up of a bony core growing from the skull. They are covered in a sheath made of keratin, kind of like your fingernails. The pronghorn, sometimes called pronghorn antelope, is a unique animal. It has horns, but as the name suggests, the male's horns have small prongs on them. Female pronghorn also grow horns, but they are short and smaller and don't show the same prongs.

Antlers are found on deer and their relatives, including elk, moose, and caribou. With one exception—Caribou—antlers are found only on the males of the species. Antlers can be single tines, usually called spikes, but they can also have lots of points. Elk and caribou have long, skinny antlers. Moose have broad, flat antlers. It is especially impressive to know these antlers grow back every year. They grow quickly during spring and summer. At this time they are covered with fuzzy-looking blood vessels, and people call them velvet. The antlers reach their peak size in the fall, when they play an important role in mating displays. The antlers fall off (called shedding) in winter. These shed antlers are often nibbled on by mice and other critters. Horns and antlers can be impressive sights. How many species can you find with horns? Have you ever found a shed antler?

MOOSE

Moose are the largest members of the deer family, but their gigantic size doesn't mean they are easy to spot. They often do a great job of hiding themselves in dense willow thickets. Or they might be swimming in ponds and you won't see them at all. The next time you're hiking in moose territory, keep your eyes peeled. Once you finally do spot one, it'll be well worth the wait. These are one cool animal!

LITTLE-KNOWN FACTS

1. The species called moose in North America (Alces alces) is actually referred to as elk in Europe.
2. Only bull moose grow antlers, which can be more than 5 feet from tip to tip and weigh more than 40 pounds.
3. The antlers are broad and flat like the palm of a hand; they have numerous points sticking off of them like fingers.
4. Moose have a strange flap of skin hanging down below their throats called a dewlap or bell. This might be used to display dominance, or it might help cool moose off in summer. Nobody is entirely sure what function it serves.
5. Sometimes moose will stop eating for a bit in winter and just stay in one spot. This is a survival method, because they'd use more energy searching

for food than the energy the food would provide.

6. Moose are very comfortable in the water. They feed on plants underwater and can remain underwater for 30 seconds or more.
7. Moose can be found in every Canadian province, so Canada is a very popular place for people who want to see moose in the wild.
8. Moose are so adapted to the cold that they sometimes overheat in summer.

Types: One species
Size: 8 to 10 feet and 600 to 1,300 pounds
Eats: Vegetation of all types
Eats them: Wolves, bears, other large predators
Range: Northern regions around the globe

GO OUTSIDE

This might be the hardest challenge in the whole book! Moose can be hard enough to see on their own, but now go on an antler hunt. Can you imagine going on a hike and finding giant moose antlers in the woods? Cool!

BISON

Historically abundant and widespread in the American Great Plains, bison were overharvested for their meat and hides in the 1800s. Now bison can be found in numerous state and national parks, including Yellowstone in Wyoming, and Wind Cave and the Badlands in South Dakota. You can also see them in Wood Buffalo National Park in Alberta. A handful of people have domesticated bison (much like ranching cattle), but there's nothing like seeing these large creatures in the wild.

LITTLE-KNOWN FACTS

1. In the early 1900s there were only about 1,000 bison left in North America. People knew they had to help, so they started working to protect them. Bison populations have increased since then, but they will never be as abundant as they used to be.
2. Bison might be big, but they can still move. They can reach speeds of nearly 40 miles an hour.
3. Both males (bulls) and females (cows) have horns. The bulls' horns are thicker and larger than the cows'.
4. Bulls will use their horns in a face-off. They will head-butt each other, trying to establish dominance or fighting for a female.
5. Even though they aren't related to the buffalo of Asia and Africa, bison are sometimes called buffalo.
6. In winter the large muscular hump and big head of bison help them plow snow from side to side to find food.
7. Bison sometimes wallow, leaving large divots of dirt where they roll around.
8. One species of prehistoric bison had horns 7 feet across.

Types: Two species—one in North America and one in Europe
Size: 7 to 12 feet tall and 800 to 2,000 pounds
Eats: Grazes grasses and forbs
Eats them: Bears, wolves, other large predators
Range: In parks, refuges, and preserves in western North America

MOUNTAIN GOAT

The mountain goat is one of the best climbers in the world of animals. Found in the mountains of the western United States, these cool animals are fun to see, often standing in groups along steep rocks. If you're going on vacation to the mountains, see if these great animals are in that area. Glacier National Park is an especially good spot.

LITTLE-KNOWN FACTS

1. Mountain goats have thick fur because they often live in cold areas. They are like the hipsters of the animal world because they have very distinctive beards.
2. Many people know mountain goats as goat-antelopes. This is because they are close relatives to both goats and antelopes.
3. Mountain goats have a cool thing called a cloven hoof. This means they have pads between their hooves that can help them balance on narrow and steep areas.
4. Impressive jumpers, mountain goats can leap up to 12 feet!
5. Mountain goats have white fur, which helps them blend in on snowy mountains.
6. Female goats have a fun name. They are called nannies. Males are called billies.
7. Billies often live by themselves. But nannies gather in groups of around twenty, including their young.
8. A group of mountain goats is referred to as a tribe.

Types: One species in North America
Size: 4 to 6 feet
Eats: Grass, moss, other plant matter
Eats them: Cougars—one of the only predators that can get to them
Range: Parts of the West and up into Alaska

GO OUTSIDE

It's easy to just pay attention to what's in front of you and not around you. But if you do, you might miss out on some pretty cool animals. The next time you're on a hike, make sure to look everywhere, including the tops of trees, the sides of hills and mountains, and around all water areas.

WHALE

Whales are some of the most beloved and celebrated creatures of the ocean. Often known for their massive size, whales are fascinating creatures that scientists are still studying and learning more about every year. They can differ a great deal, since there are many whale species in the world. This just makes them even more amazing. You could have an entire book about whales. Actually, there are entire books about whales. But we'll give you a highlight right here.

LITTLE-KNOWN FACTS

1. Many whales feed by just swimming through areas with their mouths open.
2. Gray whales are known for being great migrators. They'll travel more than 10,000 miles each year. This is farther than any other mammal. They usually feed in colder waters and mate and give birth in warmer waters.
3. Have you ever heard of whale "songs"? These are created by humpback whales. This is a form of communication, used usually during mating season.
4. Why do we often see whales at the water's surface? They are mammals after all, so they need to come up to breathe.
5. Young whales (called calves) can stay with their mom for up to a year.
6. All mammals have hair, right? This is true, and whales are no exception. Some whales have little hairs covering their bodies; others have whiskers. So they don't have much, but they do have hair.
7. The killer whale is also known as the orca. They are very popular whales with black and white markings. Orcas eat fish, sharks, whales, and other marine animals.

8. Studies show that whales make friends. Females will be apart for a while, but then they'll come back and float (or hang out) together.

9. The closest relative to a whale is a hippopotamus.

10. Sperm whales are a type of whale that sleeps completely vertical.

11. The largest animal in the world is the blue whale. It can reach more than 100 feet long and weigh 140 tons.

12. Blue whales are extremely loud. They can be heard from more than 100 miles away.

13. Others in the whale family that you might not realize are whales include dolphins and porpoises.

14. The all-white whale, the beluga, continues to be endangered. More conservation efforts are needed to save this amazing creature.

Types: Nearly 100 species of whale, including dolphins; common North American whales include the blue, killer, and humpback.
Size: A few feet to more than 100 feet
Eats: Plankton, crustaceans, fish, depending on the species
Eats them: Few predators, though some sharks will attack
Range: Off the coasts of North America

GO OUTSIDE

There's nothing like seeing whales in their natural environment. If you are along the coasts, see if you can sign up for a whale-watching tour. Or if you're taking a ferry or a boat, just look on your own.

COYOTE

Most animals in the dog family are highly adaptable, and the coyote is no exception. Coyotes are common and thrive throughout North America. Many people fear them because it's not uncommon to see them around backyards and they can look really menacing (especially if you hear stories about how they go after pets). But like most wild animals, they're relatively harmless if you give them their space.

LITTLE-KNOWN FACTS

1. Coyotes can have large litters. While the average number of pups is six, there can be as many as eighteen babies.
2. Like others in the dog family, coyotes use a pouncing technique to catch prey, where they'll jump straight up in the air and then land on their prey.
3. Coyotes can be extremely fast, reaching speeds of 40 miles per hour. This is enough to hunt down animals as speedy as jackrabbits.
4. Coyotes don't hang out in packs quite as much as wolves do, but they will form packs for hunting.
5. A female coyote will find a den to have her pups in. She'll stay in there with them until their eyes open, which usually takes ten to fifteen days.
6. It's true that coyotes have a bad reputation for eating small dogs. Yes, they will attack small animals, but there's an easy solution to this: Don't leave your small dog outside if you know there are coyotes around.
7. Coytoes can smell really well and can even detect prey buried under several feet of snow.

Types: One species in North America
Size: 2 to 4 feet
Eats: Most small animals, like mice and rabbits
Eats them: Wolves and other larger mammals
Range: Common throughout North America

RABBIT

Rabbits are familiar backyard wildlife across much of the country. You might not even think of them as wildlife at first because they are popular pets too. They are probably one of the most common types of wildlife you can find without too much looking. They are also found in diverse habitats, from swamps in the Southeast to the forests of New England to the deserts of the West. You can also see them in parks, woodlots, and farmlands.

LITTLE-KNOWN FACTS

1. Cottontails, the most common rabbits in North America, are named for their short tuft of a tail that resembles a cotton ball.
2. Male rabbits are called bucks; female rabbits are called does. Yep, it's the same names that deer have.
3. Young rabbits are usually born in burrows or thickets, where they stay for a few weeks.
4. You've heard that rabbits are good at hopping, right? Well, they do have good hopping muscles—they can jump more than 8 feet.
5. Rabbits and hares are coprophagic. This fancy word means that they only partially digest their food, so they eat their own poop as a way of getting added nutrients.
6. At only 8 or 9 inches, the pygmy rabbit is the smallest rabbit in North America. They are diggers, and they are found in the sagebrush region of southern Idaho and surrounding states.
7. Rabbits' front teeth never stop growing, but they don't get huge. They are continuously worn down, so they stay at a good size.
8. The eyesight of rabbits is unique. They can see behind their heads but not right in front of their noses.
9. Rabbits are also unique in this way: They sweat through the pads of their feet.
10. Are pet rabbits and wild rabbits the same? They look the same, after all. It's definitely not the case though. Domestic rabbits have a different number of chromosomes than wild rabbits.

Types: A few species in North America, including the eastern cottontail, swamp, and pygmy; many more species around the world
Size: 9 to 20 inches
Eats: Twigs, barks, buds, grasses, and forbs
Eats them: Numerous medium-size predators, including hawks, eagles, owls, bobcats, foxes, and coyotes
Range: Nearly anywhere, from southern Canada across the United States and into Mexico

GO OUTSIDE

Put out a rabbit feast and see if you can lure them into your backyard. Some of the items you might put out include carrots, lettuce, and any other greens you have on hand. Keep in mind that you might also attract other animals, but be especially on the lookout for rabbits.

SCIENCE Q&A: How Do You Identify Animal Tracks in the Wild?

When you're out and about or on a hike, you always want to keep an eye on the ground in case you come across cool animal tracks. All species of animals have unique tracks, and you can learn to identify them. Not only is this a cool thing to be able to do, but it can also be useful if you want to know what animals are in the area.

What's the best way to look for tracks? It helps if the tracks are in soft material like snow, mud, or sand. After it rains is also a good time to look for tracks.

How can you tell one track from the next? This can be a little tricky. In fact, there are entire books on tracks so you can study the little differences from one track to another. But there are a few things you can look at to help you out, even if you're not experienced at identifying tracks.

You'll want to get a close look. Get right down on the ground with the track, and start studying it. If you are able, take a picture of it so you can compare it later to the tracks in books or online. You can also sketch the track in a book if you like to draw.

Notice how it compares in size to something like your hand or even a dollar bill. How many toes are there? Can you see claw marks in addition to the toes? What else is unique about it?

You should remember that different animals have different prints. For instance, many animals have hooves. And birds have an entirely different track altogether. Once you learn a few basics, it gets a lot easier. But you have to start somewhere, so get out there and start looking for tracks.

DESTINATIONS: Family Farms

If you're lucky enough to live on a farm, then you already know about the great adventures you can find there every single day. But for most people, the most they know about farms comes from a song involving Old MacDonald. Don't let your farm experience be limited to "E-I-E-I-O."

WHO? If you have both young and old in your family, then this is the place for you. Little ones will love petting or just looking at the animals and hearing all the sounds of the farm. Older kids can feed the animals, ride horses, and maybe even milk some cows.

WHAT? A farm is always filled with activity, but it varies depending on what kind of farm it is. With family farms, you'll probably find a handful of animals to visit, a garden, and other activities. If you have a farm in your area that has regular business hours, call ahead to get an idea of what you can find there.

WHEN? If you visit in spring, chances are you'll get to see lots of new life—new fields being planted, ducklings, chicks, and other baby animals. In fall it's harvest time with pumpkins, apples, and more. Do a little checking with the family farms in your area to see if there are any special events planned.

WHERE? You might be surprised to find out about a family farm location. Even if you live in the city, it's probably a short drive to a local farm. Or if you live in a more rural area, you might have a few more options to choose from. Also, don't overlook all types of farms—pumpkin farms, dairy farms, horse farms—they're all great places to visit.

WHY? Getting a taste of farm life is definitely worth your time. It helps you relax, take a step back, and realize where a lot of your food comes from. It's also a great way to see animals. So take a moment out of your busy schedule and relax on a farm.

WOODCHUCK AND MARMOT

Marmots and woodchucks (also called groundhogs) are closely related. They are the largest of the squirrels in North America. Yes, they really are a type of squirrel. Powerful diggers, these ground squirrels tunnel out extensive holes and burrows. Woodchuck and yellow-bellied marmot are the most widespread species. The next time Groundhog Day comes around, remember that these little guys are also a woodchuck or marmot. Go ahead and test your friends on that fact!

LITTLE-KNOWN FACTS

1. Marmots and woodchucks all hibernate. So only a few are disturbed in an attempt to predict the spring weather. (Psst! Groundhog Day is a fun tradition, but it's not a reliable weather forecast.)
2. They are very good sleepers! Some species can hibernate for nearly ten months.
3. During hibernation their heart rates can drop to four beats per minutes and they might breathe a single breath every five minutes. Now those are some pretty amazing survival techniques!
4. All species have strong front legs and claws that help them dig.
5. The number of names for this animal seems to be never-ending. One nickname for marmots is whistle-pig.
6. The word "woodchuck" might have been derived from a similar-sounding Native American word: wuchak.
7. Marmots are sometimes called rockchucks because they tend to live in piles of boulders and rocky talus slopes.
8. The Alaska marmot was once considered the same as the hoary marmot, but it is now classified as a separate species.

Types: Six species
Size: 2 to 3 feet and up to 12 pounds
Eats: Grasses and other vegetation
Eats them: Eagles, wolverines, mountain lions, bears
Range: Woodchucks are found in the East, Midwest, and across Canada. Marmots are found in the western mountains and in pockets of Washington; Vancouver Island, British Columbia; and Alaska.

SQUIRREL

Squirrels are one of the most diverse groups of rodents. There are all types, including ground squirrels, tree squirrels, and even flying squirrels. Some squirrels aren't even called squirrels. This is the case with woodchucks and prairie dogs. They are really part of the squirrel family, but you would never know it by their names. Squirrels are common, zipping in and about backyards. They are especially popular (and sometimes greedy) if you have a bird feeder.

LITTLE-KNOWN FACTS

1. Tree squirrels, like gray and fox squirrels, are active year-round, while nearly all ground squirrels hibernate over the winter.
2. Gray and fox squirrels are common in city parks. You can hardly go to a park without seeing a squirrel. Find out what squirrel species are in your area.
3. Not all gray squirrels are gray. They can be much darker, like black or even red.
4. Tree squirrels often live in hollowed-out tree trunks, but they will also build shelters made of leaves.
5. The red squirrel is sometimes called the pine squirrel or chickaree, and it is found in coniferous forests.
6. One sign of red squirrels is a midden, which is pinecone bits that have piled up over the years.
7. Most ground squirrels are pretty plain, but some have spots, lines, or stripes.

8. Antelope squirrels and golden-mantled ground squirrels look like chipmunks, but they don't have stripes on their faces.
9. Flying squirrels don't actually fly; they glide short distances from tree to tree.
10. Squirrel babies are born with their eyes closed. They rely on their parents for a few months before they are able to venture out on their own.

Types: Dozens of species
Size: From 8 to 24 inches
Eats: Varies but can include nuts, seeds, berries, mushrooms, insects, eggs, even carrion (dead animals)
Eats them: Numerous bird and mammal predators
Range: Widespread throughout the United States

GO OUTSIDE

Squirrel nests are actually pretty easy to find. Look up in the trees for a grouping of leaves or twigs together near the base of a branch. It's tempting to think this is a bird's nest at first, but squirrel nests are much bigger. Fall is a good time to see nests once most of the leaves have fallen.

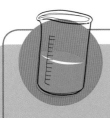

SCIENCE Q&A: How Do Animals Survive the Winter?

Winter can be a harsh season to survive. Some species migrate away from the cold in an effort to find food, but not everyone is on the move. There are lots of animals that can still thrive in winter, and they'll even use winter to their advantage.

Many species, including jumping mice, some ground squirrels and other rodents, and bears, go into varying degrees of torpor or hibernation in winter. They eat extra food in fall. Then their body functions slow down for the winter. They emerge from hibernation in the spring. How is torpor different from hibernation? It's similar but usually not as long.

You can find plenty of species that stay active all winter long. Have you ever seen mouse tracks on top of the snow? Next time you see them, follow them for a bit. Where do they go? Do they seem to disappear at the base of a tree or a shrub, only to reappear somewhere else?

It turns out that snow can make a great blanket for small mammals. They can tunnel and live underneath the snow. This is called the subnivean zone. Lots of times it is warmer near the ground and under the snow than it is out in the open. If you are a mouse, hiding under the snow is a great way to protect yourself from potential predators like owls and coyotes. It doesn't always work, though, because sometimes predators just plow through the snow after their prey.

Weasels, at least the ones living in the North, have another handy winter adaptation: They turn almost entirely white in winter. But not all weasels change color in winter. Weasels that live in the South stay brown year-round. Other animals change colors for winter survival too.

Another way to survive winter is through food storage. Some animals, like the pika and squirrels, store food that will last them all winter long. Birds will do this too. These food caches are like the kitchen pantry when it's cold.

These are just some of the amazing ways that animals are equipped to handle winter. Let's face it: Winter can be long and cold, but now you know that plenty of animals have what it takes to survive the season.

OTTER

You can't help but admire and adore otters. They are a blast to watch, swimming and diving in and out of the water. You might not think there are otters in your area, but they are pretty widespread, so you might be surprised. Go ahead and check out a river near you for the chance to observe these interesting critters.

LITTLE-KNOWN FACTS

1. Otters inhabit homes along the river, either in a burrow, den, or beaver lodge.
2. Look for otter families in spring. The young are born blind, and their eyes open after about thirty days.
3. They can come on land, but otters are best known for their strong swimming abilities and life in the water. They can swim up to 6 to 7 miles per hour.
4. Even though otters can be found in the same areas that you'd find

beavers, don't mistake them for one. In fact, otters are more closely related to weasels.

5. Otters have powerful tails that can be up to a foot long. In general, otter tails are about one-third the size of their body.
6. Sea otters are considered to be skilled animals. They have learned how to use tools like rocks, driftwood, or shells to crack open the shells of the prey they eat.
7. While they're only found along a section of the Pacific coast of North America and Alaska, sea otters deserve a special mention. They grow to up to 5 feet. They've suffered in the past because of hunting, but conservation efforts are underway to help protect them for the future.
8. Here's another really cool sea otter fact: They love to eat, and they often do so on their backs! The next time you visit an aquarium, look for the sea otters and watch them eat.

Types: Two species in North America—river otters and sea otters
Size: 25 to 60 inches long
Eats: Snakes, frogs, crayfish, lizards
Eats them: Coyotes, eagles (river otters), sea lions, sharks (sea otters)
Range: Throughout much of North America except the Southwest for river otter; northern Pacific coast for sea otter

BAT

Bats tend to have a bad reputation, but they are seriously cool mammals. A lot of people don't even know they are mammals. In fact, they are the only mammals in the world that can fly! If you've been afraid or cautious of bats in the past, then maybe it's time to give them another chance. There are oodles of interesting facts about them.

1. There are a lot of myths about bats. The biggest one is that they are blind. There's even that phrase "blind as a bat." This is far from the truth. In fact, bats actually have really good eyesight.
2. Bats use this cool thing called echolocation. This is when bats send out high-pitched sounds and listen for the sounds to rebound off surrounding objects. Bats detect what's around them and can find their next meal (mostly insects) this way.
3. There are exceptions to what most bats eat. The vampire bat (found mostly in South America but also in parts of Mexico) will bite birds, farm animals, and other mammals and lick their blood for food.
4. Young bats are called pups. And most bats only have one pup a year. This isn't much in the animal world, which is one reason some bat populations are in danger.
5. Bat moms are the coolest. Even if there are hundreds or thousands of other bats around, they can find their young because of their unique smell and sound.
6. Do you know what bat guano is? It's bat poop, and it actually makes really great fertilizer.
7. Look at a picture of a bat skeleton sometime. They are so cool! Their wings are their "hands" and "fingers" and they look a lot like yours.
8. Bats are known for gathering in large numbers. Bat colonies can reach into the hundreds or thousands of individual bats.
9. Bats will roost together in caves, roofs, hollow trees, and other areas.
10. Do you live in an area where there are lots of mosquitoes? Put up a bat

house. This will help support the bat population, and they'll eat hundreds of mosquitoes every night.

11. Bats can reach speeds of more than 60 miles per hour!
12. Bats can have a really long life—up to thirty years.

Types: More than 1,000 species around the world, with several in North America
Size: Most just a few inches
Eats: Mostly insects, fruit, pollen, nectar
Eats them: Hawks, weasels, raccoons
Range: Many species found throughout the world

GO OUTSIDE

Go out at dusk, right when it's starting to get dark. Put out a blanket and lie down to watch, because this is when the bats start coming out. As it gets darker, more will come out, swooping and flying around. Many species prefer open areas in the woods or flying over open ponds.

SKUNK

What's the first thing that pops into your mind when you think of a skunk? Is it something along the lines of ewwwww? Yes, these small mammals do have a foul reputation, but if you can look past that, you'll grow to admire these little stinkers.

LITTLE-KNOWN FACTS

1. Not all skunks are striped. Both the eastern and western spotted skunks have a more black-and-white mosaic pattern.
2. Young skunks stay with their mother for up to a year as they learn how to be on their own.
3. When threatened, skunks can omit a horrible odor from under their tail. This is what gives them such a bad reputation. They can shoot this liquid up to 9 feet! The smell can travel half a mile.
4. Some people say that the smelly liquid that a skunk omits is pee, but this is a myth. It sure is a good defense mechanism, though. Skunks have very few predators, which you have to admit is pretty impressive!
5. Skunks can adapt to a wide range of habitats. This includes mountains, prairies, forests, and even backyards. In fact, there are many stories

about skunks spraying dogs, so watch out!

6. Skunks are adaptable animals and will go after almost anything for a meal. They even attack beehives because they eat honeybees.
7. Skunks can't see all that well, but they sure do hear and smell great.
8. Skunks live in homes that are usually created by other animals, like dens and burrows. You can also find them living in old logs or empty holes of trees.

Types: Three species in North America—striped, spotted, and hog-nosed
Size: 12 inches for spotted, up to 30 for striped and hog-nosed skunks
Eats: Insects, small mammals, birds, eggs, fish, fruit, seeds
Eats them: Owls, coyotes, bobcats
Range: Skunks are found throughout North America.

WOLVERINE

The wolverine is an animal that survives and thrives in cold climates. Don't be fooled by the look of this animal. Sure, it looks like it's related to a bear, but it's actually more closely related to a weasel. It is a short, stocky animal, but it is the largest member of the weasel family. They mostly stick to themselves, making them one of the true loners of the animal world.

LITTLE-KNOWN FACTS

1. The wolverine can cover a lot of ground. In a single day it can travel 15 or 20 miles in search of food. This is quite a way, considering most animals stick to a very small territory.
2. Not all male animals are bigger than the female, and that's the case here. The male wolverine is only about one-third the size of the female.
3. They have a fantastic sense of smell. For instance, if an animal is burrowed under the snow, a wolverine can smell it 10 to 20 feet deep! This is good for the

wolverine, but not so good for that hibernating animal.

4. Wolverines have fascinating paws that are perfect for walking in the snow. When they step down, their foot presses down to nearly twice its size. This means the feet are like snowshoes, built right onto the foot. Try to find a wolverine track or look online to see what one looks like. You'll definitely be surprised.

Types: One species of wolverine in the world
Size: Up to 40 inches
Eats: Rabbits, rodents, caribou, plants and berries in summer, carrion (dead animals)
Eats them: Larger meat-eating mammals
Range: The northern parts of North America, Europe, and Asia

BADGER

American badgers have very distinct face patterns with white and brown striping (many call it their badge). They are very different from other badgers around the world, and they prefer wide, open areas where they can roam. Badgers have a fierce reputation—they're known for being aggressive and even mean. So even though they're not that big, don't let their size fool you.

LITTLE-KNOWN FACTS

1. Badgers are amazing excavators. They have long claws that are designed to dig. Then their feet in the back are almost like little shovels, pushing the dirt through and helping to create a safe haven.
2. All this digging is helpful. Badgers can both hear and smell really well. They dig in an area where there are rodents, and soon they'll have their next meal.

3. Move over, skunks! If badgers are threatened, they can also release a foul odor that warns their predators to get away.
4. It's not easy for predators to get badgers. First of all, they are very vocal and will hiss and growl to scare attackers off. Next, they have a thick and muscular neck area, so predators will have a hard time carrying one off in their mouth. So they might attack a badger, discover they can't carry it, and then leave it be.
5. You might not know it by looking, but badgers have very powerful jaws. In fact, they have thirty-four teeth, including four very sharp canines.

Types: One species, American badger, in North America
Size: Up to 28 inches
Eats: Small mammals like prairie dogs, ground squirrels
Eats them: Coyotes and other large mammals
Range: Much of the western half of the United States

ARMADILLO

The armadillo carries its own suit of armor: a hard shell that helps protect it from predators. It has some of the most natural protection around. This is good, since it doesn't move all that fast, even if a predator is after it. Most armadillos are found in South America, though there is one species you can look for when you're visiting the southern United States.

LITTLE-KNOWN FACTS
1. The middle of this armadillo species has bony bands in the center—hence the name nine-banded armadillo. In reality, they have eight to ten bands. So what's with the bands? They allow the animal to be flexible, which can come in handy when moving around or escaping predators.
2. The armor and bony skin of this animal account for about one-sixth of its overall weight, which can be up to 14 pounds.
3. Here's something unique about the offspring: This species of armadillo nearly always has quadruplets, which is four babies, and they're all the same sex.

4. All armadillos are diggers and can dig out an impressive burrow to live. Their short, powerful arms are designed to help dig. Many other animals appreciate their digging too. Rabbits, burrowing owls, and other animals will use their abandoned burrows.
5. Many people think of armadillos rolling up in a ball to defend themselves. This is true, but only for two species of armadillos, neither of which is found in North America.

Types: One species, the nine-banded armadillo, in North America
Size: Up to 22 inches
Eats: Ants, birds, fruit, roots
Eats them: Coyotes, cougars, wolves, bears
Range: Southern United States

BOBCAT

If you were to look at the face of a bobcat, you'd swear you were looking at a short-haired cat that you might see at someone's house. They do have some pretty similar catlike habits. Of course this doesn't make them a friendly cat, so it's best to stay away. Most animals are more afraid of you than you are of them. But if they have young nearby, they can be aggressive.

LITTLE-KNOWN FACTS

1. Bobcats are named for their short tails, which look like they have been bobbed (cut short). Their tails are only 4 to 7 inches long.
2. Also referred to as wildcats, bobcats are about twice the size of domestic kitties.
3. Bobcats are seldom seen. They are nocturnal, so that's one reason, but they are also stealthy, elusive travelers.

4. Like domestic cats, young bobcats are called kittens. They stay with their mother for six to nine months, learning how to hunt and survive, before they go out on their own.
5. Also similar to domestic cats, bobcats are excellent pouncers. They can leap up to 10 feet in the air, which helps them attack their prey.
6. The lynx, the closest relative to bobcats, lives in snowy regions.

Types: One species in North America
Size: From 26 to 44 inches
Eats: Rabbits, hares, rodents, deer
Eats them: Larger meat-eaters, like mountain lions
Range: Throughout Mexico, southern Canada, and much of the United States

FOX

Foxes have a reputation for being stealthy—they can come and go without you even knowing they're around. You can find five total fox species in North America, though the red fox is the most common and widespread. These small, doglike animals wander both cities and rural areas. Since they mostly hunt at night, it makes them even harder to see. If you do want to see one, you should keep an eye out around dusk.

LITTLE-KNOWN FACTS

1. Foxes are members of the dog family, along with wolves and coyotes. They're all considered canids.
2. While some members of the canids (like wolves) live in groups called packs, foxes usually live alone.
3. Female foxes are called vixens.
4. Young foxes are called kits or cubs. When they're little, they have to watch out for eagles, which might swoop down to get them.

5. The gray fox, also fairly common in North America, has unique claws and can climb trees almost like a cat!
6. Foxes make a lot of different noises—one sounds like a cross between a dog bark and a parrot squawk.
7. Foxes are among the group of mammals that use burrows. Though they can have homes aboveground, they prefer to find one underground.

Types: Five species in North America—red, kit, swift, arctic, and gray
Size: Most are 23 to 30 inches long. Swift and kit foxes can be as small as 13 inches.
Eats: Rabbits, mice, beetles, worms, frogs, birds, fruit
Eats them: Coyotes, wolves, bears, mountain lions
Range: Red and gray foxes are found throughout the lower forty-eight states. Kit and swift foxes are found only in small areas in the western and central United States. Arctic fox habitat is in northern Canada and Alaska.

GO OUTSIDE

Search for a den that looks like a fox could use it. Don't go digging around in it, but use this opportunity to think like a fox. What would make a good home? Where would you go at night? Once you start thinking like an animal, you just might see a few along the way.

OPOSSUM

You might think opossums lack that cute, cuddly look. Yes, they do look a bit scraggly, and they have a tail that looks more like a rat's tail than anything else. They are pretty fascinating nocturnal animals though. If you come across an opossum, chances are you're going to think it's dead. But don't let it fool you!

LITTLE-KNOWN FACTS

1. Opossums are in the marsupial family—the same group as kangaroos!
2. If they're threatened, opossums will pretend to be dead, hoping the predator will go away. They can stay curled up this way for several hours. This is where the phrase "playing possum" came from.
3. You can find one main species of opossum in North America—the Virginia opossum.
4. They have very impressive tails, which can be longer than their bodies at 10 to 22 inches.
5. Opossums have fifty teeth. They'll use these teeth to stop by a backyard and nibble on dog food, bird seed, or garbage.
6. When an opossum baby is born, it's about the size of a dime! They have

a lot of growing to do before they can be on their own. Following birth, they live in a pouch (similar to a kangaroo pouch) for two to three months.

7. Many people think opossums carry rabies, but actually this is extremely rare.

8. Contrary to a popular myth, the opossums of North America don't sleep hanging upside down by their tails.

Types: One species, Virginia opossum, in North America
Size: 13 to 20 inches
Eats: Eggs, frogs, insects, fruit
Eats them: Mountain lions, wolves, bears, other large predators
Range: Central and southeastern parts of the United States, Mexico, and along the West Coast

GO OUTSIDE

Everyone should see an opossum "playing possum" at least once. Now, you shouldn't approach an opossum if you see it on the ground. Always give it space. But it's a good nature goal to see this survival technique for yourself.

BEAVER

If you think you see a beaver, then you must be near the water. These critters have webbed feet, which are great for swimming. In general, water is a big part of their lives. They build their homes on lakes, ponds, and slow-moving rivers and streams, giving them some added protection from predators. So the next time you see a big pile of logs and sticks out in the water, take a second glance for a furry critter sticking up among the mess.

LITTLE-KNOWN FACTS

1. Beavers are part of the rodent group. They have large incisors, which they use for gnawing on wood.
2. These animals have a really cool third eyelid that is transparent. It comes

down over the eye when they're swimming so they can see underwater.

3. Beavers are smart in building their homes on water. For added protection, they make the entrance only accessible under the water, so it really keeps predators away.

4. Young beavers often stay with their parents for a couple of years. If you see one beaver, there's a good chance you'll see up to five more.

5. Beavers have huge, flat tails that can be a foot long or more. So what do they do with these tails? Primarily, they're used to slap the water, warning other beavers in the area of potential danger.

Types: One species, American beaver, in North America
Size: 30 to 35 inches
Eats: Leaves, twigs, bark, water plants
Eats them: Foxes, coyotes, wolves, weasels, eagles, owls
Range: Most of North America except for the Southwest and Mexico

GO OUTSIDE

Find signs of beavers. This can include a gnawed-up tree alongside the river or a group of branches and twigs damming off part of the water. It's not hard to find once you know what to look for. Then you'll know where to go if you want to spot a beaver.

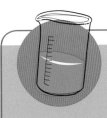

SCIENCE Q&A:
What Is a Keystone Species?

Nature is all connected. Everything affects everything else. But some animals have major impacts on the rest of nature, and these are known as keystone species. Like the top rock in a stone arch, they support a whole range of other critters. Keystone species can change the surrounding areas, and other species can be dependent on these changes.

Let's take a look at a specific animal example. Beavers are considered a keystone species. One reason is because they gnaw down trees. They also build dams that block up flowing water. Beaver dams can create a whole pond by damming up a section of river or stream. This is a big change to the landscape. Beaver pond areas can provide habitat for a wide range of species. Fish and amphibians will take advantage of these waters. So will birds and mammals. The plants will also change because of the beavers. See how their behavior is affecting many others?

Prairie dogs are another classic keystone species. Prairie dogs live in large colonies, and they dig extensive burrows in the prairies. But prairie dogs aren't the only animals that use these burrows. How many animals can you think of that live in prairie dog towns? There can be dozens of other species living in these burrows—things as diverse as badgers and burrowing owls to rattlesnakes and bison. Even spiders and toads will use these burrows. So, again, you can see how prairies dogs change the landscape, and how other animals are dependent on these changes.

While everything in nature affects everything else, the species that change things in a way that benefits other animals are the keystones.

PORCUPINE

Just take one look at a porcupine and you can easily tell that it's sending a "stay away" message. The quills that cover its body offer amazing protection from other animals. If you have a curious dog, make sure it doesn't come face-to-face with this prickly animal—your pet will be sorry it did.

LITTLE-KNOWN FACTS

1. Porcupines are actually large rodents. True, you probably think of mice or rats when you think of rodents, but now you can add porcupines to that list as well.
2. Though you can't see it very well, under all those quills porcupines are covered in fur.
3. If porcupines lose their quills—either from puncturing something or just falling out—they will grow new ones.
4. Those quills are pretty small, and they really add up. Overall, one porcupine can have 20,000 to 30,000 quills!
5. When baby porcupines (called porcupettes) are born, they have soft quills. The quills harden after a few days.

6. It's true that most animals leave porcupines alone, but it does have a few predators. How do those predators eat them? They flip porcupines over, because there aren't quills on the stomach.
7. There's a rumor that porcupines can shoot their quills. This isn't true, but you still don't want to have a run-in with these animals.
8. A group of porcupines is called a prickle.

Types: One species, North American porcupine, on this continent
Size: 26 to 32 inches
Eats: Bark, twigs, nuts, other plants
Eats them: Bobcats, cougars, fishers
Range: Throughout the top half of North America

GO OUTSIDE

Here's another item to look for outside, though this one is small and tricky. Try to find porcupine quills in nature. If you think it's like searching for a needle in a haystack, you're right. Quills are needlelike, and they can be extremely hard to spot on the ground. Still, it's a fun thing to look for when you're out on a hike.

LEARN

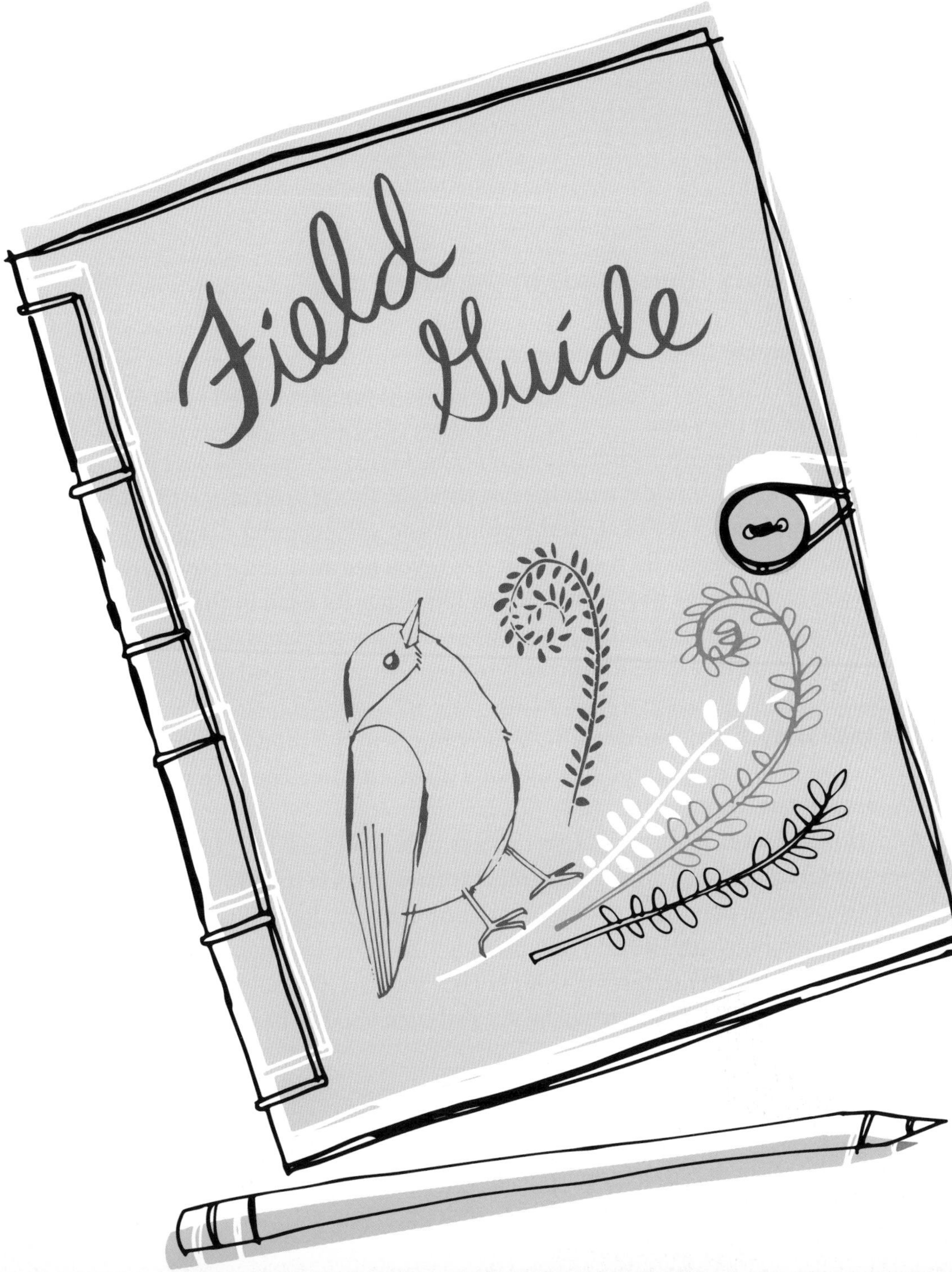

SECTION 1: THE BASICS

This section will take a look at common animal myths and bust them once and for all!

Ostriches bury their heads in the sand.

MYTH SCALE: 3

About the myth: Everyone knows this one is true. Many people have seen this one with their own two eyes. They look up to see one of these giant birds with its head in the sand.

The truth: This has been circulated for centuries, so it's one of those myths that a lot of people think is true. It's not though! This myth has a lot to do with how ostriches nest. They nest on the ground and will even dig a large hole to lay and keep their eggs. So think about it—if you see an ostrich from a distance, you can imagine how it might look like it has its head in the sand. To add to the myth, an ostrich has a pretty small head compared to the rest of its body, so it would be especially difficult to see whether its head is in or out of the sand.

The takeaway: Ostriches don't bury their heads in the sand at all. Sure, it's easy to see how it might look like that at a distance when they are nesting, but it's just not the case.

Additional facts: While they aren't native to North America, ostriches are pretty interesting birds and are common at zoos and even on farms throughout the country. They are native to Africa and are actually flightless birds. They usually weigh between 100 and 300 pounds. They also lay eggs that weigh 3 to 5 pounds. One more interesting thing is that they aren't really known for being smart birds. They have very small heads and even smaller brains!

Bees gather honey from flowers.
MYTH SCALE: 3

About the myth: We all know that bees are associated with honey in some way, right? We also know that bees go to flowers to dig out something sweet, right? Well, if you put the two together, then it's easy to think that bees are gathering honey straight from the flower and then taking it back to their hives.

The truth: Bees are not gathering honey straight from flowers. They are actually gathering nectar. Nectar in flowers is like a sugar water, mostly made up of water. But the process of making honey is just getting started. Worker bees store this sugar water in their stomachs

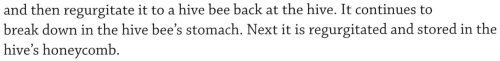

and then regurgitate it to a hive bee back at the hive. It continues to break down in the hive bee's stomach. Next it is regurgitated and stored in the hive's honeycomb.

The takeaway: This process is a bit more complicated than it sounds, but the main thing to remember is that bees are not gathering honey from flowers. They are gathering sugar water. The honey part comes later.

Additional facts: While the bees gather the nectar, they are also pollinating the flowers because they are transferring pollen grain from one flower to the next. This is really important for flowers. They need to be pollinated to grow nice and healthy. So it's okay to be cautious of bees, but don't be afraid. You should encourage them to be in your backyard!

All reptiles lay eggs.

About the myth: Lots of animals lay eggs, including birds, insects, fish, and reptiles. But do all reptiles lay eggs? Nothing is ever as easy as it seems. Of course there are a few reptiles in there that have to be different. Let's find out which ones they are.

The truth: Snakes are definitely reptiles, but not all of them lay eggs. Well, not in the traditional sense anyway. Many female snakes, including rattlesnakes and garter snakes, keep the eggs inside their bodies. So they're not really "laying" the eggs. Instead, the eggs hatch inside of the mother, and she keeps the babies in there until it's time for them to come out. Then when she gives birth, they come out of her alive! Can you imagine a female snake slithering around with eight to ten babies inside of her? It sure makes it hard to move around and catch food.

The takeaway: Don't assume that all reptiles are egg layers! You can impress your friends or even your teacher with cool facts like this.

Additional facts: Snakes aren't the only exception to reptiles laying eggs. Skinks are another reptile that sometimes delivers live babies. Skinks are a type of lizard. Yes, some lay eggs in the traditional way, but not all do!

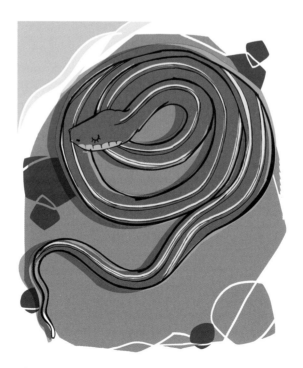

Touching a toad will give you warts.

MYTH SCALE: 3

About the myth: It's been a long-standing belief that you shouldn't touch toads because they will give you warts. The myth says that you should avoid touching toads altogether, and if you do happen to come into contact with a toad, you should wash up thoroughly.

The truth: This myth probably got started in large part because toads have dry, bumpy skin, and it looks like they have warts all over their body. So people assumed that warts came from toads because they look the same. This is impossible though. Warts are actually a type of human virus, not something you get from other animals.

The takeaway: You absolutely cannot get a wart from a toad. So feel free to pick up that little toad you find hopping along in your backyard. Feel its skin and notice how rough and bumpy it is. Then, as with anything else, wash your hands when you're done. Not because you might get a wart but because it's just a good hygiene practice overall.

Additional facts: You know those bumps that look like warts on a toad's body? Those are equipped with something called parotid glands. These release a substance that can be harmful to predators. It's not going to hurt you in any way, but it's a pretty cool tool that helps them avoid being eaten!

DESTINATIONS: Hiking Trails

Hit the trails this season, and take in some great fall color at the same time. Hiking is a year-round activity, but it's especially gorgeous this time of year. It's easy to find hiking trails in your area. There are entire magazines, websites, and stores devoted to this favorite outdoor pastime. Best of all, you can find trails with varying difficulty, so even the youngest outdoor enthusiasts can join.

WHO? Anyone can go hiking. Small trails around parks are usually short, well kept, and stroller friendly if you have younger siblings who need to go along for the ride. It's easy to find more challenging trails for older kids and teens too. Look for difficulty levels (easy, moderate, and difficult).

WHAT? In its most basic form, hiking is just walking. Hiking can be a short leisurely stroll or a multiple-day backpacking journey. Start off on beginner routes and don't try to do too much. Once you get a little experience, you can start doing more and more.

WHEN? Hiking can be done year-round (some extreme-sports people even love winter hiking). But fall is an ideal time to go because of the cool weather.

WHERE? If you're new to hiking, try going to your local outdoors store. Ask for good tips on where to go. Also, many states have hiking trails mapped out already. So check your local or state travel site. You'll soon be filled with more hiking trails than you could possibly ever try.

WHY? First off, it's a great form of exercise. You can hike for several miles and, because you're always seeing something new and different, you won't even realize it. It's also a great way to go beyond the crowds. Hiking trails are designed to go into areas where there is less overall traffic. So you're likely to see some amazing things in nature that you wouldn't see otherwise.

TIPS AND TRICKS: Many people think hiking is just walking, but it can be a lot more work than that. Be prepared—pack snacks that will keep you energized, wear good shoes, and pack plenty of water. And don't forget to take breaks if someone in your group needs a rest. You want to take it easy at first so you have energy to last the entire adventure.

Spiders are insects.

MYTH SCALE: 3

About the myth: When you think of insects, what comes to mind? You probably think of something small with little legs that crawls around. With this in mind, it would be easy to assume that spiders are part of the insect family.

The truth: Spiders have a whole category of their own: arachnids. Mites, ticks, and scorpions are some of the other crawly critters that are in this group. What are the differences between spiders and insects? Take a look. To begin with, spiders do not have antennae like insects do. They also have eight legs, compared to insects' six. Finally, insects have bodies made up of three parts, while spiders have bodies in two parts.

The takeaway: Spiders are really in a class all their own. The next time you are outside, see if you can find a spider and an insect and really try to notice the differences between the two. Don't forget to grab your magnifying glass.

Additional facts: Fear of spiders is called arachnophobia, and it affects a lot of people. Some studies say that as many as 50 percent of women are scared of spiders.

Bats are blind.

MYTH SCALE: 3

About the myth: Have you ever heard the saying "blind as a bat" before? These flying mammals are active under the cover of darkness, and it is nearly impossible for us to see anything in the dark. Seems likely that bats could be blind.

The truth: Bats don't rely on sight nearly as much as people do. That doesn't mean they are blind though. All bats can see. Some of the fruit-eating bats can see especially well. Bats that feed on insects have another adaptation to help them locate food. It's called echolocation, and it is when bats send out high-pitched sounds and

listen for those sounds to rebound off surrounding objects. Bats detect what is around them and pinpoint their insect meals this way. The echolocation sounds are too high-pitched for people to hear, but researchers can use special equipment to detect these signals. The scientists can even tell bat species apart based on their echolocation sounds.

The takeaway: Even though they are mostly nocturnal, bats are not blind. They have good vision but even better hearing. Maybe instead of "blind as a bat," the phrase should be "hear like a bat."

Additional facts: While we are on the subject of bats, let's talk about the whole rabies issue. Some people are convinced all bats have rabies. While bats can be carriers of rabies, they are no more or less susceptible than other mammals. As with all wild animals, give bats plenty of space. Especially if they are out during the day or they are acting strange in any other way.

Porcupines can throw their quills.

MYTH SCALE: 3

About the myth: Have you (or your pet) ever gotten stuck by porcupine quills? If so, it seems like the quills just reached out and grabbed you, right? Almost like you didn't even touch the animal, but instead that the porcupine threw its quills at you. But can porcupines really toss their quills like little spears?

The truth: Porcupine quills are easily dislodged from the porcupine and into whatever they come into contact with. But the animals can't throw their quills.

You should still give a porcupine plenty of space though. Porcupines can have over 30,000 quills, which are really considered modified hairs. They are extra stiff, and they come to a very fine tip. The tips of the quills have hundreds of microscopic barbs on them. This makes them extremely difficult to remove from flesh. If you are lucky enough to see a porcupine, take a couple of pictures, but then let it waddle away or climb up a tree.

The takeaway: You might not even see the porcupine quills under the rest of the long hairs, but if the porcupine feels threatened, it will raise up its quills. You might even hear the quills rattling together. Porcupines can release an odor when threatened too. This is similar to what skunks do. But no matter how cornered the porcupine feels, it can't throw the quills at a threat.

Additional facts: Porcupine quills take half as much pressure to puncture skin as needles, so researchers are examining them in an attempt to make better needles and staples for medical use.

Polar bears are left-handed.

MYTH SCALE: 3

About the myth: It doesn't matter which is your dominant hand, but are you right-handed or left-handed? It is way more common for people to be right-handed. Only about 10 percent of the world's population is left-handed. But get this: Some people are convinced that polar bears are left-handed.

The truth: It is fun to imagine a polar bear using its left paw to accomplish polar bear tasks. But really, scientists haven't observed this to be the case. If anything, polar bears are probably ambidextrous. They use both their left and right paws pretty equally.

The takeaway: Polar bears pretty much use their left and right paws the same. Most polar bear tasks require both paws anyway. Or sometimes no paws at all are needed.

Additional facts: Another rumor about polar bears is that they will cover up their noses so they can sneak up on their prey. The theory is that the black nose will give them away in the snow, but they can hide this behind a white paw. It's fun to think of polar bears playing peekaboo, but it isn't true. They will still pull a surprise attack though. When seals poke up through the ice to breathe, polar bears can be waiting there to eat them.

Mice eat cheese.

MYTH SCALE: 2

About the myth: Have you ever seen a cartoon with a mouse? Chances are there's a piece of cheese nearby because that's what it likes to nibble on. If you have cheese, better watch out, because a mouse might come along to munch on it.

The truth: It's hard to pinpoint where this myth actually started, but it's been repeated time and time again. In reality, mice will eat just about anything. They'll even gnaw on cardboard and paper if that's all that's available. If they had their choice, though, they would eat seeds, fruit, and other sweet items.

The takeaway: Mice will eat cheese if it's all that's available, but they certainly don't prefer it. Still, you shouldn't set out cheese to catch a mouse. If you really want to try to bring one in, you should offer peanut butter instead!

Additional facts: Mice tend to get a bad reputation, and lots of people are afraid of them. They are pretty harmless though. There are more than thirty species of mice, and they range in both size and color. One more fun fact about mice: Their tails are usually as long or even longer than their bodies!

Rabbits are rodents.

About the myth: Rodents are small mammals like mice, chipmunks, and squirrels. Some mammals that are small are clearly not rodents. What about

rabbits? Aren't they just squirrels with big ears and cotton-ball-like tails?

The truth: About 40 percent of mammal species are rodents, from the pygmy jerboa to the capybara. Rodents thrive around the world, but rabbits aren't in this category! Along with hares, rabbits are lagomorphs. They are different than rodents in a few key ways, especially with regard to their top front teeth. Similar to rodents, lagomorphs have a pair of top incisors. But they also have a second pair of front teeth directly behind these.

The takeaway: Even though rabbits look a lot like many of the rodents, they aren't closely related at all. Rabbits are different than hares in a few key ways as well. Hare babies are born with their eyes open and with hair. They basically hit the ground running. Baby rabbits are furless and have closed eyes. They develop more in a nest before they are able to move about. Some hares, including the snowshoe hare, turn white in the winter and brown in the summer.

Additional facts: Pikas are also lagomorphs. These small mammals look like rabbits with smaller ears. They live in talus slopes or boulder fields in the mountains or the far north. They will gather and store vegetation to eat all winter long.

Flying squirrels can fly.

About the myth: When you think of animals that fly, you mostly think of birds, right? Maybe even insects, but what about mammals? Most mammals can't fly, but there are a few that can—like bats. What about flying squirrels though? They

can fly, right? They are called flying squirrels after all.

The truth: Flying squirrels are small mammals that live in holes in trees (called cavities, just like holes in your teeth). They come out at night to feed. Despite their name, flying squirrels can't really fly. However, they do have remarkable adaptations that allow them to glide from tree to tree. Flying squirrels usually glide less than 20 feet. An impressive glide can go well over 100 feet, but no matter how hard they try, flying squirrels can't fly up.

The takeaway: Flying squirrels have flaps of skin between their front and back legs called patagium. A squirrel will climb high up in a tree and then jump off. The patagium acts like a parachute as the animal "flies" to another tree. The long tail acts like a rudder, so the squirrel can steer a bit.

Additional facts: North America has two species of flying squirrels. They look pretty similar but are found in different regions. Flying squirrels are active at night, so they have large eyes to help them see in the darkness.

Feeding birds in fall stops their migration.
MYTH SCALE: 3

About the myth: Some people say you should take down your bird feeders in the fall. The theory is that if birds can still find enough food, they won't migrate south before winter hits.

The truth: Migration is about finding food, but that doesn't mean if you provide food, the birds will stick around. It helps to understand a bit more about migration. Migratory birds experience a sort of restlessness known as Zugunruhe. Migration is triggered by photoperiod (the amount of sunlight each day). Migratory species head south as the days get shorter. Each bird species is different, and some don't ever migrate. You can always find some bird species all year long, even in the far north.

The takeaway: The migration cycle is something birds know naturally. Based on natural signals, including the length of the day, migratory birds fly between winter and summer homes. Feeding the birds during migration can help them fuel up for their journey, but it won't keep them from migrating onward. Birds will build up fat reserves before tackling the challenge of migration. Some species can nearly double in weight. This fat provides them the energy they need on these long-distance flights. It is like filling up your gas tank before a long road trip.

Additional facts: Some birds may use the earth's magnetic field to help them navigate, while others might use the night sky as a reference.

Hummingbirds migrate on the backs of swans or geese.
MYTH SCALE: 3

About the myth: There are many stories out there to explain where birds go in winter and how they get there. One of the more entertaining stories is that hummingbirds will hitch a ride on the backs of larger birds like geese to get where they need to go.

The truth: Sometimes smaller birds will chase larger birds, but this doesn't mean they are trying to get a ride. For one thing, geese and hummingbirds aren't usually found in the same types of habitats. Also, they migrate at different times, and they fly to different locations for the winter. This myth is just a bit of folklore that mistakenly gets passed around from time to time.

The takeaway: It is pretty incredible that something as tiny as a hummingbird can make an epic migration, but they do. Ruby-throated hummingbirds can even fly for 18 hours nonstop to get across the Gulf of Mexico to their wintering grounds. Not all hummingbirds have to migrate though. Anna's hummingbirds and other species in California and the Southwest aren't migratory at all.

Additional facts: Hummingbirds can flap their wings over sixty times per second. Go ahead and try to flap your "wings" that fast!

Owls are wise.

MYTH SCALE: 3

About the myth: The thought that owls are wise has been around for hundreds of years. From folklore to blockbuster movies, owls have often been used to depict intelligence and wisdom.

The truth: Owls are animals that seem to have a gaze when they are looking around. Owls aren't the only animals with eyes, but very few species have eyes that stare back at you like these species. The oversize, forward-facing owl eyes might have led to the false notion that these are the wisest of birds. This comes down to something called anthropomorphism. It's a big word, but it basically means you give human thoughts and feelings to nonhuman things like animals. These are usually traits that humans can relate to or are often viewed positively. So it looks like people have been saying owls are wise without having much to back it up.

The takeaway: Measuring intelligence is tricky business. Owls are pretty great at being owls. Just because you can look into their big owl eyes doesn't make them smarter than hawks, eagles, warblers, or sparrows. It also doesn't make them any smarter than the mice or rabbits that they eat. It just makes them owls.

Additional facts: Owls' eyes give them incredible vision, but the hearing of these hunters is even more impressive. The feathered tufts on some owls aren't ears. (They aren't horns either.) Owls don't have external ears, but what is really unusual is that their ears aren't directly opposite of each other. One ear opening is higher up on the side of the head and the other one is lower down. This helps owls pinpoint the exact location of a sound.

A snail is a slug with a shell on its back.

About the myth: Snails and slugs look almost exactly alike. They seem like they are pretty much the same thing. Do you think a slug could find a shell, crawl up inside, and turn into snail? Or if a snail gets tired of hauling around a bulky shell, could it set off for the freestyle life of a slug?

The truth: They look like the same thing, but they're not. There are numerous species of both snails and slugs. Most are aquatic (live in water). Others are terrestrial (live on land). The terrestrial ones secrete slimy mucus. This helps them slide along. It also helps them retain moisture so they don't shrivel up and die. As long as nobody pours salt on them, snails and slugs can live up to twenty-five years in the wild.

A fundamental difference between snails and slugs is the shell, so let's focus on it. Snail shell formation is a pretty complicated process. The snails are born with their shells, although it isn't quite the full shell you're picturing. The shell continues to grow throughout the lifetime of the snail. Both snails and slugs need to maintain a certain amount of dampness about them. In addition to secreting mucus, they tend to hang out in cool, moist environments.

The takeaway: Snails and slugs are related to each other. Despite many similarities though, no matter how hard they try, slugs will never become snails. And snails will never become slugs. They'll always be different critters. Both are considered mollusks, but so are octopuses, squids, clams, and oysters.

Additional facts: Snails and slugs are both known as gastropods, a term that combines the Greek words for stomach (gastros) and foot (podos). There are also species of gastropods known as semislugs. These have reduced shells that are usually softer than the shells of true snails.

Snapping turtles can't let go after they bite.

MYTH SCALE: 3

About the myth: Snapping turtles have strong jaws and are quick to bite, but can they let go? Some people think they can't let go until they hear thunder.

The truth: Snapping turtles have reached near-mythical status. They are elusive creatures by nature and are most active at night. Spending much of their lives in water, they often prefer to sit and wait for their prey to pass by. They can be most visible in the spring when the females search out sites to dig nests. This journey might take  them across busy roads, so snapping turtles can unfortunately become roadkill victims. Also, you should resist any temptation to pull a turtle by the tail, as this can damage the spine.

Some people claim that once a snapping turtle bites, it can't open its mouth again. But it would be awfully hard to eat if you could only bite one time. Another popular claim is that once a turtle bites, it won't let go until it thunders. This isn't true.

The takeaway: You certainly don't want to get bit by a snapping turtle, but claims of their jaw strength have been stretched over the years. The jaw strength for snapping turtles is impressive, and their ridged shells and pointed mouths make them look much more intimidating than many other turtles.

Additional facts: Alligator snapping turtles of the southeastern United States have an appendage they use as fishing bait. They dangle this "worm" out of their mouths and then snap up fish that come in close to investigate.

Raccoons wash their food before eating it.

MYTH SCALE: 2

About the myth: If you've ever seen a cartoon with a raccoon in it, there's a good chance it shows the raccoon washing its food. This has been the belief for years—that before eating their food, raccoons will go and wash it in some kind of water because they prefer to eat it when it's clean.

The truth: Raccoons have very small, almost humanlike hands, and they have been observed putting their food in water before they eat it. So this is probably where the myth got started, but it's not really washing. Scientists still aren't sure why some raccoons like to wet their food before they eat it. Maybe they just like it that way. But even then, they don't always wet their food. Raccoons will raid bird feeders and garbage cans for food at night, and they aren't washing that food prior to eating it.

The takeaway: It looks like a raccoon is washing its food, but this isn't the case. Even if you see a raccoon holding food at a stream or underwater, it's not "washing" it like we do or how we might think.

Additional facts: Raccoons really do eat almost anything. They will eat eggs, garbage, fish, mice, and lots of other things. They come out at night to feed, so keep an eye out in your backyard for the chance to see a raccoon.

DESTINATIONS: Campgrounds

Ah, camping. You can hardly find a cheaper family trip. You can get as involved as you want—packing dozens of supplies to make your own meals, building your own campfire, etc. Or you can also take an easier route and just focus on the basics. Camping is a good reminder to unplug every once in a while—take a book or board games and just enjoy the time in the great outdoors with your family.

WHO? People camp with kids at any age—even babies. However, kids ages 5 and up are probably going to do best out in a tent. They can stay up later, roasting marshmallows on the fire, and they won't mind sleeping on the ground in a sleeping bag. Make it an activity for the entire family. Or if you're not seasoned campers, try camping in your backyard before you hit up a campground.

WHAT? You can find very simple campgrounds with almost no amenities or you can find elaborate sites with activities, water play areas, grill areas, and more. Decide what amenities you'd like to have, and then do a little bit of research before you go. The areas with more activities are naturally going to be a bit more crowded, but it's worth it if you're looking for things like beach areas and showers. If you like being secluded, find an area that's more remote.

WHEN? Many campgrounds are open year-round, but late spring to early fall is when they are most popular. You really can't pick a wrong time to go, but keep in mind that you don't want it to be too hot or cold. And plan accordingly depending on what time of year you're going—don't forget things like bug spray and extra blankets.

WHERE? It's never been easier to find campgrounds near you. Not only does every visitor center and travel website have a specific section for campers, but there are also dozens of resources online to choose from. Just type in "camping" along with your destination (by city or state) and see what comes up. Chances are you'll have results in an instant.

WHY? Nothing makes you appreciate nature like being out in it 24 hours a day. When you go camping, nature is all around you. Even if you don't think you're the camping type, give it a try for at least a night. You might like it more than you think.

TIPS AND TRICKS: Start off small—if you haven't been camping with your family, just do an overnight trip. If they love it, keep increasing the length of time you go. You might soon be going for weeklong trips all over the country. But it's important not to overdo it right away. One night sleeping in a wet tent because of rain could make someone never want to try camping again, and you don't want that.

All bugs are bad for the garden.

About the myth: It can take a lot of work to make a garden look beautiful, so if you go outside to find a bunch of bugs destroying your plants or eating your veggies, you want them gone. You might do anything to get rid of them so you can have a bug-free backyard.

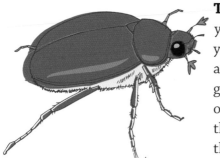

The truth: Before you grab that bug-killing spray, you should really look at the bugs you're getting in your backyard. Most bugs you find in the garden aren't actually bad bugs at all. In fact, many of the good bugs will actually get rid of the bad bugs without you having to do a thing. If you just spray something, there's a good chance you're going to kill all the bugs in your backyard, including good spiders, caterpillars, and more. Think about that for a second. If you kill all the caterpillars in your backyard, you're not going to have butterflies either. And what about bees? Flowers need bees to pollinate them, so you don't want to go and kill them.

The takeaway: All good gardens have bugs. Yes, there are some bad bugs out there that you can control on a case-by-case basis, but don't try to get rid of all the bugs. You need them to have healthy plants. Before you go eliminating bugs, do a little bit of additional research to see if you can figure out what you have.

Additional facts: Beetles are one of those bugs that often get a bad reputation. In some cases, as with Japanese beetles, they can take over backyards and kill plants. But in many other cases, beetles are part of a healthy backyard. For instance, ladybugs are beetles, and they are a good bug to have because they will help get rid of bad bugs.

Skunk spray is pee.

MYTH SCALE: 3

About the myth: It isn't smart to mess with a skunk—you could get peed on. And the smell of skunk pee is the worst. And once it gets into your clothes or on your dog's hair, it is nearly impossible to remove.

The truth: Skunks eat just about anything, and they can show up in even the most urban of settings. Make no mistake: You want to give skunks plenty of space whenever you see one. If threatened, skunks will hiss and stomp their feet. They might even lift their tail up as a warning sign. As a last resort skunks will fire off a cloud of spray in self-defense. It isn't pee though. It is a separate spray made up of irritating and stinky chemical compounds.

The takeaway: Skunk spray is a unique compound that is squirted out of specialized glands. It isn't pee, but that doesn't make it any more appealing if you get some on you.

Additional facts: So how do you get rid of skunk smell? It is a myth that tomato paste or juice is the trick. Hydrogen peroxide is your best bet. It is most effective at neutralizing those stinky thiol chemicals that cause that rotten smell.

Rabbits love carrots.

MYTH SCALE: 2

About the myth: "What's up, Doc?" asks a certain cartoon rabbit. If carrots are Bugs Bunny's favorite snacks, aren't they the favorite food for the cottontails running around your neighborhood as well?

The truth: Bunnies will nibble on carrots, but they can't live on carrots alone. In the wild, rabbits tend to eat vegetation. This can include veggies but consists of mostly grasses and herbs. Rabbit teeth grow throughout the animal's entire life, but they are worn down by all of the chewing that rabbits do. Rabbits have two sets of upper front teeth. The second pair is directly behind the front pair. These small teeth are sometimes referred to as peg teeth. The peg teeth are one way scientists determined that rabbits weren't closely related to rodents like mice and rats.

The takeaway: Both celery and broccoli growers tried to convince the creators of Bugs Bunny to switch to these vegetables, but thanks to that cartoon, rabbits will always be associated with carrots. Even though rabbits would rather eat the leafy green tops than the orange carrots.

Additional facts: Another myth about rabbits is that if you plant a bunch of marigolds around your vegetable garden, it'll keep the bunnies out.

Lobsters are red.

MYTH SCALE: 2

About the myth: Lobsters are a tasty treat for many people. They are a classic menu item in Maine. In addition to being found on dinner plates, they are also featured on some Maine license plates. The red crustacean is an icon for the state.

The truth: In the wild, lobsters come in a lot of different colors. They can be brownish to olive green. Some might have hints of red that you can see, but they certainly aren't bright red. They only turn that way after being heated up—like in a pot of boiling water. The red pigments in lobsters are stable in heat, so while the other colors fade away, the red intensifies. It can take a lobster many years before it grows large enough to be harvested. They can live to be over 100 years old and grow to over 3 feet long. As they grow bigger and bigger, they molt out of their shells. This happens about once a year. It takes a while for the new shell to harden up. They spend most of their lives near the ocean floor, and during their soft phase, they try to hide under rocks even more than normal.

The takeaway: Lobsters are red, but only after they've been cooked. They are usually brownish or green when they are alive.

Additional facts: Not all lobsters have claws. The clawed lobsters, including the American lobster in Maine, are generally found in colder waters. Spiny lobsters (also called rock lobsters) tend to be found in warmer waters.

A snake in the water can't bite.

MYTH SCALE: 3

About the myth: Even if you love snakes, you sure don't want to get bitten by one. Have you ever heard that a snake in the water can't bite? The story goes one of two ways: Either a snake can't bite when it is underwater or a snake can't bite while swimming on the water because it can't coil up and strike.

The truth: There are numerous species of snakes that are excellent swimmers—not just water snakes and water moccasins (cottonmouths). Many snakes will eat frogs and minnows. It'd be hard to eat a minnow if you couldn't bite underwater! Snakes can't lunge very far on land, and even less so on water, but that doesn't mean they can't bite if something or someone gets too close. Lots of times snakes will be sunning themselves along the edge of the water, perhaps on a rock or a log. If they sense something approaching, they'll often get in the water and swim to safety. You might not even know they were ever there.

The takeaway: Snakes in the water, just like snakes on the land, tend to retreat from people if they have that option, so you should be cautious but not scared. If they feel cornered and are harassed, they will bite in self-defense.

Additional facts: In 1999 the Lake Erie water snake was protected as a threatened species under the Endangered Species Act. Through conservation and education efforts, the species was removed from the list by 2011.

Baby animals are fuzzy.

MYTH SCALE: 2

About the myth: If you've ever held a little kitten or puppy, then you know they are just about the softest and fluffiest things imaginable. You just want to cuddle them as much as possible because they are so nice to touch. Other baby animals like rabbits and even baby birds must be just as fuzzy.

The truth: Are you ready to never think of baby animals the same again? OK—most baby animals are born just like you are: totally, 100 percent naked! So a lot of them start off with hardly any hair on their bodies at all. Or if they have some hair on their bodies, it's just small little bits, and it's certainly not what you would call fuzzy. For animals that have fur (or even feathers when it comes to birds), it takes a while for them to completely fill in and get that soft animal fuzz that you're thinking of. And then think about other baby animals like reptiles, frogs, and so on. When is the last time you heard someone talk about a frog being soft, fuzzy, and cuddly? No way!

The takeaway: Even baby animals that do have fur don't start off that way. Check out a book about baby animals in the nonfiction section of your library. Then you can see for yourself through a few pictures.

Additional facts: Have you ever held a baby chick or a baby duck? They are just about the softest animals you can find. While they grow up to develop large feathers that really aren't cuddly at all, it sure is fun to hold them when they're little.

SECTION 2: THE NEXT LEVEL

If you touch a baby bird, the parents will abandon it.

MYTH SCALE: 3

About the myth: You come across a baby bird that hasn't learned to fly yet. It's hopping about and seems scared. You look around and see a nest nearby, just at the crook of a tree. You want to help the baby, but then you remember some advice you heard about touching birds. It makes sense. You don't want the mother to abandon her baby because of you.

The truth: Bird parents have a strong instinct to care for their young, and they are not going to suddenly abandon it. For starters, a quick human touch doesn't actually transfer a very strong scent, so the parent bird probably won't even know you helped the baby back into its nest. Second of all, there are several examples of birds helping to care for young that aren't their own. For instance, brown-headed cowbirds will lay their eggs in another bird's nest, and then those birds feed and raise the young. Similarly, with bluebirds and others that nest more than once a season, juvenile birds will sometimes pitch in and help raise their siblings. So the bottom line is that a mother bird won't abandon her baby just because a human touched it.

The takeaway: If you find a baby bird on the ground, it's not necessarily hurt, lost, or abandoned. If you happen to see a nest nearby from which it likely fell, go ahead and put it back inside. Of course, you shouldn't linger too long, because predators could pick up your scent and the parent is probably waiting to return. Otherwise, leave it alone and keep an eye out. Chances are its mom or dad will be back for it.

Additional facts: Most young birds don't actually spend that much time with their parents. You might think about young geese (goslings), and it certainly seems like they follow their mom around for weeks or even months. But this isn't the case for most young. Songbirds, which include most backyard birds, hatch and then leave their nest after only two to three weeks. Some of the bigger birds (owls, hawks, eagles) need to rely on their parents longer. Shorebirds often hit the ground running, leaving the nest as soon as they hatch.

Bees die after they sting you.
MYTH SCALE: 2

About the myth: No one likes to get stung by a bee—ouch! But isn't it just a little bit satisfying to know bees are done after stinging you once? Then they'll never sting anyone again! Well, that's how the myth goes at least.

The truth: Yes, this myth is partly true, because honeybees can only sting once. This is because when their stinger goes into your skin, they can't pull it back out again without ripping out part of their abdomen. Ouch for you and them! So they die shortly after. Honeybees are not the only bees out there though. There are about 20,000 different species of bees in the world, and many bees can sting you over and over and over again.

The takeaway: It's true that honeybees can only sting you once, but all the other bees out there, including bumblebees, can sting you multiple times. So can wasps and hornets. Most insects won't bother you unless they feel threatened though. Leave them alone, and chances are they'll leave you alone too.

Additional facts: Another bee-related myth is that bumblebees can't sting at all. This is not true. They can sting but rarely do. Just leave them alone, and you shouldn't have to worry about them. Instead, enjoy watching them fly around your flowers.

Animals can smell fear.
MYTH SCALE: 3

About the myth: If you've ever been around a dog and are a little nervous (maybe because it's big or it doesn't look friendly), you know that it's nerve-racking. You try to make yourself calm down and act like the dog doesn't bother you, but that doesn't seem to work. It's like the dog can smell your fear.

The truth: It is true that all animals, including humans, have chemicals that come out of their bodies called pheromones. But the thing is, research shows that pheromones are something that only animals of the same species detect. This doesn't mean that the dog you're scared of doesn't know you're scared though. Chances are you are giving off other signs of being nervous, and it's picking up on physical clues instead.

The takeaway: The bottom line is that animals can't smell fear. Yes, they can detect when you are afraid, but that's probably because they can see it in your eyes, hear it in your voice, and detect it in your body language. Just try to act as confident as possible, and you'll be just fine!

Additional facts: Horses are another animal people say can smell your fear. This is not true either, but it's easy to see how someone might think so. When you're trying to ride a big horse, it can feel if you're nervous when you're sitting on top of it. It's how you hold the reins, kick your feet, and everything in between.

Baby animals are helpless.
MYTH SCALE: 2

About the myth: Imagine you're outside going for a hike and you see a little bit of movement in the grass. You peer a little closer and see a baby deer (called a fawn) tucked down low. You worry a little bit, wondering if the parents have abandoned the baby. How is it supposed to survive all on its own? Shouldn't you help it?

The truth: It's easy to look at a baby animal and think it's helpless and abandoned, but this is not usually the case. For instance, a mother deer will find her baby a place to sit and hide from predators, but she's usually not very far away. You might find other animals like baby rabbits or birds this way too. Don't think they have been abandoned though. Keep an eye out, and you'll probably see the parents pretty soon.

The takeaway: Even if you don't see parents nearby, babies aren't necessarily helpless. There's often an awkward stage where young animals aren't babies anymore, but they're not adults yet either. They still have ways of protecting themselves though. It's best to just leave them alone and let nature take its course.

Additional facts: Some baby animals don't stay with their parents very long at all. Birds are on their own at a young age, and so are rabbits. Rabbits are only with their parents for about six to eight weeks, and then they're all alone!

Male mosquitoes don't buzz.
MYTH SCALE: 3

About the myth: Bzzz, bzzz, bzzz. You know that annoying bzzz around your ear? It's like the mosquito is just hanging out there, teasing you and waiting to swoop in and bite you. Is it really a female mosquito? Are they really the only ones that bzzz?

The truth: It's pretty silly to think only females have a bzzz sound. This is not true at all. However, the females are probably the ones buzzing around your ear, and here's why: Only female mosquitoes can bite. They need your blood for protein for their eggs, while the males feed on flower nectar instead.

The takeaway: While both males and females buzz, the females are the ones to blame for biting you. Don't think you can get away from them though. Mosquitoes can detect you from far away just based on your breathing.

Additional facts: Believe it or not, they say mosquitoes are one of the most deadly animals in the world. This sounds pretty strange, right? It's not because they are all that dangerous by themselves, but they carry a lot of diseases like malaria, yellow fever, and others that can lead to death.

Fish either live in freshwater or in salt water.

MYTH SCALE: 2

About the myth: If you have pet fish, then you know that you either have a freshwater tank or a saltwater tank, but you can't mix them. Many of those beautiful tropical fish you see at the fish store need a special saltwater tank. So it should be the same for fish in the wild, right?

The truth: It's true that in many cases, fish either live in fresh or salt water. For instance, catfish and bass tend to be freshwater lake fish, while marlins and swordfish are in oceans (salt water). There are fish that will cross between freshwater and salt water though. They are called euryhaline species and can adapt to many conditions. For instance, salmon are born in freshwater but spend most of their lives in salt water. They just return to freshwater when they spawn (when they go to lay their eggs). In other examples some fish spend most of their time in freshwater but then go to salt water to spawn. This is the case with eels.

The takeaway: Most fish don't go back and forth between freshwater and salt water because they can't survive very well, but there are a few exceptions to the rule.

Additional facts: While most bass are freshwater fish, there is one exception to this too. Striped bass are found along the Atlantic coastline, and they will go between freshwater and salt water.

DESTINATIONS: Lakes

Lakes are one of the hottest spots to be in summer. No matter where you live, there's probably a lake within driving distance. You might not even know it existed. Make sure it's not a private lake, and then make plans to go for the day. Lakes are also the perfect place to take your boat, canoe, or kayak.

WHO? Everyone can go to the lake, but the ages of those going will determine what you need to bring. Babies will probably need something to ride in if they're going in the water. Older kids will probably want to bring water toys or even skis or a tube to pull behind a boat. Remember that if you go on a boat of any sort, you'll need life jackets for everyone. So bring those along unless your area lake has a public beach area where you can rent them.

WHAT? Lakes vary a great deal as to what's offered, so do a little research before you go. Some have campsites and entertainment areas with games, water toys, food, and more. You can even rent boats or pontoons at some locations. Even private lakes could still have public access areas. You can spend a whole day fishing, boating, playing water games, or just relaxing.

WHEN? The best time to go to the lake is when it's hot and the water is cool and refreshing. If you live in northern areas, you might want to wait until later in the summer to go to the lake because it'll take a while for the water to warm up. Or if you live in a hot area, you might want to go earlier before the water gets too hot! Either way, sunny days are the best. Don't forget the sunblock!

WHERE? This is where it varies quite a bit by where you live. There are areas that have huge natural lakes that go on for miles and miles. Other areas have much smaller lakes, but they're everywhere. Go online and do a search for lakes in your area. Chances are, you have one by you. And don't worry if you don't have a boat. There are still plenty of things to do.

WHY? Lakes are often near forests or other natural areas that you wouldn't otherwise discover. It's a great excuse to get outside and go swimming or fishing. And because lakes often have campsites nearby, those are two good experiences to combine.

TIPS AND TRICKS: You don't have to have a boat to enjoy a day at the lake. Just pack up your swimsuits, lunch, a cooler, and some fishing gear, and you'll have plenty to keep you busy. And don't overlook rivers. You can have a lot of fun along the river, enjoying many of the same activities as on a lake.

All spiders make webs to catch food.
MYTH SCALE: 2

About the myth: What makes a spider a spider? It's the ability to make a spiderweb, right? It just makes sense that all spiders know how to make webs. How can you be a spider if you can't make a web?

The truth: Scientists are still learning lots about spiders. There are over 40,000 described species, but they say the actual number could be three to five times higher. There are numerous styles of spiderwebs out there too. But the bottom line is, not all spiders build webs. While we think of many spiders using webs to catch food, spider silk can serve many other functions too. Spiders can also wrap their prey up mummy-style with their silk without needing a web at all. They can also use it to line burrows where they live or make egg sacks.

The takeaway: Even though not all spiders make webs, they can be an effective way for spiders to catch food. But it isn't the only way. Many species, especially jumping spiders, fishing spiders, and wolf spiders, stalk their prey. They don't need webs and instead sneak up on their meals. Other spiders wait for their dinner to come to them. Crab spiders, for example, sit camouflaged on flowers, snapping up unsuspecting insects as they pass by.

Additional facts: Spiders use spider silk for one more thing: ballooning. Ballooning is like a hot-air balloon ride for young spiders as they relocate to new areas.

Turtles have teeth.
MYTH SCALE: 3

About the myth: Turtles have sharp teeth and can bite a broom handle right in half. They also have an egg tooth when they are born to help them break out of the egg, so turtles must have teeth, right?

The truth: The bite of a turtle can be something fierce, and a couple of species of turtles might be able to put a hurting on a broom, but turtles don't have teeth! Some species of turtle have a diet heavy in meat and live animals. They don't need teeth though. A turtle mouth is sometimes referred to as a beak. The turtle beak has sharp ridges and bony plates to help grasp prey and tear off bits of meat. As far as the egg tooth goes, this is partially true. However, it isn't a real tooth. This structure is more like a miniature rhino horn. Baby turtles use this egg tooth to bust out of their shells, and then it falls off shortly after hatching.

The takeaway: Turtles don't have teeth, but this doesn't mean they can't bite! The mouths of turtles are quite varied from one species to the next. Yes, some have sharp edges, but none have teeth.

Additional facts: If you look at the fossils of some turtle species that are now extinct, you can see that many did have teeth.

Owls can spin their heads all the way around.

MYTH SCALE: 2

About the myth: Even if you haven't seen an owl in person, you've probably seen books or movies where the owl is looking straight ahead and then it rotates it's head all the way around. It seems to rotate in a full circle. Now that's like having eyes in the back of your head!

The truth: Owls can rotate their heads a lot—most species can make it about 270 degrees! However, they can't quite rotate their heads all the way around (which would be 360 degrees). There's a good reason owls can rotate their heads so much. The way their eyes work makes it very difficult for them to see things around them. You know how you can keep your head still and move your eyes around to see what's around you? Owls can't really do this, so they rely on moving their heads instead. It works great—owls are known for being good hunters, and a lot of that is because of their great eyesight.

The takeaway: It might look like owls can rotate their heads all around—after all, 270 degrees is pretty impressive. It's not quite all the way around though. If you get the chance to see an owl in person—either in the wild or at a zoo or something—take a close look to see how far they rotate.

Additional facts: Want another quirky fact about owls? Many owls have feathers on the top of their head that look like ears, but they're actually called tufts! Look up a picture of a great horned owl to see an example of this.

A turtle on its back can't flip back over.
MYTH SCALE: 3

About the myth: Think about a turtle for a second. Its body has a big job in holding up its shell. So what happens when a gust of wind comes along and knocks that turtle right over on its back? It doesn't seem like it'll ever be able to flip back over, does it?

The truth: This theory has been tested, and while it might seem next to impossible, turtles can flip themselves back over. Much like a little baby is learning to flip itself over or crawl, a turtle does so a little bit at a time. It just takes a couple of good moves to get the right angle and the right motion to flip back. You can even find videos online to show how turtles can flip from their backs.

The takeaway: You should never turn a turtle over to perform this test for yourself because it's not very respectful to the animal, but you don't need to worry about turtles either. They have grown accustomed to hauling around those big shells, and they'll be just fine if something happens.

Additional facts: Turtles have a reputation for being slow, but is that really the case? The short answer is yes. Turtles are very slow, in part because they have a big shell to haul around and little legs that don't move very fast. If you see a turtle on the side or middle of the road, go ahead and move it so it doesn't get hit by a car.

Male animals are bigger than female animals.
MYTH SCALE: 2

About the myth: It's easy to think that males of most species are bigger than females. We live in a culture where men, on average, are taller than women. So it's easy to think of all males as the larger, bigger, more dominant ones, even in the animal world.

The truth: It's true that with mammals, the males are often bigger than the females because they usually have the job of offering protection. But that's definitely not the case with all animals. With most insects, the female is actually bigger than the male. This is the case for a lot of birds, especially raptors, too. This is because females have the job of carrying young, so they need bigger bodies for this.

The takeaway: You can't assume that males are actually bigger. Even for mammals, you might come across a female that is bigger than her mate. Challenge yourself by observing animals at the zoo or on a farm or even the smaller animals like insects in your backyard. See if you can figure out which one is male and which is female by using a good guidebook.

Additional facts: Here's a fun phrase to learn: sexual dimorphism. When sexual dimorphism exists in species, it means that males and females have distinct things that make them look different. When it doesn't exist, it means they look exactly the same and it's hard to tell the difference between them by appearance only.

Sharks kill a lot of people.

MYTH SCALE: 3

About the myth: As you're splashing in the ocean, you see the hint of a shark fin in the distance. It starts to circle someone out in the water. If you believe what you see in the movies, this person is about to get attacked and could be this shark's next meal.

The truth: Most sharks do not attack. In fact, they don't even come near shore where they would come in contact with humans. Out of all the shark species out there (there are more than 300), only a very small handful will even attack a person. And even in those few instances, it's usually because they are confused, not because they are out to eat them. (Humans are not really part of a shark's diet.) There are many other animals that are considered more deadly to humans than sharks, including horses, cows, ants, deer, bees, and hippopotamuses.

The takeaway: We actually do more harm to sharks than they do to us. By fishing the ocean, it's taking away their food supply. The next time you have a chance to see a shark (probably in an aquarium of some sort), take a closer look at it, and try to gain a new appreciation for sharks. They are pretty cool animals. They just get a bad reputation because of a few movies out there!

Additional facts: Sharks have a lot of teeth! They lose them a lot too, but they can quickly grow replacements. Some studies show that sharks can have as many as 30,000 teeth during their lifetimes.

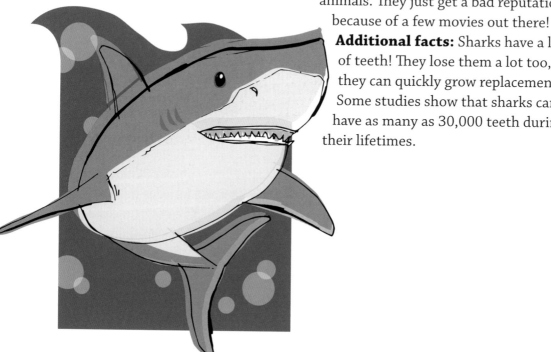

You can tell how old a ladybug is by the number of spots it has.

MYTH SCALE: 3

About the myth: This one makes a lot of sense, right? As a ladybug gets older, it gains more spots. So if you count them up, you can tell how old it is.

The truth: The number of spots a ladybug has actually has nothing to do with its age. Spots do matter though. There's more than just one kind of ladybug out there, and the pattern of spots can tell you what kind it is.

The takeaway: It's a lot of fun to count a ladybug's spots, so count away! But the number isn't actually a way to predict its age.

Additional facts: The red and black color combination is one that many insect-eating animals have learned to leave alone. The colors are like a big warning sign to say stay away!

You can tell how old an animal is by counting its antler points.

MYTH SCALE: 3

About the myth: Antlers come in many shapes and sizes. Antlers are impressive headgear. You can't really compare antlers from species to species. Elk have long thin tines, while moose have flatter antlers. Most things start off small and they get bigger and bigger as they grow up. Antlers could be that way too. They do fall off and grow back every year, so maybe animals grow one new antler point for every year of their lives.

The truth: The first set of antlers can be a single pair of spikes, and it is true that antlers can grow larger year after year. But some really old animals can have smaller antlers again. A lot of other factors go into antler growth too. Things like age but also genetics, disease, and animal nutrition.

The takeaway: You can't simply count the antler points to age an animal. If you find a skull to examine, ignore the antlers and look at the teeth. Teeth wear down over the years, so you can get a rough estimate of the age of an animal by simply examining a jaw.

Additional facts: Horns are another structure grown on the heads of some animals, like bighorn sheep, bison, and cattle. Horns are made up of a bony core and covered in a keratin sheath. Unlike antlers that have multiple tines, horns don't branch.

Starfish and jellyfish are both types of fish.

MYTH SCALE: 3

About the myth: Starfish and jellyfish—they both have fish in their name. Even though they're a little different than a lot of the typical fish you know, they have to be some type of fish, right?

The truth: A lot of people will tell you that starfish and jellyfish are actually the wrong names and you shouldn't be using them. They will tell you to instead use the terms "sea star" and "sea jelly." This is because they aren't really fish at all! They are actually more closely related to sea creatures like sand dollars and sea urchins. Starfish, for example, don't have gills, scales, or fins. And while jellyfish float around in the water more like fish do, they are made up quite differently as well.

The takeaway: Names can easily fool people, and in this case, it's not hard to see why. Starfish and jellyfish might have fish in their names, but they aren't types of fish at all.

Additional facts: The sea stars that you are probably familiar with are part of a family called the echinoderms. This is the same family to which sea dollars belong. (A lot of people don't realize sea dollars are animals. They think they are just shells.) Go ahead and surprise your friends and the adults in your life with that one!

All woodpeckers peck wood.
MYTH SCALE: 2

About the myth: When it comes to woodpeckers, you just have to look at their name to understand them. The first part is wood. The second part is pecker. So they must peck wood. It's part of their name after all.

The truth: There is some truth to woodpeckers pecking wood, but do you know why they do it? There are a few reasons. First, they'll peck at wood to get at the insects hiding behind the bark. They'll also peck wood to carve out (also called excavate) a hole so they can nest there. And they will peck at wood to hide (also called cache) their food. But do all woodpeckers peck wood? No! In fact, some woodpeckers will peck at cacti instead.

The takeaway: Not all species of woodpeckers peck wood, but many do. There is a difference between holes that are carved out for nesting versus those for digging for insects or hiding food. Go on a hike to see if you can find a few holes in the trees that look like they came from a woodpecker.

Additional facts: Related to woodpeckers are a group of birds called sapsuckers. No, they don't necessarily suck up sap—don't be fooled by their name! Instead, they tap rows of sap wells into trees and then they dip their tongues into the sap that oozes out.

Baby sea turtles hatch during the full moon.

MYTH SCALE: 2

About the myth: Baby sea turtles hatch out at night. They need to have a full moon so they can find their way to the ocean.

The truth: Sea turtles hatch out of eggs on land, but they spend much of their lives at sea. The funny thing is, after the female comes to shore to lay her eggs, she heads right back out to the ocean. The eggs are left to incubate in the sand for a couple of months. Then when the babies hatch out, they are on their own. It is pretty crazy to think that baby sea turtles never see their parents. They do hatch out at night, but it doesn't have to be during the full moon. Hatching can be during any phase of the moon. Instinctively the young sea turtles head for the horizon that is more lit up. This should be toward the water, but with artificial lighting they can get turned around and head inland instead.

The takeaway: If you are walking along the beach at night, perhaps you'll be lucky enough to see the remarkable sight of baby sea turtles scrambling down the beach and off to sea. Even if it isn't on the night of a full moon.

Additional facts: All of the species of sea turtles found in North America are threatened or endangered.

Only male animals grow antlers.

MYTH SCALE: 1

About the myth: In the animal world males and females are sometimes called different things. For example, moose and elk males are called bulls and the females are called cows. It is buck (male) and doe (female) for deer. The easiest way to tell the males from the females is to look for antlers, right?

The truth: Antlers are bone-like structures that are grown annually. Every year they are shed off and then regrown. That means at certain times of the year neither males nor females have antlers. You can still see the pedestal where the antlers grow, though, if you look closely. Also, female caribou (reindeer are technically the same thing) grow antlers. Female caribou antlers tend to be smaller than male antlers.

The takeaway: It is only the males that grow antlers in most species, but the one exception in North America is the caribou. It is extremely rare, but once in a while a female deer can grow antlers.

Additional facts: For all species, antlers grow quickly during the summer months. They are covered with blood vessels (called velvet) and have a soft, fuzzy appearance as they grow. Male antlers are important during the rut or breeding season. Large antlers can intimidate other males. There are also occasional pushing matches between two males to sort out disputes and to try to impress the females.

SECTION 3: CHALLENGE YOURSELF

Birds have no sense of smell.

MYTH SCALE: 2

About the myth: Many animals have a reputation for having a great sense of smell, but birds aren't really one of those animals. A lot of animals need their sense of smell to help them eat, but birds don't need that. They can just use their sense of sight instead.

The truth: For years scientists have thought that birds can't smell. Some people even suggest that if you want to keep squirrels away from your bird feeder, you can put hot pepper on your birdseed because birds can't smell it anyway. Recent studies, though, have suggested that we might not know as much as we thought. Scientists now have evidence that shows many examples of birds being able to smell to locate food. They also think birds can use their sense of smell to select mates, find nesting spots, and find food in the wild.

The takeaway: Scientists are always learning and studying animals, so what was true a few years ago isn't necessarily true today. Sure, they thought birds couldn't really smell much, but it's not the case. They're still learning about a bird's sense of smell and how it varies from one species to another, but they can smell!

Additional facts: Turkey vultures definitely use their sense of smell to locate food. One of their primary sources of food is roadkill and other decaying carcasses, which smell pretty awful to most people. If they couldn't smell, they wouldn't be able to locate this food.

There are penguins in North America.

MYTH SCALE: 3

About the myth: Penguins are iconic birds of the cold. They survive in cold and blustery conditions in places like the Arctic and Antarctica.

The truth: Of the nearly 700 species of birds that are found regularly in the United States, penguins aren't one of them. If you've ever seen pictures of penguins hanging out with polar bears, you'll know they are fake. Penguins and polar bears live in different parts of the world. Polar bears are in the north and penguins are in the south. (Arctic comes from the Greek word for "bear," and Antarctic means "without bears.") No penguins live in Alaska or Canada. Come to think of it, polar bears would probably think penguins taste pretty good for lunch, so maybe this is a good thing.

The takeaway: You can't find penguins anywhere in North America, except in zoos. There is just one species of penguin that lives north of the equator, the Galapagos penguin. Humboldt penguins live along the western coast of South America. The rest of the species live along the southern coasts of South America, Africa, and Australia as well as along the Antarctic coast.

Additional facts: Penguins can't fly, but they are excellent swimmers. They flap their wings similar to flying birds, and this propels them along underwater. Penguins' main food sources are fish, so being great swimmers is key. A final burst of speed helps launch penguins out of the water and back up onto the ice or land. It's like a reverse dive.

Bald eagles are rare.
MYTH SCALE: 2

About the myth: Back in the 1970s eagles were almost wiped out! Pesticides were causing eagle eggshells to break before the babies could hatch. This led to population declines, and they were put on the endangered species list. This means it's pretty rare and unique to see a bald eagle, so you should treasure those moments if you spot one.

The truth: You definitely should treasure a bald eagle sighting—that's cool! But these great birds are no longer endangered. Conservation efforts over the past several decades have helped them prosper. Now bald eagles are thriving across the country. Areas that haven't seen bald eagles for years are now having these birds nest and come back year after year. Back in the 1970s, they said there were fewer than 500 nests in the lower forty-eight states. In 2007 they removed the bald eagle from the endangered species list, and now it's estimated that more than 10,000 eagle pairs are nesting.

The takeaway: This is a true success story of people who set out to save the bald eagle. This bird is the national symbol of the United States after all, so it was definitely a worthwhile effort. The next time you spot an eagle, remember that it took a lot of work to get the population strong again. Maybe you can be a part of helping an endangered species make a comeback!

Male birds are brighter colored than females.
MYTH SCALE: 2

About the myth: Have you ever looked outside to see a bright-red cardinal perched on a branch? Keep looking and maybe you'll see a bird that looks like a cardinal nearby—except there's a big difference because it's not as colorful. It has some red on it, but it is not nearly as bright as the first one. You're looking at a male and a female cardinal. It must mean all male birds are brighter than the females, right?

The truth: In several cases male birds really do have brighter feathers than the females. Examples of this include male ducks, cardinals, bluebirds, and lots of warblers. But this isn't always the case. In many instances males and females look exactly the same. For example, blue jays, chickadees, titmice, and wrens all look alike. It's almost impossible to tell from a distance whether you're looking at a male or a female. With shorebirds called phalaropes, the females are brighter than the males.

The takeaway: Don't assume you're looking at a male! As you learn the birds in your own backyard and beyond, take the time to look them up and figure out if there are differences between males and females. It makes it a lot more fun when you spot one out in the wild.

Additional facts: Woodpeckers are a bit tricky. Some woodpecker species look exactly the same between male and female, and others have just small differences. It might be just a matter of one having a small red patch on the back of its head and the other not. Get a good field guide and see if you can pick out the differences between woodpeckers.

Snakes can't hear because they don't have ears.

MYTH SCALE: 3

About the myth: Snakes don't have outer ears like many traditional animals, so for years scientists thought that they couldn't hear at all. They believed snakes used their other senses to get information about their surroundings.

Then scientists who study reptiles (called herpetologists) started learning new things.

The truth: Snakes do have inner ears. You just can't see them. But how does the noise travel to the inner ear? Scientists think that the sound travels there through the jawbone! The way their jaw moves from side to side makes it possible for sound to transfer up to their inner ears.

The takeaway: Snakes can hear even though they don't have distinct outer ears. Maybe this means you shouldn't go sneaking up on a snake!

Additional facts: Here's another fun fact about snakes and their senses—they can actually use their tongues to smell things! You know how snakes stick out their tongues a lot? Turns out there are reasons they are doing this. They're using their tongue to help them gather important information about their surroundings.

To live underwater requires gills.

MYTH SCALE: 2

About the myth: It's common knowledge that fish have gills. In fact, it's those gills that allow them to live and breathe underwater. So it must be common for other animals that live underwater to have gills as well, right? Not so fast!

The truth: Lots of animals live underwater without having gills. To start with, dolphins and whales don't have gills at all. They both have lungs and blowholes. They can stay underwater for long periods of time. Then they come to the surface to breathe in new air through the blowholes on the tops of their bodies. Another underwater creature that doesn't have gills is the frog. Several species of frogs live around and under water, yet they come to the surface to breathe as well.

The takeaway: Fish definitely have gills and need them to breathe underwater, but there are actually lots of other animals that can live in oceans and lakes that do not breathe in this way. In general, water animals are fascinating. Get a good nonfiction book from the library about animals that live in water. Learn which ones have gills and which ones don't. You might be surprised!

Additional facts: There are some pretty impressive animals that can stay under the water a long time without having to come to the surface to breathe. For example, the hippopotamus stays underwater for 5, 15, or even 30 minutes at a time. Sea turtles can stay underwater for up to 5 hours if they need to. And some species of whales can stay under the water for a couple of hours!

Moths are always nocturnal.

MYTH SCALE: 1

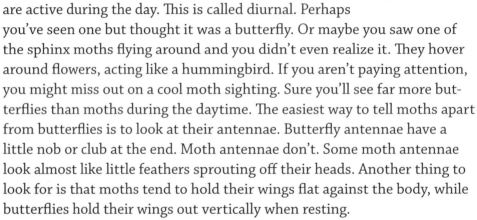

About the myth: Moths are creatures of the night. You can see them swarming around your porch light after the sun goes down. When morning rolls around, they hunker down for the day.

The truth: Most moths are nocturnal, or active at night, but there are some exceptions. Some of the most spectacular moths are active during the day. This is called diurnal. Perhaps you've seen one but thought it was a butterfly. Or maybe you saw one of the sphinx moths flying around and you didn't even realize it. They hover around flowers, acting like a hummingbird. If you aren't paying attention, you might miss out on a cool moth sighting. Sure you'll see far more butterflies than moths during the daytime. The easiest way to tell moths apart from butterflies is to look at their antennae. Butterfly antennae have a little nob or club at the end. Moth antennae don't. Some moth antennae look almost like little feathers sprouting off their heads. Another thing to look for is that moths tend to hold their wings flat against the body, while butterflies hold their wings out vertically when resting.

The takeaway: You'll see the most moths after dark, but don't forget to look for moths during the day too.

Additional facts: Moths and butterflies are closely related. They are both classified as Lepidoptera. Moths make up around 90 percent of this group, while butterflies and skippers are just 10 percent.

DESTINATIONS: Local, State, and National Wildlife Refuges

You're never far from a great adventure when it comes to the National Wildlife Refuge System. Today, there are more than 500 refuges all across the country, and they do a great job of preserving our plants, wildlife, birds, and more. All together, these refuges cover more than 150 million acres (that's bigger than the whole state of California), yet many people don't even realize they exist. National Wildlife Refuge land is protected so people can't build on it or develop it. And since the government owns it, you technically own part of it too. The phrase from the famous Woody Guthrie song "this land is your land; this land is my land" certainly rings true for refuges. Get out there and enjoy!

WHO? Refuges are for the entire family. Most have great paths even for strollers. Or, for older kids, check out the biking trails or hiking along refuge trails that are a little less traveled. You will also find that many locations have auto tours as well, which is a great way to cover a lot of ground in a short amount of time. Best of all, refuge activities are usually free or are very inexpensive for families, so you don't have to worry about spending a lot to have a fun day out.

WHAT? First off, refuges are a great place to find native plants, insects, and wildlife. Take a magnifying glass, camera, and/or binoculars. You can do a variety of activities at refuges, including hiking, fishing, bird watching, and more. Many refuges even have special activities or programs throughout the year. So get in touch with your local refuges, check out their visitor centers, and support them and their local programming.

WHEN? While you can go to refuges year-round, many people overlook going in winter. Don't make that mistake! Pick a sunny day, bundle up, and head out to explore. You don't have to go out for long or for very far, but winter is one of the most peaceful times to visit. Plus, you'll see plenty of animals out looking for food. To learn about events in winter and beyond, sign up for their newsletters or get on their email list. Then they can stay in touch and keep you informed.

WHERE? They're everywhere. Go online to www.fws.gov/refuges and you can search for refuges by state or using your zip code. Most states have several to choose from, so chances are there's one just a short drive away. Remember: Refuges are in areas that often have marshes, are on water, or are off the beaten path. So even if you have to go a little out of your way, it's worth it.

WHY? It's hard to find a better setting that's so close to home and celebrates your area's best features. The job of refuges is to preserve the land around us, so it's like seeing your own backyard in all of its natural glory. In addition, many of the people who work at refuges are volunteers. So get out and support these local programs. It helps ensure that they'll be around for generations to come.

TIPS AND TRICKS: Duck Stamps will get you free admission into National Wildlife Refuges. Learn more at www.fws.gov/duckstamps.

Did You Know?

President Theodore Roosevelt and the US Fish and Wildlife Service helped get this program started way back in 1903. Roosevelt saw the importance of preserving America's most valuable natural land, and he named Florida's Pelican Island as the first official refuge.

All animals naturally have the ability to swim.

MYTH SCALE: 2

About the myth: A lot of swimming has to do with instinct. Have you ever seen dogs go in the water? Somehow they seem to just know to wiggle their front legs and swim to shore. After all, it's not called the dog paddle for nothing!

The truth: For the most part, animals are pretty good swimmers. A lot of animals are even able to swim within hours of being born. Not all animals have these same instincts though. For instance, people, apes, and chimpanzees have to learn how to swim. Did you learn how to swim? Do you remember how long it took? It's no easy task!

The takeaway: Swimming abilities differ from one animal to the next. If you happen to be at the zoo or somewhere in the wild where you see animals swimming, take a look at their different styles. Observe how some species differ from others.

Additional facts: All ducks are great swimmers, with their webbed feet, and wood ducks are some of the most impressive. A wood duck will jump out of its nest from high up in a tree within just a few hours of being born. Now that's impressive!

Animals sleep with their eyes closed.

MYTH SCALE: 2

About the myth: When you go to sleep, you close your eyes. This function seems pretty common and well known. How else are you supposed to sleep?

The truth: Animal sleep is fascinating. If you ever get the chance to check out a book about animal sleep from the library, you'll learn all kinds of things! But no, not all animals close their eyes when they sleep like we humans do. Lots of birds and fish sleep with their eyes open.

The takeaway: Sleep varies a great deal from one animal to the next. Some sleep standing up. Some sleep during the day. Some even sleep with their eyes open. But one thing is similar—all animals need sleep!

Additional facts: Dolphins are one of the most fascinating sleepers. They actually sleep with one eye open and continue to swim while they're sleeping! They will put part of their brain to rest while closing just one eye at the same time. It's pretty impressive.

Groundhogs can predict the weather.

MYTH SCALE: 3

About the myth: Groundhogs have been predicting the weather for years. The way the story goes is that a groundhog comes out of its burrow and looks for its shadow. If it sees its shadow, it goes back inside, and we will have six more weeks of winter. If it doesn't see its shadow because it's a cloudy day, it stays outside, and that means spring is just around the corner!

The truth: This folklore dates back to the 1800s and the Pennsylvania Germans. It originated in Europe, where history says they would often use a badger instead of a groundhog to predict the weather. While lots of people look to animals to be weather predictors, this one doesn't have much credibility. You can't plan for six weeks of weather based on a single day of whether or not it's cloudy.

The takeaway: You don't need to believe the groundhog, but it's still fun to join in the celebration. Groundhog Day is on February 2 every year, and lots of people treat it like a holiday. People often hope for a cloudy day because by early February, they're sick of winter and would like an early spring.

Additional facts: Groundhogs are a type of rodent, and some people also refer to them as woodchucks. They are a type of ground squirrel, mostly found in the eastern half of the United States, but they also extend into Canada and parts of Alaska. They have powerful claws that are perfect for digging their burrows, where they sleep, raise their young, and hibernate during winter.

Wolves howl at the moon.

MYTH SCALE: 3

About the myth: One of the most typical and picturesque night scenes related to animals is that of a wolf and a moon. The wolf usually has its nose pointed up at the sky where there's a full moon, and it's letting out a long, soulful howl.

The truth: This myth has been circulated for years and years. No one is exactly sure where it got started, but there are a lot of ancient stories, pictures, and art related to wolves from all over the world. Wolves are pretty common—you can find them all over the world except Antarctica and South America, so it's no wonder so many cultures have embraced this animal. But the truth of the matter is, they don't really howl at the moon. **The takeaway:** Wolves might howl at night, and they might even howl when there's a full moon. But they are not purposefully howling at the moon. It's still fun to hear wolves howling at night though. What do you think they're howling at?

Additional facts: Wolves are actually very similar to dogs, and they communicate in a lot of similar ways. They will howl, bark, whine, whimper, and more. Another important thing to note about wolves is that some populations are expanding while others are on the endangered species list.

Animals can only see in black and white.
MYTH SCALE: 2

About the myth: You might have heard that dogs only see in black and white. Then this must be true for other animals too!

The truth: Let's start with dogs—they don't just see black and white. Dogs, like many animals, see colors but don't see as many colors as humans do. Animal eyes have fewer cones than most humans. For instance, they are missing the red cone, so red and green look the same to them. All animals are different though. For instance, deer don't see orange like we do—this is why hunters in the woods can wear bright orange and the deer don't seem to notice.

The takeaway: It can vary a lot from one animal to another, but the bottom line is that most animals can see colors.

Additional facts: Some animals can even see better than humans because they have more eye cones. For instance, some snakes, butterflies, and birds are believed to have excellent eyesight and might be able to see colors that we can't.

You can't wake a hibernating animal.
MYTH SCALE: 2

About the myth: Hibernation is common in animals during winter. It involves animals going into a deep sleep, so for several weeks they can go without food. Even if you tried to wake up an animal, it would just keep right on sleeping.

The truth: Hibernation varies so much from one animal to the next. And for most animals, if you tried hard enough, you could wake them up. Still, it's a pretty amazing thing in general. Hibernation involves an animal usually going into a protected space like a burrow or a den and then lowering its metabolism. Animals don't necessarily sleep away the whole winter like some people think, but they are able to go long periods of time with relatively little food. Other species will go into a daily torpor, which is kind of like an overnight hibernation.

The takeaway: The bottom line is that you shouldn't disturb an animal at all, whether it's hibernating or not! And if you did, the animal would probably wake up. There's so much more to learn about hibernation and how it's different from one animal to the next. Do some more research on your own so you can amaze your friends!

Additional facts: Some species automatically go into a seasonal hibernation, while other species might just slow down their metabolism during harsh conditions.

Birds only nest in spring.

MYTH SCALE: 2

About the myth: Spring signifies new life. It's the time of year for birds to start building their nests. You can see them out and about, singing and flitting from one tree to the next as they gather nesting material and prepare to lay eggs and raise babies.

The truth: Spring does mark the start of nesting season for many birds, but the truth is that some birds start earlier, even in winter! Owls are especially known for this. They will start nesting as early as January or February, depending on the area. They start building their nests and laying their eggs even when there's snow on the ground in some cases. Although they don't nest until later in the year, ducks are birds that start choosing mates in winter as well.

The takeaway: Spring isn't the only time for nesting birds. When you're out and about this winter, keep an eye out for owls and ducks to see if you notice them exhibiting signs of nesting. These might include males and females hanging out together more, or the birds gathering nesting material. You can also listen for owls calling to one another.

Additional facts: Most owls and ducks don't use birdhouses, but a couple of them do. Screech owls and wood ducks both will. Of course, you'll need the right habitat. Owls need wooded areas, and wood ducks need to be by water. If you don't live in these types of areas, don't be discouraged. Use it as an excuse to go out looking for birds.

DESTINATIONS: Zoos and Aquariums

Zoos and aquariums are some of the most popular destinations for families. It's no wonder why—they showcase the world's amazing biodiversity, capture the imagination, and generate a lifelong interest in nature. The really good zoos and aquariums go beyond just highlighting animals. They also foster meaningful conservation work on a local and global scale. So check out and support those near you.

WHO? These destinations are great for all ages. Often, the organizations even offer discount rates for youngsters, so even the smallest of naturalists will enjoy a visit to a zoo or an aquarium. Look for educational programs and day camps throughout the year. Some zoos and aquariums even offer internships for high school students.

WHAT? Zoos and aquariums have educational exhibits, but they also provide critical conservation efforts, including captive breeding of numerous endangered species. Ask about what kind of efforts are involved in your area and how you might be able to help. Often zoos and aquariums will have special events where you get more of a behind-the-scenes look. If you're offered this opportunity, take it.

WHEN? Winter can be a great time to visit zoos and aquariums. A few animals might be moved into indoor enclosures, but some other animals will become more active as the weather turns cooler. Indoor aquariums can keep you in touch with nature all winter long too. Plan ahead and you might be able to catch feeding time for some of the species.

WHERE? While many of the most famous zoos and aquariums are found in larger cities, smaller-scale operations can be equally as impressive. Look to your state or city visitor center to be your guide, and look for these types of places when you're traveling too.

WHY? Zoos and aquariums offer close views of some of nature's most fascinating critters. Most of us don't live in areas that have a lot of these creatures naturally. Where else can you learn about so many different animals in such a short amount of time?

TIPS AND TRICKS: Many zoos and aquariums offer seasonal discount rates. Visiting in the winter might just save you a buck or two. You can also gather up a bunch of friends and get a group rate in some instances.

Pelicans live by the ocean.

MYTH SCALE: 2

About the myth: Pelicans are the ultimate beach bums. They chill on the coast, feeding on fish, living their lives near the ocean.

The truth: There are two different species of pelicans that live in the United States. The brown pelican is common along the California coast as well as in the Gulf of Mexico and up the Atlantic as far north as the Chesapeake Bay. The American white pelican spends the winter in these coastal waters as well. But during the summer breeding season, American white pelicans move north. They nest on large bodies of water in the central and western United States and Canada. One of the largest colonies of American white pelicans nests on Yellowstone Lake in Yellowstone National Park. That's about as far from an ocean as you can get. There are eight different species of pelicans in the world, and they all generally nest in large colonies. The four brownish species usually nest in trees, and the four species of whitish pelicans prefer to nest on the ground.

The takeaway: All pelicans are fish eaters that live near water. Brown pelicans live by the ocean, but American white pelicans nest along waters far inland.

Additional facts: Pelicans have different fishing styles. American white pelicans swim together to round up fish for eating, while brown pelicans plunge-dive out of the air to catch a meal.

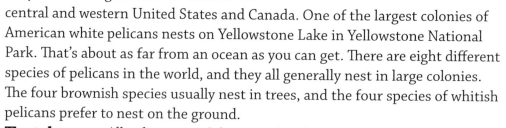

Damselflies are female dragonflies.

MYTH SCALE: 3

About the myth: Males and females of the same species can look similar but slightly different. Damselflies and dragonflies look almost the same. Damsel is a term for females, even when they aren't in distress. That makes damselflies girls. By default that makes dragonflies males.

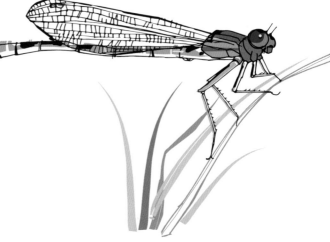

The truth: As logical as all of that sounds, it couldn't be further from the truth. First off, damselflies and dragonflies aren't the same species. There are actually loads of different species of each, and each of these species has males and females. Even though they look similar, there are a few different ways to tell damselflies and dragonflies apart. You can start by looking them in the eyes. Damselflies have eyes along the sides of the head, and these eyes are separated by a little bit of space. The eyes of dragonflies nearly touch each other and are closer to the top of the head. Another way to tell them apart is how they hold their wings. Damselflies hold their wings along their bodies, while dragonflies keep their wings held open.

The takeaway: Damselflies and dragonflies do have many things in common, including big eyes, long, skinny bodies, and those cool wings. They aren't the same species though. And all of the different species of damselflies and dragonflies have both males and females.

Additional facts: In total there are about 5,000 species of damselflies and dragonflies. Together they make up the order called Odonata, which means "toothed ones." Here's the thing though: They don't have teeth.

Snakes and lizards are slimy.

MYTH SCALE: 3

About the myth: If you've never touched a snake or a lizard, how do you think it would feel? They don't have any hair, so they must be cold and slimy, right? They sure aren't warm and fuzzy like mammals.

The truth: Snakes and lizards aren't slimy at all. None of the reptiles are. They are all covered in scales. Sometimes these scales can be quite small and smooth. This can give them a shiny appearance, so it is understandable that people would think snakes and lizards would be slimy. But they aren't. Amphibians like frogs and salamanders can have a bit of mucus on the skin that gives them a slimy feel. Amphibians lack scales, so they use mucus to keep themselves from drying out too much. But not all amphibians are slimy either. Toads have pretty dry skin, kind of like snakes and lizards.

The takeaway: Snakes and lizards are reptiles. They are covered in scales, but they aren't slimy. Remember a few snakes and lizards could potentially be dangerous, so use caution. Also, if you do handle one for a quick inspection, be gentle, and always put them back where you found them.

Additional facts: A cool thing about reptile scales is they are made up of keratin, much like fingernails.

Frogs ribbit.

About the myth: For years kids have been learning animal sounds, and the one long associated with frogs is the traditional ribbit, ribbit, ribbit. Movies, books, and all kinds of other media use the ribbit, ribbit sound of frogs in nearly everything they do, so it must be the sound that most frogs make.

The truth: First of all, there are a lot of different kinds of frogs out there, and there's no way they all make the same sound. Second of all, you'd probably be pretty surprised to hear the different kinds of sounds frogs can make. Chances are it's not what you're thinking. American bullfrogs have a very deep sound that doesn't sound like a ribbit at all. And many other frogs don't sound very froglike either. Now, the one frog that produces a sound most like a ribbit is the Pacific tree frog. This is probably where all those ribbits come from, but this is just one type of frog!

The takeaway: You can have a lot of different sounds when it comes to frogs. Take this opportunity to do some searching online to find out what frogs sound like. You could even put together a little test or quiz for your friends or parents to see if they can tell the differences between frogs. Now when you're out in the wild and you hear a funny noise, you might be able to identify it as a frog and teach others too.

Additional facts: We can probably blame Hollywood for the whole ribbit, ribbit thing. It makes sense: The Pacific tree frog is found all along California, where lots of movies and TV shows are made. So it's only natural that people there use it for the frog sounds.

All birds can fly.

About the myth: Birds fly. It's just what they do. It doesn't get much simpler than that.

The truth: Most birds do fly, but there are a few exceptions. Penguins and ostriches are two exceptions to the "birds can fly" rule. Both of these birds can't fly at all, yet they are still birds. Other birds that cause a lot of confusion regarding whether they can fly are chickens and even turkeys. You usually see these birds grounded, but they can fly if they want to. Turkeys spend the night roosting in the tops of trees. They might not go great distances, but they still have what it takes to fly.

The takeaway: See if you can dazzle your friends with the fact that not all birds fly. It's one of those trickier ones because most do in fact fly. But you'll look even more impressive when you can tell them exactly which ones can't.

Additional facts: For birds that migrate in the fall, you might be surprised to find out that many young birds are all on their own! Yep, their parents aren't necessarily showing them where to go or fly. They have to figure it out all on their own even though they've never done it. So for birds that migrate hundreds of miles to the tropics for winter, they are figuring out how to get there without any help!

Opossums hang by their tails.

About the myth: Animals as different as monkeys, anteaters, tree porcupines, and lizards can hang from tree branches with their prehensile tails. Many marsupials also have this distinctive skill. Having a tail is cool enough, but being able to hang from a tail is a really awesome trick. But can opossums hang by their tails?

The truth: The opossum species found in the United States

and southern parts of Canada is the Virginia opossum. While many species of opossum can have fully prehensile tails, adult Virginia opossums can't hang from their tails. Their bodies are too heavy and their tails are too weak. They can twist their tails around branches to use like an extra leg. This helps them balance.

The takeaway: Virginia opossums can climb trees, but they can't hang by their tails. But that doesn't make them any less cool. They still have distinct marsupial adaptations, including a pouch. Young opossums are quite small when they are born. They stay in the pouch for two months as they continue to grow. Once they leave the pouch, young opossums sometimes can be seen riding along on their mother's back.

Additional facts: Opossums have a highly variable diet. They'll scavenge up almost anything to eat. For example, insects and worms . . . eggs and baby birds . . . plant matter . . . roadkill . . . even garbage. The habit of eating roadkill leads many opossums to unfortunately become roadkill themselves.

Butterflies come from cocoons.

MYTH SCALE: 3

About the myth: Butterflies start off as caterpillars. And caterpillars transform into butterflies in cocoons right? Seems pretty clear. How is this even a myth?

The truth: It is almost as simple as that. Except butterflies don't make cocoons, they make chrysalises. Moths are the ones that make cocoons. It takes butterflies four stages to become adults: egg, larva, pupa, adult. Adult butterflies lay eggs on specific host plants. Caterpillars (the larva stage) emerge from the eggs, and then they eat. And they eat. And they eat. As caterpillars continue to eat, they outgrow their skin. They'll shed their skin multiple times. The final molting of skin is what forms the outer shell of the chrysalis (the pupa stage). The pupa stage lasts around a week or two for most butterflies. The transformation from caterpillar to adult butterfly is called metamorphosis. The chrysalis splits open and the adult butterfly emerges. After unfolding and drying the wings, it takes off for the first flight.

The takeaway: Metamorphosis happens for both butterflies and moths. Just remember that butterflies hatch out of chrysalises and moths from cocoons.

Additional facts: Metamorphosis is when an animal goes through a huge change in shape and structure during its lifetime. Insects aren't the only animals that can experience it. For example, tadpoles changing into frogs is also called metamorphosis.

SECTION 1: BEGINNERS

Splash in a puddle.

ADVENTURE SCALE: 1

The basics: April showers don't just bring May flowers. They also bring instant smiles. Slip on your galoshes and take a rainy day walk. Splashing in puddles will bring a smile to anyone's face. It's freeing to let yourself get a little wet and muddy.

Challenge: Everyone sings in the shower, but now it's time to get out and sing in the rain. Make sure there's no thunder and lightning, then go outside and belt out a tune. Umbrellas are optional! It's fun to get wet (though you might want to have a warm shower or bath waiting for you when you're done).

Did you know? Deeper and bigger doesn't necessarily equal better splashes when it comes to puddles. For best results, go along the edges of puddles and stomp in the more shallow spots.

Animal sighting: When it rains, worms underground like to crawl to the surface. After the rain stops keep an eye out for worms as well as birds—they'll be out looking to eat those worms!

Listen for birds on a sunny day.

ADVENTURE SCALE: 1

The basics: A lot of people think birds only sing and make noise in spring, but this isn't the case at all. Go outside in winter when a sunny day hits, and the birds will be out, celebrating the warmth with the rest of us.

Challenge: Learn how to whistle a bird song yourself.

If you do it in the right way, you just might be able to attract a bird. Or a bird might hear you and decide to sing back at you.

Did you know? A few birds have winter themes in their names. Have you ever seen a snow bunting or a winter wren? How about a snowy owl? Look them up in your field guide. If they live in your area, see if you can spot one.

Animal sighting: One bird you can always count on singing outside is the American robin. Try to learn its song!

Watch the tide come in.

ADVENTURE SCALE: 2

The basics: Go to the beach in the evening and just wait for the tide to come in. It's impressive to see the water splash up higher and higher on the beach, and it's fun to run through the edge of the waves too.

Challenge: Watch the tide go out in the morning, and find a tide pool to explore. Tide pools are where pockets of water gather and sea creatures like to live. Horseshoe crabs are one thing you might spot. Go see what else you can find.

Did you know? The tide comes in twice a day: morning and evening. Why? It's because of the gravitational pull of the earth. And since the earth rotates, you get it twice. Try timing the tide coming in to see how long it takes. It happens a lot faster than most people think.

Animal sighting: There are all sorts of little animals living in those tide pools, but they're not always easy to see! Be patient and watch for movement.

Listen to the night sounds.

ADVENTURE SCALE: 2

The basics: This is the perfect excuse to stay up late. Wait until it's completely dark out, and then go outside and just listen to the sounds of the night. What will you hear—an owl, crickets, toads, wolves? See if you can pick out the different sounds and figure out what they are.

Challenge: You can hear them, but can you see them? Try to spot one of these critters making the sounds as well. They often get quiet when you shine a light, so you might have to be a little sneaky. Practice seeing things in the dark. Once your eyes adjust, it's pretty easy.

Did you know? Toads don't just croak, they also squeak. If you catch a toad, hold it up and listen closely to hear it squeak as well.

Animal sighting: Owls, like the great horned owl, are common to hear at night. Listen carefully to see if you can find out which tree an owl's roosting in at night.

DESTINATIONS: Your Own Backyard

Some of the best nature finds ever are right in your own backyard. You might not think your backyard has much to offer, but it does. Nature is everywhere— you just have to look. Of course, the phrase "backyard" means something different to everyone. For those with lots of space, you probably see wildlife and nature every day. But for those who don't, challenge yourself to expand "your own backyard" within a mile or two from your house. There's probably more around than you thought.

WHO? Challenge your entire family to discover the backyard together. It doesn't matter how old you are—there's something to see. Sometimes it's the youngest explorers who find the little details that others miss. Make this a regular family experience. Go out as an entire group and just look at and appreciate your own backyard.

WHAT? Try a little bit of everything in your backyard—from watching birds and looking for bugs to playing games and just relaxing, you can do it all. Take a weekend and see just how many things you can accomplish in your backyard. With a little creative planning, you can do a lot.

WHEN? It's good to keep a journal of what you can find in your backyard during every season, but winter is an especially good time to check it out. Here's why: You might think winter is cold and inactive, but it's not. You'll have to search a little harder, but bundle up and check things out. Perhaps you'll find animal tracks in the snow. Maybe different birds will visit your feeders in the winter than in the summer.

WHERE? After you've explored your immediate backyard, start expanding. What's within a mile of your house that you can check out? What's within 5 miles? While they aren't right outside your back door, it's pretty cool to say it's in your neighborhood.

WHY? Sometimes we get so focused on going to destinations that we forget about the things that are right at our fingertips. Don't overlook these. It's easy to go somewhere and spend money to be entertained. But the backyard offers free enjoyment, and you don't have to get in a car to go.

TIPS AND TRICKS: Rather than planning a vacation, try a staycation. You'll have a new appreciation of where you live if you treat your hometown as a destination. There are bound to be places you've yet to explore in your own area. Make a list of places you want to check out in your neighborhood, and then start checking them off the list.

Wake up before the birds.

ADVENTURE SCALE: 2

The basics: You've heard the phrase "the early bird catches the worm," right? Well, the early birder hears the birds. The dawn chorus of birdsong is an experience anyone can appreciate. While it's mostly males singing during this time to proclaim a territory or attract a mate, females of certain species (like vireos or cardinals) will also add to the chorus line.

Challenge: Bird songs can be fun to learn, but don't get overwhelmed. Set a goal to learn songs from ten to twenty species of common birds in your area. It will add fun to your day, and spring is the perfect time to learn them.

Discover more: Cornell Lab of Ornithology has some of the best bird songs around. Go on their website, allaboutbirds.org, where you can find bird profiles and listen to their songs. The songs and calls on there are real recordings from nature.

Animal sighting: All birds can be up early in the morning, but a few species you might look for include the American robin, black-capped chickadee, American goldfinch, or eastern or western bluebird.

Celebrate Earth Day.

ADVENTURE SCALE: 2

The basics: Earth Day, April 22, is one of the most celebrated nature days all year. You're bound to find places in your area celebrating this iconic day. Go to a preplanned celebration, or create your own by exploring your own backyard and neighborhood. The bottom line is: Get outside!

Challenge: Another iconic nature celebration is Arbor Day, held the last Friday in April. Plant a tree on Arbor Day and watch it grow year after year. If you don't have room to plant a tree yourself, see if you can plant one in a local park or somewhere else to support your local community.

Discover more: Earth Day gets bigger and better every single year. See how you can be involved on a local level by going to earthday.org. If there's nothing scheduled, see if you can put something together at your school or library. They'd probably love to have someone get something going.

Animal sighting: Earth Day is in April, which is a great time for bird migration. Look for birds like the yellow-rumped warbler, brown creeper, or ruby-crowned kinglet.

Celebrate International Migratory Bird Day.
ADVENTURE SCALE: 2

The basics: International Migratory Bird Day (IMBD) is a day in May that celebrates birds around the world. Many nature centers, Audubon groups, and bird observatories plan special programs in honor of this day. It's a great opportunity to get outside and learn something new about the birds in your backyard.

Challenge: Attend a local bird walk. There are birding groups all over the country, and they'll often hold family bird walks. Find one to go on— you're sure to learn a lot. And don't worry about being an expert. The group will often supply binoculars for you to use, and no one expects you to know all the birds.

Discover more: You can get involved in this very cool event. Start by going to the website birdday.org. Before you know it, you'll be making IMBD an annual tradition.

Animal sighting: Here's another opportunity to look for migrating birds. Keep an eye out for the indigo bunting, rose-breasted grosbeak, and scarlet or summer tanager.

Go to a petting zoo
ADVENTURE SCALE: 2

The basics: Local farms often put
together petting zoos featuring
friendly farm animals like chickens,
goats, ponies, and potbellied pigs. This is an
easy way to experience farm life up close.
Look for a petting zoo at a festival, neighborhood party, or farm near you.

Challenge: Feed the animals from your
hand. The people running the petting zoo
will often have food you can buy or use. Sit
back and let the animals come to you. Don't
be scared. Just hold still, and you'll make a new
friend.

Did you know? Don't assume the best animals at the petting zoo are the
fuzzy little ones. Potbellied pigs and goats are some of the friendliest animals
around.

Animal sighting: So many good animal opportunities like goats, cows, and
chickens. Remember to move slowly and don't be too loud. You don't want to
scare the animals!

Make sugar water.
ADVENTURE SCALE: 2

The basics: Spring is the time orioles and hummingbirds start coming around,
so invest in a sugar-water feeder to attract these colorful birds. Sugar water is
four parts water to one part sugar. Boil until it all dissolves. Let
cool and fill feeders. Be sure to change out the water every
few days so it stays fresh.

Challenge: Put up a hanging basket near your feeder. This
will give hummingbirds an extra source of nectar, and it creates a
more natural setting. This will increase your chance of success in
attracting these cool birds.

Did you know? A lot of people think you have to add red food
coloring to sugar water to attract hummingbirds, but that's not

the case at all. In fact, it's best to leave it plain, which means fewer steps overall.
Animal sighting: If you're in the East, look for the ruby-throated humming-bird. In the West look for the Anna's, rufous, and others like the broad-tailed.

Look closely at a spiderweb.
ADVENTURE SCALE: 2

The basics: Spiders are some of nature's true engineers. Their web silk is some of the strongest material in the world. Study the construction of spiderwebs closely. What is the web attached to? Is the web simple or complex in design?

Challenge: Look at a spider under a microscope or magnifying glass to examine its distinctive anatomy. When you get an up-close look at spiders, you'll see that they're not scary at all and are really pretty cool.

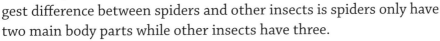
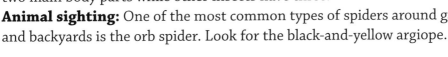

Did you know? Spiders are not insects. They are in a family all on their own—arachnids. The biggest difference between spiders and other insects is spiders only have two main body parts while other insects have three.

Animal sighting: One of the most common types of spiders around gardens and backyards is the orb spider. Look for the black-and-yellow argiope.

Find a turtle.
ADVENTURE SCALE: 2

The basics: Some turtles like to hang out near the water while you can find others in the woods. Most turtles are easy to handle, and you can take a close look at them. But watch out for snapping turtles—you'll want to keep your distance.

Challenge: Spot a turtle with its young. You can often find young turtles lined up on a log near the water. They can be hard to spot—they often camouflage themselves against the park—but once you spot them, they're hard to miss.

Did you know? What's the difference between a tortoise and a turtle? Both are reptiles, but there are many differences. For instance, turtles have webbed feet while tortoise feet are short and sturdy. Tortoises also have heavier shells while turtle shells are more lightweight.

Animal sighting: If you go for a hike in the woods, look for a box turtle or its shell. Otherwise, painted turtles are common to find sunning themselves near water areas.

Collect your own chicken eggs.
ADVENTURE SCALE: 2

The basics: Fresh farm eggs are yummy, and they're even better when you collect them yourself. If you don't have chickens yourself, find a local farm or egg supplier. Ask them if you could stop by sometime to visit the chickens and help collect the eggs. They'll probably be happy to show you around.

Challenge: Have you ever held a baby chick? They're so soft and fuzzy. Petting zoos might have baby chicks, or ask a farm that has chickens. It's a great experience.

Discover more: Have you heard of CSAs? Community-supported agriculture is when you can sign up to get a crop share from a farm. This can include everything from fruits and veggies to farm-fresh eggs. Learn how to sign up for a CSA by going to localharvest.org.

Animal sighting: Not all farm chickens are the same. Ask your local farmers if they know what types of chickens they have. Chances are they have many different types. One of the most common is the Cochin chicken.

Find an anthill.
ADVENTURE SCALE: 2

The basics: Ants are some of the hardest-working insects around. They're always on the move, building and gathering food. Established anthills can be years old and huge. Keep an eye out to see if you can find one in your area.

Challenge: Follow an ant back to its home or see where it's going as it leaves the anthill. It'll take a little patience.

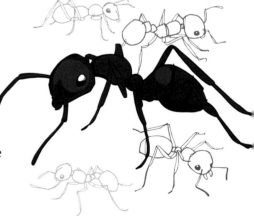

Did you know? Around the world, there are thousands of different kinds of ants. They work hard and carry things on their backs that weigh more than twenty times what they do.

Animal sighting: Are those all ants you're looking at? Look very closely to see what other little bugs might be hanging out as well.

Flip over a rock.
ADVENTURE SCALE: 2

The basics: When you flip over a rock or a log, you never know what you might find underneath. Keep an eye out for any critters that might be mad and defensive that you're disturbing their home, but for the most part, it's a good way to explore nature. Don't forget to put it back where you found it after you're done having a peek.

Challenge: Find a hollow log and take a look inside. Turtles, butterflies, or other bugs and critters could be using it as a home. Just look carefully. You don't want to startle the critters.

Did you know? Piles of rocks, logs, and debris all provide great homes for living creatures. If you're out for a walk or on a hike, remember this, and you'll discover even more. Or create your own pile in the backyard to give animals another habitat source.

Animal sighting: The pill bug (some call it a roly poly) are common bugs you'll see under a rock. You'll need to look quickly because as soon as you lift it, they're going to scatter.

Soak in a hot springs.
ADVENTURE SCALE: 2

The basics: Hot springs are geothermal features most abundant out in the West. Some are commercial operations, while others are more natural. Some of the best require hiking to. They all have comfortable warm waters that are especially relaxing as the cool temperatures settle in.

Challenge: Experience hot springs on a cold day. The change from cold to hot is shocking yet relaxing. Once you step into the water, you'll forget all about the frost and chill.

Did you know? Hot springs are a result of geothermal heated groundwater. This sounds complicated, but they're just bodies of water that are heated from the Earth's crust. Still, it's pretty amazing that it doesn't take any machines or electricity to make this natural hot tub.

Animal sighting: You might not find many animals coming up to drink the water out of a hot springs, so instead, look up while you're soaking. See if you can spot hawks or eagles soaring in the sky.

Count the arms on a starfish.

ADVENTURE SCALE: 2

The basics: While many species of starfish have five arms, some can have more. In fact, lots more! What is the highest number of arms you can find? Did you know that some species of star- fish can even grow their arms back if damaged?

Challenge: Have a starfish challenge and see who can spot the most starfish in an hour. Hit the beach and start looking. You're going to find them along the water's edge.

Did you know? Right now, scientists are trying to change the name of the starfish to sea star because it's not actu- ally a fish at all. Starfish are more closely related to sea cucumbers, sea urchins, and sand dollars.

Animal sighting: After you've found your starfish, see how many sea urchins you can spot nearby.

Take a snowshoeing hike.

The basics: Snowshoeing is as easy as walking. The snowshoes help distribute your weight, so you can walk on top of the snow. It's something everyone should experience at least once.

Challenge: Snowshoe racing generally uses a smaller snowshoe. Have your own race with your friends, or participate in a sanctioned event. Popular distances include 5 and 10 kilometers.

Did you know? Traditional snowshoes were made with a wooden frame and rawhide webbing.

Animal sighting: A fresh layer of snow is the perfect time to look for animal tracks. As you're snowshoeing, try to find tracks and identify what could've made them.

DESTINATIONS: State and National Parks

The state and national park systems are some of the best resources in the country for nature lovers. There are thousands of parks scattered all over the country, so stake out the closest ones to you, and then make a goal to visit at least three this year. They're also good places to visit while on a vacation, even if you're vacationing for the weekend only a few hours away. They're set up for visitors, so take advantage of these great sites in your own backyard.

WHO? Parks are especially appealing to older kids. Get a good daypack with lunch, a camera, and whatever else you enjoy. You can even take turns choosing what you want to do. No matter who goes, make sure everyone dresses comfortably and wears good walking shoes.

WHAT? Go hiking, biking, running, walking, birding, animal watching, fishing, exploring, and more. The parks are filled with things just waiting to be discovered. They usually have lots of brochures and ideas with things to do as well. Go out and discover what's available.

WHEN? Most parks are open year-round, though you'll find extended hours in summer. While many areas are easy to get to, don't be afraid to go off the beaten path to explore the lesser-used trails. As long as there's not a sign that it's closed off to the public, feel free to look around.

WHERE? Your state is your best resource. Look for your local or state tourism website. Chances are they've highlighted the parks across the state and even have information about what resources are available at each one. If you're visiting some place new or are on vacation, be sure to keep state and national parks in mind. You're bound to discover something new.

WHY? State and national parks are owned by the people. Yep, that includes you as well. Here's why—it's usually tax money that keeps these places up and running, so you should visit. You really are part owner of these places, and it's good to see what you're contributing to.

TIPS AND TRICKS: Parks are especially great places to visit at dawn and sunset. The crowds tend to be fewer, and there's often great activity with birds and wildlife. So get up a little bit early to make it worth your while or wait to go later after everyone else has gone home for the day.

Make a winter feast for the birds.

ADVENTURE SCALE: 2

The basics: You can use inspiration from our DIY wreaths project in the "Projects, Games, and More" section to start off with, but don't stop there. Put out seed, suet, fruit, fresh water, and several other food offerings for your birds. Then see who shows up for dinner. (A lot of people put out their old Christmas tree after the holidays to make a bird feast area.)

Challenge: Set a goal of how many different types of birds you want to attract to your feast in a single day. Twenty is a good starter goal. If you don't meet it, try again the next day or week. And if you hit it, increase your goal.

Discover more: Project FeederWatch is a winter citizen science project of the Cornell Lab of Ornithology. It is fun and easy to participate in your own backyard. Learn more about it at birds.cornell.edu/pfw/.

Animal sighting: Woodpeckers are some of the best visitors to winter bird feasts. Look for the downy, hairy, red-bellied, and other woodpeckers.

Look for winter berries.

ADVENTURE SCALE: 2

The basics: Many plants, like juniper, chokecherry, and holly, keep berries all winter long. These can provide essential food for birds. Gather them and hang them up around your feeders to bring in birds. This is a great activity to add to the bird feast (see above).

Challenge: With a little patience and a few tips from our DIY wreaths project (see page 264), you can make a whole wreath out of berry vines. It'll be pretty too. Don't worry if you mess up—just keep working and reworking it until you have it the way you want it.

Did you know? Many garden centers sell berry vines by the bundle. Buy some to add to your wreath project. Or if you have a neighbor or friend that has berries, ask if they'd like to share.

Animal sighting: Here are some of the birds that will stop by for berries: cedar waxwings, American robins, gray catbirds, northern mockingbirds, and northern cardinals.

Put out a birdbath.
ADVENTURE SCALE: 2

The basics: Not only will birds bathe in the birdbath, they'll also drink up the water. They will love having a fresh water source since most water in winter is frozen. If it's especially cold out, you might have to melt the water a few times a day so the birds can still get at it.

Challenge: Add a heater to your birdbath. You'll have to invest a little bit of money in this, but then you don't have to worry about melting the ice all the time.

Tips and tricks: Flowing water will help keep the birdbath from freezing and will also attract more birds. This is a trick for bringing in more birds year-round. Birds are attracted to things they can hear.

Animal sighting: All birds will come to birdbaths, including gray catbirds, juncos, and goldfinches.

Take winter nature photos.
ADVENTURE SCALE: 2

The basics: Snow and ice are both gorgeous. And best of all, they don't move much, so it's easy to capture great winter photos. Look for a day when the sun is out, because it'll really make the snow and ice sparkle.

Challenge: Capture a picture of a bird at a feeder. You can set up in a window inside so you don't get too cold. Then open the window and snap a shot when the birds stop by for a treat.

Tips and tricks: Snow makes the landscape brighter. Be careful not to overexpose your photos. Even on automatic digital cameras, take a look at the photos right after you take them to make sure they look good.

Animal sighting: It can be hard to catch an animal photo in winter. One of your best options will be getting a bird picture. Try going to a pond or lake where you'll likely see ducks on the open water.

Go to a butterfly house.

ADVENTURE SCALE: 2

The basics: Indoor butterfly houses are the perfect spot to visit in winter. The butterflies will make you think it's summer. You can check out a butterfly book at the library to learn more about these amazing fliers.

Challenge: Get a butterfly to land on you. To give yourself a better shot, wear bright colors so they'll think you're a flower. But above all, you have to be patient. If you wait long enough and don't move around too much, you'll get one to land on you sooner or later.

Did you know? Mourning cloak butterflies will overwinter as adults in the wild and can become active in late winter and early spring.

Animal sighting: One of the coolest things about butterfly houses is that you get to see colorful species. Look for blue butterflies like the blue morpho!

Put up a roosting house.

The basics: Most people think of putting up birdhouses in spring, but you can put them out in winter too. Then birds will have a place to roost (sleep and rest) during cold days and nights. It's a great way to offer them protection.

Challenge: Offer a feeder near the roosting house. Then the birds won't have to travel far for food. Make sure you keep it filled throughout winter.

Did you know? Flying squirrels will also use boxes to roost in all winter long. So hang one up—you never know what you'll attract.

Animal sighting: If you get an owl house, you might be able to attract a screech owl to your backyard!

SECTION 2: ADVANCED

Catch a frog or toad.

ADVENTURE SCALE: 3

The basics: Most frogs and toads like to be near water, so that's a good place to start looking if you're trying to catch one. When you find a frog or a toad, be gentle with it and then let it go.

Challenge: Build a toad abode for your little friend. Make one using an old terra-cotta pot or container. Make sure to leave an opening so the toad can come and go as it pleases. You can even decorate the outside area with rocks and such to make it more like a natural setting.

Did you know? Frogs and toads are not the same thing at all—they even come from different scientific families. Frogs have bulging eyes and webbed feet. (These are just a couple of differences. Look up more online or in a book.) Toads have stubby legs, short hind feet, and often have dry, warty skin. But don't worry—you're not going to get warts from them. That is a myth!

Animal sighting: Bullfrogs are so cool to see because they are big. Go find one!

Find a bird's nest.

ADVENTURE SCALE: 3

The basics: As the days get longer, migratory birds return north for the breeding season. If you pay attention, there's a good chance you'll spot birds building a nest out of sticks, grass, hair, or even spiderwebs. A handful of backyard birds will use birdhouses while others build their nests anywhere they can, including trees, hanging baskets, and even the tops of lampposts.

Challenge: Put up a birdhouse this year and see what you attract (try our vintage birdhouse project on page 291. And if you want to take it one step further, monitor the nests by keeping a journal and making notes of how the fledglings grow.

Did you know? Some birds nest high while others nest low. Others even nest in silly places like lampposts.

Animal sighting: American robin nests are some of the most common you can find. Maybe you can even spot a mother bird sitting on one!

Bike to a nearby destination.
ADVENTURE SCALE: 3

The basics: Biking is great exercise and it's fun too. Instead of getting in a car for everything, try biking to a local park or playground instead. You might be surprised at how fast you get there and how much fun you have. Plus, bikes are often allowed in areas that cars aren't.

Challenge: Check out a local bike trail. Many communities have bike trails to get you around town. It's also a popular activity at many national parks and national wildlife refuges. So check one out near you.

Discover more: Go to your local bike shop. Often, they'll have free maps of routes to explore in your area. You might be surprised to find out just how many biking options you have.

Animal sighting: While you're biking, look for animals around the trails. Chipmunks and squirrels are two that you'll definitely see.

Find animal tracks.

ADVENTURE SCALE: 3

The basics: As snow melts away and spring showers fall, it can get a little sloppy outside. These conditions are ideal for finding animal tracks. Follow an animal trail through the meadow, or seek out tracks near water. Based on the tracks, see if you can find any clues about what the animal was doing.

Challenge: It's simple to make plaster casts out of animal tracks. You just need some plaster and a container to stir it up. Deep tracks dried in mud are the best impressions to capture in plaster. Start with a good plaster mix, available at craft stores. Next, pour the plaster in the track and then just let it dry.

Discover more: If you really want to ID tracks, pick up an animal-tracks book at your local library or bookstore. Also check out the array of nature guides at Falcon.com. Once you study up a bit, you'll be able to identify tracks right away.

Animal sighting: Three types of animal tracks that you should be able to see and identify are rabbit, coyote, and squirrel.

Dig your own worms for fishing.

ADVENTURE SCALE: 3

The basics: A couple of shovels of dirt can yield enough worms for an entire day of fishing. Pretty much all fish can be coaxed with worms, including trout, sunfish, bass, walleye, and catfish. For best results, dig for worms right after a spring rain.

Challenge: Catch grasshoppers for fishing instead. Grasshoppers are especially popular for bait on western trout streams. Watching a fish slurp up the grasshopper as it floats on top of the water is fun.

Did you know? Night crawlers are the most common worms sold for fishing, but that's not all you can use.

If you find another worm while digging, give it a try. You never know what'll work.

Animal sighting: While you're digging for worms, look at the grass and plants nearby to see what other critters you can see crawling around.

Find your state bird.
ADVENTURE SCALE: 3

The basics: Every state has a state bird. Which species represents your state? Once you find out, grab a pair of binoculars and get out there to find it!

Challenge: The bald eagle is our national symbol, so go out and see if you can spot one of these magnificent fliers. If you like eagles, you might also go online to check out some of the famous eagle cams where you can watch the eagles raise their young.

Did you know? If you're looking for your state bird (or flower, tree, and more for that matter), go to 50states.com. This is a great website with lots of good information divided by state.

Animal sighting: While you're out searching for your state bird, keep track of the others birds you see too.

Catch a dragonfly.
ADVENTURE SCALE: 3

The basics: Dragonflies often patrol the edge of water or open meadows. They are agile fliers and can be difficult to catch in a net. If you manage to scoop one up, gently hold the wings back and look at it closely. After a few minutes be sure to release it.

Challenge: Find a damselfly. Damselflies are closely related to dragonflies. You'll recognize them because they hold their wings behind them when they are perched.

Did you know? Huge, dinosaur-like dragonflies used to exist. There are fossil records of one dragonfly that had a wingspan of more than 2 feet.

Animal sighting: Fish will sometimes leap out of the water to try to catch and eat bugs like dragonflies. Watch for this!

Build a sand castle.

ADVENTURE SCALE: 3

The basics: You need some buckets, a good sand shovel, and a few good sculpting tools for added details. Be sure to find good packing sand—you might have to dig a little to find sand that is a little bit wet so it holds together better. Start the castle small with a couple of towers, and then solicit some help from friends to grow it bigger.

Challenge: Create a sand village. You can make several homes, a river, a moat, and more. Then if you'd like, you can even add people, cars, and other toys to make it into a big game.

Did you know? Around beach communities, you can often find sand castle competitions, which are fascinating to watch. Look for one to attend if you live near the beach or plan to go on vacation when one of these takes place.

Animal sighting: Look for sea birds like gulls, terns, and plovers while you're hanging out on those sandy beaches.

Find a young bird.

ADVENTURE SCALE: 3

The basics: Summer is a great time to spot young birds. You might see them up in trees or on the ground, chirping and hoping that their parents will keep feeding them. They don't look like adult birds—their markings might be a little different. So keep an eye out.

Challenge: It's going to be difficult, but see if you can watch a young bird learn how to fly. Observing a nest daily will help increase your chance of seeing that first flight. Research how long a particular bird species stays in the nest; then you'll have a better idea of when the birds might fly.

Did you know? One of the easiest young birds to spot is the American robin. They almost look like full-grown robins at first glance, and they are as big. But juveniles have spots on their breasts, making them easy to pick out. You can find them hanging out on the ground in mid- to late summer.

Animal sighting: If you see a baby bird awkwardly stumbling around, chances are the mom isn't too far away. Give it space and wait around to see if the mother comes back to feed it.

Find caterpillars.
ADVENTURE SCALE: 3

The basics: The good thing about finding caterpillars is you know just where to look. They'll be on plant leaves, often on the underside. Go to your garden or a nearby park and gently lift up the leaves. Remember, they might not be very big. Caterpillars start off very tiny.

Challenge: Find a monarch caterpillar. Monarch butterflies only lay their eggs on milkweed. So first find out what milkweed looks like, then look for the yellow and black stripes of monarch caterpillars.

Did you know? Monarch Watch is a wonderful organization that is working to increase the monarch population across North America. Learn how you can help their efforts to increase the monarch population by going to monarchwatch.org. You can even track monarch migration online, which is cool to follow.

Animal sighting: Get out a magnifying glass while you're searching for caterpillars. You never know what other tiny bugs you'll find crawling up and down the plants.

Find a fox or a bunny hole.

ADVENTURE SCALE: 3

The basics: Foxes and bunnies are both animals that use burrows. A burrow is just a fancy word for a home that is in the ground. You can often find foxes and bunnies around small hills, which are easy for them to dig out. Don't get too close though. You still want to respect the burrow. It's an animal's home after all.

Challenge: This will take a little bit—no, a lot—of patience, but see if you can spot a bunny or fox going in or out of that hole. You might have more luck spotting one early in the morning or later in the day just before it gets dark. Don't give up—they have to come back sooner or later.

Did you know? Desert tortoises, prairie dogs, and badgers are three other animals that live in holes. Can you do a little looking to see what others do as well?

Animal sighting: Look for both a baby bunny and a mother bunny. They'll likely be close to each other if the baby is young.

Go butterfly watching.

ADVENTURE SCALE: 3

The basics: On a nice summer day, butterflies are busy flying from flower to flower looking for nectar. Use a soft butterfly net to carefully capture one for a few minutes, but then be sure to be gentle. Butterflies are fragile, and you want them to be in good shape when you let them fly away.

Challenge: Try to spot five different butterflies in half an hour. If the butterflies are out and about, it shouldn't be too hard. You can even use binoculars to get great views as butterflies settle onto flowers.

Discover more: Every summer you can help researchers by counting butterflies in your area. Learn more at butterflycount.org. Your participation will help conservation efforts around the country.

Animal sighting: Look for swallowtails, which are big and bold with their yellow-and-black coloring. Also look for smaller yellow butterflies, which are probably members of the sulphur family.

Find snakes sunning.
ADVENTURE SCALE: 3

The basics: Even if you don't like snakes, it's still cool to find them sunning. Snakes often soak up the rays in open areas along trails, on the road, or even on a rock along a river. Observe the snakes from a distance—they like to be left alone.

Challenge: See if you can find a snake's dried-up old skin sometime while you're exploring outside. You might either find a whole skin or just part of one. Look at it and observe it. How fresh is it? How much of it is intact? How big is the snake? These are some of the questions to think about.

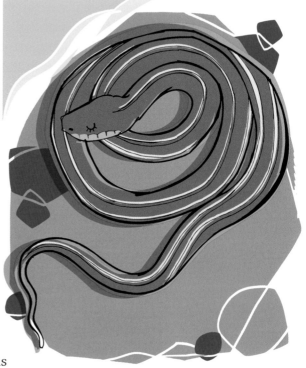

Did you know? Snakes shed their skins as they outgrow them. Some snakes shed them every few weeks and others don't shed but once a year. As snakes get older, they shed their skins less.

Animal sighting: Garter snakes are some of the most common snakes in backyards and gardens. They are generally black and yellow, and you can find them lying on rocks in the sun.

Go fishing.

ADVENTURE SCALE: 3

The basics: Get your fishing license, gather up your equipment, and then hit your local lake, pond, or stream. If you don't have your own gear, rent it from a local shop. Many states offer free youth-fishing days on occasion or host workshops to teach beginners how to fish.

Challenge: Put the timer on and get ready—you must catch ten fish in half an hour. So that's a fish every 3 minutes. Bait, hook, release. Don't waste time. If that's too much of a challenge, start off smaller (maybe five in half an hour) and then keep increasing your goal.

Did you know? National statistics estimate more than forty-four million Americans fish every single year!

Animal sighting: Look for little bugs flying around the top of the water while you're fishing. Dragonflies are always flying to and fro!

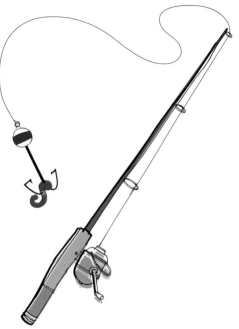

Find your own fossils.

ADVENTURE SCALE: 3

The basics: Did you know you can find your own fossils just like the paleontologists? Many paleontologists are eager to have visitors on fossil digs. Maybe you can even help dig a little.

Challenge: Go out fossil hunting on your own. You might have to do a little research ahead of time to know what you're looking for and where to look, but it's satisfying to know you did it all by yourself.

Discover more: Head out to a local museum to get an up-close look at fossils. Public museums usually have great fossil collections, and they can help you get started in finding your own.

Animal sighting: Don't forget to keep an eye out for bugs and other crawlers as you're digging in the earth.

Go on a hike.

ADVENTURE SCALE: 3

The basics: Sometimes it doesn't matter where you go—just getting outside on a hike and enjoying the world around you is a great way to see your area. Look for hiking trails near you. You'll probably discover something that you never even knew existed.

Challenge: It's easy to hike for an hour or two, but make a whole day of it. Pack your lunch, make sure you have good hiking boots on and any other supplies you might need (like water), and then get going.

Did you know? Some of the most famous hiking trails in North America include the Continental Divide, the Appalachian Trail, and the Pacific Crest Trail. Hikers will sometimes hike these for months at a time, going thousands of miles.

Animal sighting: There are so many great animals to see on a hike. For woodland animals, keep an eye out for raccoons, squirrels, birds, chipmunks, skunks, and many others.

Search for an arrowhead.

ADVENTURE SCALE: 3

The basics: Native Americans created arrowheads hundreds or even thousands of years ago. You can find them all across the country, as long as you know where to look. An easy place to look is along rivers and streams. But do a little investigating in your area to learn where other people are finding arrowheads. Then go to those places to look.

Challenge: Look for other Native American artifacts. Pretend you're an archaeologist and see what you can discover. Go to a state or local Native American museum to see all the things that have been found over the years.

Discover more: Look at your local museum for arrowheads or other artifacts found in your area. You can learn a lot about your state and the people that settled there just by checking out a museum.

Animal sighting: While your eyes are glued to the ground, keep an eye out for other animal signs. For instance, you might see the markings of a snake slithering through the grass or dirt. You might also see ants marching along to their anthill.

Try car camping.

ADVENTURE SCALE: 3

The basics: You don't always need a tent to go camping. Instead, just sleep in your car. Find a campsite to go to, unpack everything you need, and then make a bed in the back of your car. (It helps if your seats fold down.) It's a quick and easy way to enjoy camping. And you'll stay dry even if it rains.

Challenge: Try backpack camping. You'll need a good, solid backpack that can carry everything you need, from a tent to campfire supplies. Load everything up, head into the great outdoors, and camp out of your back-pack. (Make the oldest or strongest person carry the heavier supplies.)

Discover more: Every year, the National Wildlife Federation leads the Great American Campout. This usually takes place in June, and they encourage the whole family to camp together. Learn more about this cool event at nwf.org.

Animal sighting: Right at dusk, when you're sitting around the campfire, look around for nocturnal animals about to come out at night to eat. This could include bats, owls, raccoons, and more.

DESTINATIONS: Public Gardens

Gardeners are some of the friendliest people around. They just want to share the beauty of their work with others. You can find hundreds of public gardens around the country, and often nonprofit groups or volunteers run them. Seek out a couple public gardens in your area or when you're traveling. It's impossible not to appreciate the gorgeous scenes.

WHO? Most public gardens are set up for strollers and wheelchairs, so it's really an activity for anyone. Go for an hour or go for the whole day. If the garden you're going to isn't free, check to see if it has a membership you can be a part of. Usually, after only one or two visits, it pays off.

WHAT? Public gardens are made for viewing. So expect a lot of walking and watching. If this isn't enough to keep you happy, look at the calendars of public gardens. They often have events, family days, and other special activities. Make plans to go during one of those days for even more excitement.

WHEN? Check the bloom times in your area. Public gardens often have different waves of peak blooming seasons. You might see apple blossoms peak in late spring while the perennials are in their prime midsummer. Ask the staff or volunteers at the garden. That's what they're there for, and they really do know best.

WHERE? Botanical gardens are everywhere—so do a search and see if you can find a botanical garden near you. Arboretums or indoor gardens are also something to look for. Of course, you should also explore places like libraries, zoos, and other public places, as garden plots are often maintained at these locations too.

WHY? Public gardens are a good way to learn about plants and flowers, and you can also see what grows well in your area. Many public gardens plant natives, so go to public gardens for ideas on what to grow in your own backyard. Public gardens often have programs available for locals as well—some are free while others have a small fee. These programs are a good way to learn gardening in your area. Sign up for a couple that interest you.

Don't overlook cafes, restaurants, and other similar locations that might have great gardens. It might not be a public garden in a traditional sense, but it's still worth checking out. You never know where you'll find a great space. If you see a nice garden, ask if you can check it out. They'll probably be thrilled to show you around.

Watch bats at sunset.

ADVENTURE SCALE: 3

The basics: Just as the sun begins to set for the day, the bats come out, zooming about and looking for mosquitoes and other bugs to eat. They like to zip in and out of open areas, often over water. Put out a blanket to lie down. Then kick back and watch these amazing little creatures.

Challenge: Build or buy a bat house to put up. Yes, they really will use them. Just make sure you hang it high enough in a tree. It might take them a year or two to really find it, so don't give up.

Did you know? Bats have gotten a bad rap over the years. Relatively good eyesight and echolocation (a fancy word for a type of hearing bats use) will help keep them from swooping down into your hair or face. And they're pretty harmless overall.

Animal sighting: In addition to bats, look up for birds zipping all about before darkness hits.

Find cocoons or chrysalises.

ADVENTURE SCALE: 3

The basics: Caterpillars are getting ready for winter in last summer and early fall. While some will go underground, you can find those that hide in cocoons and chrysalises in fall. Look under eaves, inside sheds, under limbs, and in other protected spots. It's not going to be easy to find them, but it's a great treasure hunt.

Challenge: Don't just find those hidden caterpillars, keep track of them. Write down where you found them and then be sure to go back in spring to see if you can figure out what they have transformed into.

Did you know? There really is a difference between cocoons and chrysalises. Do you know what it is? Moths make cocoons and butterflies make chrysalises.

Animal sighting: If you're looking for cocoons and chrysalises, be sure to find an adult butterfly and moth as well. Remember, a lot of moths (but not all) come out at night, so be sure to look at all times of the day.

Listen to the howl of a wolf.

ADVENTURE SCALE: 3

The basics: Perhaps nothing is as iconic as a wolf howling in the wild. The upper Midwest, including areas of northern Wisconsin and Minnesota, offers up the chance to experience a wolf howl, as do small pockets of the Southwest and Southeast, and a few national parks in the West.

Challenge: Do a little wolf research—Yellowstone National Park has many packs, and it's one of the best places to see (and hear) this great animal. These are some pretty amazing animals.

Discover more: Some of the most studied wolves in the world can be found on Isle Royale in Lake Superior. Learn more about this important study at isleroyalewolf.org.

Animal sighting: Closely related to the wolf is the coyote. Keep an eye out for them because they can look a lot alike!

Volunteer for a local nature group.

ADVENTURE SCALE: 3

The basics: Nature is everywhere, and so are nature organizations. From a small downtown urban metropark to an expansive wilderness area, volunteers are useful to most every nature group. While some of the tasks will be indoor duties, dedicated volunteers often get to experience some amazing outdoor activities. Perhaps a local bird bander could use assistance. Maybe you'd enjoy leading a nature walk to share your love of nature and inspire others. Or you could take part in the annual cleanup efforts in your area.

Challenge: Take part in a fund-raising effort for a nature organization. It might be more work, but then you can see the money go right back into the community. It's one of the best ways to give back on a local level.

Did you know? Most of these nature groups run on very small staff and budgets. They couldn't survive without volunteers, so take a minute to see what you can do. They'll probably help you as much as you help them.

Animal sighting: While you're volunteering, play a little animal game with the other volunteers. Keep a list of all the types of animals you see.

Find migrating monarchs.

ADVENTURE SCALE: 3

The basics: While some butterfly species overwinter in caterpillar form, a few species actually migrate. The monarch migration is a multiple-generation affair. While ranging from southern Canada and much of the northern United States during the summer, the monarch's communal wintering grounds are found in the highlands of Mexico and sections of California.

Challenge: Grow your own milkweed, the monarch host plant, to encourage these delicate friends to visit your backyard. This is very important to keep the monarch population alive—they've actually been declining. So do your part and plant milkweed.

Did you know? Butterfly weed is a popular garden plant, and a lot of people don't know that it's part of the milkweed family.

Watch bugling elk.

ADVENTURE SCALE: 3

The basics: The second-largest member of the deer family in North America, male elk have a unique fall tradition called bugling that you can hear if you're in the right place at the right time. The species is abundant in many of the national forests and national parks of the West, but it has also been reintroduced into many central and eastern states including Kentucky, Michigan, and Pennsylvania.

Challenge: Learn to make the elk bugle with your own voice or with an elk call. Resist the temptation to bugle at wild elk unless you are a licensed elk hunter.

Did you know? Male elk will use their huge antlers to challenge one another during mating season. Chances are you won't get to witness it in the wild yourself, but you could look up a video of it online with your parents.

Animal sighting: If there are elks around, there are probably moose nearby too. They can be harder to see, but they are amazing!

Sketch in winter.

The basics: You know those finger-less gloves you can buy? They make the perfect sketching glove in winter. Take a pad of paper outside and let nature inspire you. Too cold? Sit by the fire and sketch from inside instead. As the snow gently falls, it'll inspire you.

Challenge: Sketch a different thing from nature every day for a week. Make sure it's something different each time. It'll make you look at winter in a whole new way.

Did you know? If you use a water-proof field notebook, you can even sketch when it is snowing outside. Wouldn't it be cool to be sketching while the flakes land on you?

Animal sighting: What animal are you going to sketch in winter? How about a majestic hawk, eagle, or owl sitting on a snowy tree branch.

Go for a night walk in the snow.

The basics: The stillness of the night is especially evident during the winter. If you take a nighttime stroll during a bright moon, the light reflecting off the snow can make it feel like daytime. Keep your eyes peeled to catch a glimpse of nocturnal creatures.

Challenge: Make a list of five different things you want to see at night, and then head out to see them all. It might take you one or two walks on different nights to spot them all, but don't stop until you do.

Did you know? The sun doesn't rise in Barrow, Alaska, for about two months each winter. This makes for a pretty long and dark winter. So be thankful of any sunshine you get in winter.

Animal sighting: Keep an eye out for nocturnal animals like opossums or raccoons.

Feed a bird up close.
ADVENTURE SCALE: 3

The basics: When it's cold, birds will often come in close to feed. Sit out by your feeder area with the feeder in your lap or in your hand. Then wait for the birds to come up and eat. You'll love this up-close look at birds. Remember, you're going to have to be patient for this to work, so bundle up. You could be sitting there for a little while.

Challenge: Chickadees are fairly easy birds to attract up close, so challenge yourself to attract two or three other species while you're out there. You might even be able to get a squirrel to pay you a visit.

Tips and tricks: Feed the birds at about the same time each day. This will help establish a routine for you as well as the birds. So when the feeder is empty and you come out to fill it, they'll be ready. Hopefully they'll be feeding out of your hand in no time!

Animal sighting: Chickadees and nuthatches are two birds that are fairly common to see up close. If it's summer, you can also try getting goldfinches to come up to a finch feeder if you hold it really still.

Go animal tracking.
ADVENTURE SCALE: 3

The basics: Winter is a great time for finding animal

tracks. You can follow the path through the snow. What was the animal doing? Searching for food? Running quickly away from a predator? Don't just think of traditional prints though. It is especially neat to see wing prints in the snow as a bird flies away.

Challenge: Find some scat. Animal scat is the science term for poop. (Isn't it cool to be able to tell your friends you know a word for poop?) You can often tell what species of animals are in an area simply by looking for their scats. If you follow animal tracks long enough, you'll be able to find some scat.

Did you know? Some species mark their territory with scat. Also, you can sometimes tell what an animal has been eating if you look at the scat really closely. You're just like a scientist now.

Animal sighting: Try to see both the tracks of an animal and that actual animal. A squirrel would be a good choice and fairly easy too.

Write a nature haiku.
ADVENTURE SCALE: 3

The basics: Haiku are poems that contain three lines. The first line contains five syllables, the second line contains seven syllables, and the final line contains five syllables. Let nature inspire you to write something.

Challenge: Write a new haiku every day for a week. Find something about nature and winter to write about every day. No two poems can be alike—so don't write about snow twice. Be imaginative!

Did you know? Haiku is a traditional form of Japanese poetry that usually has a focus on nature. Be sure to take part in this historical pastime.

Animal sighting: Let the first animal you see today inspire a poem. How about a poem about a squirrel, chipmunk, rabbit, or bird?

SECTION 3: THE PROS

Keep a journal of "firsts."

ADVENTURE SCALE: 4

The basics: This one sounds like it might be easy, but it can actually take a bit of work. It has a cool payoff if you keep after it though. Make a list of nature "firsts," like first robin to show up in the backyard, first grasshopper you see, first tulip to bloom, first day to ride your bike outside in spring, etc. Write down the date and any other details that are important. Then in a year, you can read back in your journal and compare dates from one year to the next. It's a bit of a science experiment and journal all rolled into one.

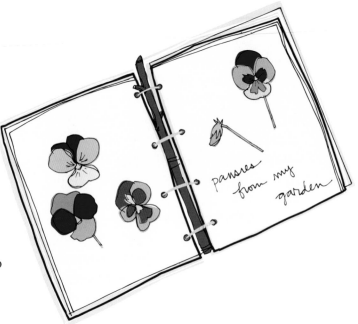

pansies from my garden

Challenge: Take pictures of as many "firsts" as you can and add them to your journal. Then you can see how one year differs from the next. Be sure to take pictures of yourself as well, so you can see how you change from one year to the next too.

Discover more: Instead of writing a traditional journal, try taking it online. Blogger.com and wordpress.com are both good blogging tools, and you can set them to be public or private.

Animal sighting: Pick an animal that you see regularly to journal about on a daily basis for a week. It'll be fun to see how they change little by little.

Raft down a river.

The basics: A leisurely rafting trip is a lot of fun, and you can even fit the whole family in the same boat or raft if you plan it right. Either enjoy the river ride as a passenger or grab a paddle and help navigate the water. But make sure to take a minute to check out your surroundings. Floating down a river gives you a new perspective on nature and wildlife.

Challenge: Hold on tight and raft through some whitewater rapids (with the proper safety gear on, of course). You might want to check on the river's level of difficulty before you commit, but there are hundreds of options all across the country.

Did you know? Whitewater rafting is actually considered a competitive sport. So if you really love it, keep practicing. You could be on the national team.

Animal sighting: While you're rafting, look for fish jumping and birds like the belted kingfisher or the great blue heron.

Find antlers in the woods.

The basics: Male deer, elk, and moose all grow antlers to intimidate the other males and to impress the females. Covered in "velvet," these antlers can grow quickly and become large throughout the spring and summer. Since they are often shed in winter, spring is a great time to go antler hunting. It's illegal to collect antlers in certain areas, so check with wildlife officials before bringing them home.

Challenge: Find a complete pair. Antlers don't always fall off at the same time, so sometimes the right antler is miles away from the left one. If you can find a complete pair, that's even more rare.

Did you know? Caribou and reindeer are the same thing, and both male and female reindeer have antlers. So don't assume a reindeer is a boy just because it has antlers.

Animal sighting: On your hike in the woods, look at the trees and try to find signs of deer rubbing their antlers on a tree. Once you see the markings, you'll start to really notice them when you're out hiking.

Dig clams.
ADVENTURE SCALE: 4

The basics: Many people like to dig clams and eat them, but you don't have to like the taste of clams to enjoy digging for them. Wear your boots, bring a shovel, and prepare to get muddy. You can often dig clams from the mud exposed during a low tide. And if you're in an area where a shellfish license is required, be sure to get one.

Challenge: It's a specific taste and some people think they're a little slimy, but be brave and give a clam a try. Who knows, maybe you'll end up loving them. Be sure all clams are properly prepared before eating them.

Did you know? Clams are living things, but they have no head, arms, or legs. Their shell is what protects them from predators.

Animal sighting: Look down and you can easily find bird tracks in the sand. Compare different tracks for size and shape. They probably came from different birds!

Inspect a lizard.
ADVENTURE SCALE: 4

The basics: There are dozens of lizard species north of Mexico and most are harmless to handle. (The Gila monster and a handful of other species are poisonous, so if you're not sure, inspect from a distance.) After you check them out, be sure to return them where you found them.

Challenge: Find a horned toad. A handful of horned lizard species go by the nickname horny toad. These lizards have spines coming out of their heads and squat round bodies. They are especially common in the Southwest.

Did you know? Lizards and salamanders are the same, right? No way! They're very different, but here's one of the basics: Lizards tend to have dry, scaly skins like snakes. Salamanders range from a bit moist to downright slimy.

Animal sighting: Here's a tip when it comes to searching for lizards. Watch closely! They can be extremely still and then suddenly they'll move. It's better to keep a little bit of distance. This way you can watch for movement and then move in for a closer look.

Catch a crawdad.
ADVENTURE SCALE: 4

The basics: Also called crawfish or crayfish, crawdads are freshwater creatures that you can often find in shallow areas. (They are closely related to lobsters.) Be careful when you're trying to catch one—they do have little pinchers.

Challenge: Devise a crawdad trap. If you want to catch a few dozen crawdads (some people like to eat them), you're going to need a trap. Look online for specifications for building your own, or buy one instead.

Did you know? There's a reason the South is known for crawfish. They have more species there than anywhere. Crawfish rely on clean water to survive and thrive.

Animal sighting: While you're looking for crawdads, look for salamanders. They often like to bury themselves in mud, and they are so cool when you finally see one in person!

Jump into the middle of a lake.
ADVENTURE SCALE: 4

The basics: It can be scary to jump in water and swim when your feet don't touch the bottom, but face your fears and take the leap. Go out to the middle of a lake in a boat or canoe, and jump. Of course, always wear a life jacket, especially if you're not a strong swimmer.

Challenge: Do a cannonball in the middle of the lake. Challenge your friends, and see who can make the biggest splash.

Did you know? You know how they say wildlife is more scared of us than we are of them? It's

true, and it's no different with fish. Think about it: If something huge splashes into the water around you, wouldn't you swim away?

Animal sighting: Look for fish doing a little bit of jumping themselves! You might also see a turtle's head poking out of the water. Don't worry—they're harmless. They'll quickly swim away if they see you coming.

Pitch a tent.
ADVENTURE SCALE: 4

The basics: It's harder than you think, but it's a little bit like riding a bike. Once you get the hang of it, it's pretty easy. Follow the instructions carefully, and make sure you secure your tent at the corners. You don't want all that hard work to be ruined by a big gust of wind.

Challenge: Get one of those huge tents with multiple compartments. They're a challenge to set up, but once you do, they're so cool. You can have a whole party inside.

Discover more: If you love camping, be sure to check out gocampingamerica.com. It has plenty of camping destinations to keep you busy for years.

Animal sighting: Before you pick a tent site, look around for signs of animals like anthills or other holes in the ground. These are things you don't always notice, and you definitely don't want to set up camp on someone's home!

Go mothing.
ADVENTURE SCALE: 4

The basics: The first thing to know about searching for moths is that you'll get the best results if you go at night. Put out fruit or a sugary "moth bait" at a simple tray feeder or smear it on a tree in the late afternoon or early in the night. After that wait for a while. Once it's good and dark, get a flashlight and head out to check your feeders.

Challenge: Get a moth book and try to identify some of those moths. Pick up a book at the local library. Either look for a book that's just about moths or see if there's moth information in a butterfly book.

Animal sighting: When you set up a light to attract moths, chances are you'll attract lots of other bugs as well. Take a close look and try to figure out what they are.

Try fly fishing.
ADVENTURE SCALE: 4

The basics: You might think fly fishing is just like regular fishing, but it's not. Fly fishing uses artificial "flies" to catch the fish. It'll take a little bit to get the hang of it. Be patient, and get lessons from someone who knows what he's doing. It will definitely take practice.

Challenge: Catch a fish. Sure, you've finally mastered the technique, but now it's time to put those skills to good use. Set a goal of catching at least a 1-pound fish.

Did you know? Fly-fishing flies are made of hair and feathers and mimic stoneflies, caddis flies, mosquitoes, grasshoppers, or other insects. Some flies can even imitate minnows or mice.

Animal sighting: The streams of fly fishing are usually shallow enough that you can see little minnows swimming near the banks.

Catch a crab.
ADVENTURE SCALE: 4

The basics: Catching fish is called fishing and catching crabs is called crabbing. You can use a piece of string with bait to go crabbing or try a crab cage instead. Either way, it's best to go with someone who has a little bit of experience.

Challenge: Now that you've caught the crab, it's time to eat it. Yes, there is a technique involved, and it might be best to solicit the help of an experienced cook so you can turn it into a tasty meal.

Did you know? Crab festivals are very popular in and around ocean-side communities where crabbing is popular and crabs are plentiful. These are great family events, so look for a festival near you.

Animal sighting: This might not be easy, but as long as you're out trying to catch crabs, try for a whale or dolphin sighting!

Go owling.

ADVENTURE SCALE: 4

The basics: Get your binoculars, bird book, and some flashlights and go out in the woods at night to search for owls. Owls are nocturnal, so the best time to look for them is at night. Gather up some friends and look for an organized owl hunt at a local nature center or bird observatory to make it even more fun.

Challenge: Train yourself to listen first and decipher what owl you're hearing. If you can hear an owl first and figure out where the noise is coming from, this will also help you in your search.

Did you know? Learn how to mimic their calls, and you can bring some owls in close. Use this on a limited basis, though. You don't want to confuse the owls.

Animal sighting: A few other birds you can see at night are night heron, nighthawk, and woodcocks if you go out right when the sun is starting to go down.

Go on a full-moon hike.

ADVENTURE SCALE: 4

The basics: The harvest moon is the full moon closest to the autumn equinox. The bright light of the full moon makes it a great time for a walk. Pack a flashlight and bug spray and go exploring. Of course, it's best to go with a small group, not on your own.

Challenge: Camp out under a full moon. You'll be amazed at how light it really is outside. You might not even need a flashlight at all, especially if it's a clear night. Be sure you have a nice thick sleeping bag since it can start getting pretty cool at night in fall.

Did you know? The website stargate.org is a great place to check out for a moon schedule. Most calendars also list when a new moon and full moon take place during the month.

Animal sighting: One of the coolest sights you can see is the shadow of an owl in front of the glow of a full moon. Make it a goal to see it!

Witness shorebird migration.

ADVENTURE SCALE: 4

The basics: While many species of birds migrate, many of the shorebird species are champions of long-distance travel. You'll have to be on the ball to see this—most start their migration in later summer. So have your binoculars ready.

Challenge: See if you can ID some of these birds. It can be a bit tricky, but a good field guide can help. Don't just look for specific marks—make sure you look at body size, wing shape when flying, and other similar details.

Did you know? You're not just going to see birds near the shore. Go inland a bit and you'll find dozens of other migratory birds passing through. They might not be their traditional coloring as some birds molt (change feathers) in fall. But it's still amazing to see some new or unusual fliers.

Animal sighting: When you're at the shore, don't forget to look for ducks too. They like to have open water to swim. You should definitely be able to see mallards at most shores across the country.

Go spelunking.

ADVENTURE SCALE: 4

The basics: Find yourself a cave to explore. Cave tours are offered in many parts of the country, from the karst caves of the Pacific Northwest to the limestone caves of the Ozarks. Find one in your area that offers exploring. To learn if your state has any, go to your state tourism website to start.

Challenge: Some cave tours are wide-open paths that lead in and out. Others are more challenging adventures. Shimmy under a low overhang. Weave in between stalagmites (growing up) and stalactites (growing down).

Did you know? Carlsbad Caverns in New Mexico is one of the most famous caves in the world. You can hike on your own into the cave via Carlsbad Caverns National Park. If you're ever in the area, definitely check it out.

Animal sighting: It's true that bats will go into caves. Don't be afraid! It's cool to see bats swooping!

Paddle a canoe.
ADVENTURE SCALE: 4

The basics: Canoes offer plenty of legroom, so they are fairly stable on the water. Canoeing is a two-person activity, and for safety reasons it's a good idea to always take at least two canoes out. Practice getting in and out of the canoe while still on land. The person in the front is the motor of the canoe, while the person in the back is the steering wheel. A third person can sit in the middle of the canoe and enjoy the ride.

Challenge: Go on an overnight canoeing adventure. The Boundary Waters, Okefenokee Swamp, and the Everglades are all classic canoe-trip destinations, but you can also find a body of water close to home.

Did you know? Historically people hollowed out logs to use as canoes. Now canoes can be made of wood, plastic, or fiberglass.

Animal sighting: Try to paddle into smooth, clear waters where you can look down and see the fish swimming.

Go ice fishing.
ADVENTURE SCALE: 4

The basics: Make sure the ice is thick and safe. If you go with experienced anglers, they'll know. Ice fishing is great fun. It might take a little more patience than regular fishing, but don't give up.

Challenge: Find an ice hut to fish in (i.e., find a friend who has one). It's also called a shanty in some areas. This will keep you protected from the winter winds. Some ice huts are even heated, so you don't have to worry about bundling up too much.

Did you know? Ice conditions vary, but generally clear ice is stronger than cloudy ice. Either way, don't go on the ice unless you know it's definitely thick and strong. Looks can be deceiving.

Animal sighting: As you're fishing, keep an eye out for birds soaring over your head. They're probably hoping you'll throw a fish their way!

DESTINATIONS: Mountains

Hop in the car and head for the mountains. There are numerous mountain drives you can find. While these auto tours offer stunning views and pullouts for pictures, be sure to venture beyond the pavement too. Mountain destinations offer up numerous opportunities for exploring. From the Appalachian chain to the Tetons, every mountain range tells a unique story. Learn a bit about the local geology to reveal these tales, and then go check them out for yourself.

WHO? Whether you'd like to stay at a fancy lodge or spend days hiking in the backcountry, you can find a mountain destination right for you. Mountains are a common destination highlighted by visitor centers, so look for information there or online. You can find something that appeals to you. Don't forget, it's higher elevation than what most of us are used to, so pack plenty of water.

WHAT? Recreation opportunities are boundless in the mountains. While climbing to the top of a mountain can be rewarding, there are plenty of other fun things to explore. For example, try fishing in the mountain streams, hiking through the forests and meadows, or just enjoying a peaceful mountain vista.

WHEN? Fall is a favorite time to visit the mountains, though you can really visit the mountains during every season. (It's fun to compare the differences between seasons.) Visitors flock to the mountains for fall foliage. As the days get shorter and the nights get cooler, the leaves of the deciduous trees change to the bright yellows, oranges, and reds that are synonymous with fall. Where? North, south, east, and west—there are mountains throughout North America. With an elevation of over 20,000 feet, Mount McKinley (also called Denali) in Alaska is the highest peak on the continent.

WHY? The fall mountain air is crisp and refreshing. Grab a light jacket and get out there and enjoy the final days of fall before winter sets in.

Do a little research ahead of time and it'll really pay off. Find out if there are special events being held, and then visit the mountains around this time. Or if you're pressed for time, look into a local tour service. Many of these services employ local, independent people who just love sharing their area with others. You might even find an organization that offers up volunteers to take you around for free. They'll help you get the most out of your mountain experience.

Find at least five new animals in the wild.

ADVENTURE SCALE: 5

The basics: There are all kinds of animals out there, and most of the time, you just need to look. Do a little research and make a list of animals that are in your area. Then set a goal to find at least five new ones this spring. Animals that might be on your list could include opossum, raccoon, beaver, porcupine, bear, deer, and more. Remember to keep your distance, and respect the animal's habitat.

Challenge: Don't stop at just five. Challenge yourself to see at least twenty new animals this spring. This will really make you get outside and explore beyond your own backyard. Keep a journal to keep track of your sightings.

Discover more: The Kaufman Field Guide series is one of the best around. Look for the Field Guide to Mammals of North America and Field Guide to Birds of North America. The books are friendly, compact, and useful. Learn more at kaufmanfieldguides.com or Falcon.com.

Animal sighting: If you want to make it even harder, try to find five different animal types. This means you can only count one mammal! You have to also look for insects, birds, amphibians, reptiles, fish, etc.

Create a fort.

ADVENTURE SCALE: 5

The basics: A fort can be as small or as big as you want. You can create one in the woods or just out in your own backyard. Have fun with it—create secret rules, make a sign, and invite your friends to join. You can even buy garden frames where you can grow your own fort! The plants will grow up the frame, creating walls.

Challenge: Create a tree house. This is a lot more work, and you'll probably need someone to help. But a tree house will offer up fun for years. If it's out of the question to have your own, try to find a tree house that you can visit. Perhaps a local park or botanical garden has one built.

Did you know? You can create a fort with a large sheet hung over a big branch in your backyard. You can make the edges stay down with heavy rocks.

Animal sighting: Once you have your fort in place, look around to see what animal neighbors you have around you.

Harvest honey.
ADVENTURE SCALE: 5

The basics: Try to find a beekeeper in your area or look for a bee program at a nearby nature center. See if you can help process the honey that has already been gathered from the bees. It's cool to see the magic happen, and tasting fresh honey is so yummy.

Challenge: Help gather the honeycomb from the hive. You'll need to make sure you wear protective gear and work with a beekeeper who knows what he's doing, but it's an amazing experience.

Did you know? Have you heard the term "queen bee"? Well, it really does relate back to bees. The queen bee is the one in the hive that is the dominant female. She's usually deep in the hive, protected. Her job is to lay eggs so there are more bees to keep working the hive.

Animal sighting: It's fun to look for bees in the wild, too. You'll likely find them buzzing around flowers!

Go geocaching.
ADVENTURE SCALE: 5

The basics: Geocaching is a modern-day scavenger hunt. People hide caches and then others use GPS to find the cache. With a quick Internet search, you can find countless geocaches near you. Plug the coordinates into your GPS, and you are ready to go.

Challenge: Create your own geocache. Just make sure you follow regulations when hiding geocaches. They are prohibited on some public lands, and you should always respect private property rights. Local nature centers are often encouraged to have geocaches located on their preserves.

Discover more: To get involved in geocaching, you'll probably find yourself at geocaching.com at some point or another. It's a good way to get started and an impressive site.

Animal sighting: Look up, down, and all around while you're geocaching! Make a list of animals while you're out exploring.

Go rock climbing.

ADVENTURE SCALE: 5

The basics: You can practice on an indoor climbing wall, but you should eventually take it outside to the rocks. Of course, you'll need to make sure you have the right equipment and are being safe. Start off small, and master those steps first before moving on.

Challenge: Don't forget to enjoy the view out there. Take a moment to just relax and take it all in from the top of the rocks. You can stay up there for a few minutes before you rappel down.

Discover more: If you want to get involved in rock climbing and meet others like you, get a parent and check out the website rockclimbing.com. You can also check out your local climbing club or wall to get tips from them.

Animal sighting: Look for lizards scurrying in an out of the rocks. They're great climbers.

Go cross-country skiing.

ADVENTURE SCALE: 5

The basics: Cross-country skiing is one of the best winter exercises around. The skinny skis are a little tricky at first, but with a little practice, you'll be kick-gliding along like an Olympic champion. Don't get discouraged if you fall—that is half the fun. You'll get the hang of it eventually.

Challenge: Once you master the basics of cross-country skiing, invite your dog along for the trip. Skijoring is like dog sledding without the sled. Instead you harness up dogs (or sometimes a horse) to pull you along on your skis.

Did you know? Most local nature centers either rent out or lend cross-country skis. It's a great way to try this sport out without buying a ton of equipment.

Animal sighting: Look for animal homes hidden in snow burrows, trees, and other places.

BONUS: PROJECTS, GAMES, AND MORE

GAME: Nature Bingo

Nature Bingo is just like regular bingo, except instead of numbers, you have a board filled with nature objects. It's a good way to make a nature hike even more fun and interesting. You can also take it on the road, especially if you're going to be driving in the country at all. You can have a game of Nature Bingo right outside your window.

Ages: 4 and up

Materials: Cereal boxes, stickers or magazine cutouts, markers, glue

Length: 10 minutes or more

Number of players: 2 or more

1. First you need to create some bingo cards. This is easy enough to do. Recycle old cereal boxes (or use any other cardboard) to make your own. To start, cut out four equal squares, roughly 6 inches by 6 inches. If you're going to have more than four players regularly, cut out more.

2. With the squares, draw a grid of four spaces across and four spaces down. You can put the name of your game, NATURE BINGO, across the top. Then fill in the squares with nature items—use stickers, magazine cutouts, or draw your own pictures of items you find in nature. Be sure to have a mix of easy, medium, and hard things to find. Good examples include a bird, an orange flower, a frog, a large rock, a ladybug, a pine tree, and a birdhouse.

3. Remember, no two bingo cards are alike. So when you draw or glue the items onto the cards, be sure to mix them up. This way, it's luck of the draw on who will bingo first.

4. Now go exploring. Every time you see something on your bingo card, mark it off. The first one to get a horizontal, vertical, or diagonal straight line is the winner.

TIP

You can create several different Nature Bingo themes. Make it a project for the entire family. For example, put together a bird bingo, flower bingo, or leaf bingo. It's a good way to learn more about a specific thing in nature.

ANIMAL TWIST

Create a bingo board with just animals. Try to focus on those in North America when you're out exploring.

PROJECT: Nature Scrapbook

From the first sunny day of spring to the last big flakes of snow falling in winter, sometimes nature is so impressive that you just want to capture it. With a scrapbook, you can! Gather up some of your favorite photos from outside or use it as an excuse to go out and take some new ones.

Supplies: Scrapbook, camera, glue, markers

Ages: Any age

Time: 30 minutes

How-To:

1. If you already have some photos that you took, gather them up and decide how you want to group them together. Do you have flower photos that you want on the first few pages? Do you want to organize it by season? Don't worry if you don't have everything figured out right away—you can always change or add on later.

2. Find a scrapbook at a local craft store that's a good fit for how many pages you want to have. You can also make your own scrapbook by putting colored pages together or taking a plain blank-paged journal and covering it with a fun design.

3. Don't spend a lot of extra money on cute stickers and designed cutouts. Make your own instead! Also look at old calendars, magazines, and even books you can pick up at rummage sales and thrift stores for inspiration.

4. Add a border to your pictures if you'd like, and then glue your pictures on to the new pages.

5. Don't forget to write a little note or journal entry for the picture, especially if you took it in or around your backyard. You might think you'll remember the picture now, but you might not. So take a little extra time to write about it now, and even add a date. Next year at this time when you're looking at it, it'll be nice to have.

6. Add to the scrapbook as you see fit, and use it as inspiration to go outside and explore more.

TIPS AND TRICKS

If you're keeping a scrapbook or journal, consider adding an entry each week for an entire year, starting with the first day of spring. It's a good way to see what's happening in your own backyard year-round. Also, give it a theme. Maybe instead of one huge scrapbook, you'd like to keep separate ones for the flowers you see, the bugs, wildlife, etc.

ANIMAL TWIST

Create a scrapbook of all the animals you've seen in your area. Even if you don't have pictures, find some online instead.

PROJECT: Rock Art

It's time to take that rock collection and do something fun with it! Here are two easy projects to make the rocks stars. Good luck, and hopefully these inspire you to create even more unique projects with rocks. Or maybe it'll inspire you to go outside and look for those perfect project rocks.

ROCK SIDE TABLE

Supplies: Side table, rocks, grout, clear glue
Ages: 7 and up
Time: 45 minutes, plus overnight drying time
How-To:

1. Find a table first. A small end table can be picked up at a secondhand store or rummage sale for as little as $2. Clean it up and paint it your favorite color or leave it as is. If you do paint it, it might take a few layers of paint to really show.

2. Using strong-adhesive clear glue, attach your rocks to the top of the table. It helps if the top of the table is even, so you might want to choose rocks that are the same width. This will ensure your top is nice and flat. Make sure all your rocks are stuck on before you move to the next step.

3. Pick up a grout from your local craft store and mix it according to the back of the package. Apply it between the rocks, let dry for the recommended time (usually 15–20 minutes), and then wipe clean with a wet washcloth.

4. Let the table dry overnight. You can fill in gaps as needed.

5. Now you have a unique table you can use, and best of all, it came from nature.

ROCK NAME FRAME

Supplies: Picture frame, rocks, clear glue

Ages: 5 and up

Time: 20 minutes

How-To:

1. Small rocks work best for this project. Use this excuse to go on a rock hunt and look for tiny rocks that you can arrange in any way you want.

2. Take apart your picture frame and remove the glass. Paint the background (if you want) so the rocks will show up better.

3. Position your rocks before gluing them. You want to make sure you have enough space in the frame.

4. Once you have the rocks where you want them, use a strong adhesive that will dry clear. Apply the glue directly onto the rock and place firmly onto the background of the frame.

5. Let the rocks dry for at least half an hour, and then you'll have a great piece of art. This is a great idea for personalizing a gift too.

TIPS AND TRICKS

Smooth, even, flat-bottomed rocks will be easiest to work with, especially on the table project. And it's even better if you can find them around the same width so that whatever you set on the table will stay nice and flat. You can often find these kinds of rocks along a stream or a shoreline.

ANIMAL TWIST

Try painting your rocks in different colors to make an animal mosaic out of it. For instance, you could create a raccoon by painting different rocks black and brown. Then make your raccoon shape and you have a cool design!

BE A SCIENTIST: Take Nature Rubbings

Don't just pass this off as an activity for little kids. It's a lot of fun to make nature prints with paper and crayons, no matter how old you are. You could even turn it into a game to see if you can guess what each print is.

Supplies: White paper, crayons, a clipboard

Time: 20 minutes

Observe and learn: Study the different textures in nature. Compare different leaves to see if some are smoother than others. Try to find unique objects and shapes that others might not notice.

How-To:

1. You can either do this experiment by hiking and then bringing the objects back to do a rubbing, or you can take your clipboard along with you and do the rubbings right there in the natural setting. So decide which way is right for you. You need to do a little preparation first. To get your crayons ready, you'll want to peel the paper off them.

2. As you're on your hike, you should look for both big and small items to do rubbings with. Once you find an item, place your paper on top of it. Then gently rub back and forth with your crayon on its side. As you rub, a print of your object should come through onto your paper.

3. If the print didn't come through well, try pressing a little harder on the crayon. A different color might show up better as well.

4. Once you have one print, go to the next object and make a print from it. Set a goal of collecting at least five to seven different prints. Then let everyone try to figure them out.

Be respectful of nature. It's OK to collect leaves or tree bark from the ground, but it's a good rule of thumb not to forcefully pull anything up, out, or off.

ANIMAL TWIST

Specifically look for unique items or markings in nature that have likely been made by an animal. Make this a learning opportunity!

GAME: Duck, Duck, Goose

Ages: 3 and up
Materials: None
Length: 15 minutes
Number of players: 5 or more
How to:

Duck, Duck, Goose is one of the most classic childhood games of all time. Anyone can play, young and old alike. You just need to be able to run. In Duck, Duck, Goose, there's no exact winner per se, but it's a fun way to get an entire group up and moving.

1. The bigger the group, the better with Duck, Duck, Goose. So gather up as many friends as you can. Then have them all sit in a giant circle. One person is chosen to be "it." He is the designated goose for now.

2. The goose walks around the circle, gently tapping people on the head as he passes. As the goose taps them, he chants "duck, duck, duck, duck." Once this person is ready to choose someone else to be it, he will tap the person on the head and declare "goose!"

3. The goose jumps up and chases the person who was it, trying to tag him. The original goose has to run all around the circle and try to get back into the spot of the person tagged before that person catches up to him.

4. If the new goose reaches the original goose before he takes his spot, that person has to go into the middle of the circle. Then he has to stay there until another person gets caught and has to go in the middle.

5. The new goose goes around the circle again and the game continues.

TIP

Duck, Duck, Goose doesn't have a lot of rules, but here's a good one to enforce if you can. Make it a rule that you have to choose a new person each time. This way, everyone will get a turn, and you won't get people picking the same ones over and over again.

DID YOU KNOW?

In some areas of the country, the game is called Duck, Duck, Gray Duck instead.

ANIMAL TWIST

What other animal variations of this game could you do? How about Moose, Moose, Bear. Or Bluebird, Bluebird, Chickadee. Have fun with it.

PROJECT: DIY Wreaths

Nothing says winter and the holidays like a wreath, and it's even more satisfying when you can make your own. It's not as hard as you might think. Don't worry about it being perfect—just give it your best shot and hang it with pride. You'll love being able to tell people that you made it yourself.

EVERGREEN WREATH

Supplies: Wire hanger, evergreen branches, twine, berries, red bow
Ages: 5 and up
Time: 15 minutes
How-To:

1. Bend your wire hanger until it's a large round shape. By using a hanger, you'll have a nice built-in hook too.

2. Look for long evergreen branches. If you don't have any yourself, you can buy some long boughs at your local garden store. They sell them around the holidays for decoration.

3. Wrap the evergreens around the hanger, securing with twine as needed. For best results, you'll want to wrap the hanger several times to cover it fully and completely.

4. Tuck branches with berries in the evergreen, securing them one at a time. This will add great color to your wreath and will also attract birds.

5. Add a red bow to the top of your wreath. It looks great, and it will also help hide the hook of the hanger.

GRAPEVINE WREATH

Supplies: Grapevine or other woody vine, twine, birdseed ornament
Ages: 7 and up
Time: 20 minutes
How-To:

1. Working with grapevine or other woody vines takes a little practice, but if you can master it, you can make some cool wreaths. Start shaping your wreath using a thicker, sturdier section of the vine. Tie it together tightly at the top.

2. Continue wrapping the wreath in layers of vine, using twine to secure when necessary. You'll want to create several layers of vine for the best look. Remember that no two wreaths will be alike. The best part about working with vine is you get a unique look each time. Often, the wreath will take a shape and life of its own.

3. At the top of the wreath, make a large loop. This will be used to hang your wreath.

4. Finally, get one of those decorative birdseed ornaments you see at the store. They're often in the shape of bells or stars around the holidays. Hang one in the center of your wreath, and put it out in a tree to feed the birds.

ANIMAL TWIST

Wreaths make a great place to attract birds. You already know you can add berries and birdseed ornaments to wreaths, but don't stop there. String popcorn and cranberries to hang on your wreath too. Attach fresh fruit slices like oranges or apples. You can even attach little bowls with wire and place seed or suet inside. Also, who says wreaths have to be round? Try shaping your wreath into a square, star, or triangle.

GAME: Kickball

Kickball is a lot like baseball except anyone can play it, and you don't need a lot of equipment like bats or gloves. You just need a ball (the size of a basketball works well, but it should be softer and bouncier so you can easily kick it) and lots of players. This is one of the greatest things about this game—you can have twenty people or more. So gather up kids in the neighborhood or start up a friendly match at the family reunion. Keeping score is optional.

Ages: 4 and up
Materials: Ball
Length: 30 minutes to an hour
Number of players: 10 or more

1. Kickball follows most of the same rules as baseball, though you probably don't want to allow stealing. So to get started, set up the bases. You can use things like trees or bushes or make your own bases out of cardboard.

2. Next, choose teams and settle on some basic rules. Are you allowed to get people out by hitting them with the ball (it might depend on how hard

of a ball you are using)? Are you playing three outs to an inning like traditional baseball? Will you have traditional strikes?

3. Once you have your rules set, team names set, and positions figured out, start playing. Remember, there are a few differences in kickball. For instance, the pitcher rolls the ball to the batters rather than throwing it.

4. Cheering is encouraged! Keep in mind that this is a friendly game, but it's okay to do a little smack talking as long as it's all in good fun. If you do want to keep score, decide how many innings to play and then have someone be the official scorekeeper. You might have an impartial umpire keep score and be the one to call close plays.

TIPS AND TRICKS

With kickball, you don't need a lot of space because the ball doesn't tend to go that far. Test out several different types of balls—you might find that it's more fun to play with a larger ball, but it's harder to handle.

ANIMAL TWIST

First, when you divide up the teams, make them animal themed. Then when ever someone gets out, they have to make their animal's sound!

PROJECT: Twig Art

As you're out hunting for gorgeous leaves that have fallen to the ground, keep an eye out for the perfect sticks to use for some art projects. Generally, you want to find twigs that aren't too thick and are less than a foot long. You don't want them to be too short either. The perfect sticks would be about 8 to 10 inches long. Gather up a few dozen, and then try one of these projects.

TWIG PICTURE FRAMES

Supplies: Twigs, picture frame, glue
Ages: 3 and up
Time: 20 minutes
How-To:

1. It's easiest to use a picture frame you already have at home. Chances are you have one that has an old picture or another one in a cabinet somewhere that you've never used.

2. Cover the top of the picture frame with a thin layer of glue. You don't

need much. Just gently smear the glue over the frame with your finger.

3. Fill the frame with layers of twigs. You are making a twig mosaic, so you'll have to trim the twigs a little bit to make them all fit perfectly.

Don't have a frame? Here's an alternative: Create your own frame out of cardboard. Then you can hang it with string from the back. If you're really feeling creative, don't use a frame or cardboard as a base at all. Find four twigs and brace them together using string or wire to make a square frame.

TWIG COLLAGE

Supplies: Twigs, art canvas or picture frame, glue

Ages: 6 and up

Time: 15 minutes

How-To:

1. Decide what you want your art to be displayed on. You can pick up an art canvas from an arts-and-crafts store. Or take the glass out of a picture frame and use that background (it's usually some sort of thick cardboard).

2. If you choose, paint your canvas or background a solid color. This will help the sticks show up better. You could also paint it in two tones—perhaps a green on the bottom quarter and blue on the top three-quarters would help create a grass-and-sky scene.

3. Using your twigs, create a piece of art. Secure the twigs with glue that will dry completely clear. You can either make your art abstract (meaning you're not really trying to create specific objects) or try creating a scene.

4. Once your piece of art is done, hang it inside or out to enjoy nature. If you do hang it outside, make sure you hang it under an eave so it's protected.

TIPS AND TRICKS

You might want to pencil out your design first before gluing on the twigs. You could also lay out all of the twigs first and then glue on the pieces one at a time.

ANIMAL TWIST

What kind of animal can you create out of twigs?

BE A SCIENTIST: Raise Your Own Butterfly

One of the most fascinating life cycles you can watch up close and personal is that of a butterfly. It's amazing to see a little caterpillar grow bigger and bigger each day before it forms a chrysalis and turns into a butterfly. Now it's time to watch and study this transformation for yourself.

Supplies: Caterpillar, caterpillar food, plastic container

Time: 2 to 3 weeks

Observe and learn: Study even the tiniest of details as you watch your caterpillar grow. How long does it take for it to double its size? How long is it in the chrysalis stage? Watch each stage carefully to better understand how the whole process works.

How-To:

1. First you're going to need a caterpillar. The easy way to get a caterpillar is to order a kit online. Chances are it'll be a painted-lady caterpillar and will come with its own food. If you're adventurous, set out to find a caterpillar on a plant instead. Then place your caterpillar in a large clear container where you can observe it. Make sure there are air holes in the container.

2. Now that you have a caterpillar, you need to make sure it gets plenty of food. If you have a kit, it'll come with food. Otherwise, you need to feed your caterpillar lots of leaves of whatever you found it on. Many caterpillars need specific plants to survive (called host plants). So if you found your caterpillar on a specific plant, it's probably the right food.

3. Watch and observe as your caterpillar forms a chrysalis. Don't be discouraged if you don't see it doing anything for a while. It needs time to make that transformation into a butterfly.

4. Once your butterfly emerges, let it go so it can fly away and continue the cycle.

The entire process of caterpillar to butterfly usually takes anywhere from two to three weeks.

ANIMAL TWIST

This is such a cool experience. Don't forget to document the whole process through journaling and photos.

GAME: Marco Polo

Marco Polo is a fun water game, and you don't need any equipment to play. You just need a group of people that like the water and can swim. This is basically a game of water tag, yet the person who is "it" has to keep her eyes closed, so it makes it even more challenging.

Ages: 5 and up

Materials: None

Length: 20 minutes

Number of players: 5 or more

How to:

1. To start, you have to set the rules and make sure that everyone understands them. So first things first—set the boundaries for the swimming area. It works well to make it where everyone can still touch the bottom. Keep in mind that it's better to be too shallow than too deep.

2. Think about what other rules you might want to set. For example, maybe you want to create rules about whether or not people can go underwater, and if so, for how long. You might also want to set a time limit as to how long one person can be "it." It's no fun having the same person chasing everyone else for the whole game, so if after 10 minutes she hasn't tagged anyone, it's time to rotate.

3. So now that you have the rules set, it's time to start. Choose someone to be it. This person must close her eyes and count to twenty. No peeking allowed at all! (You're playing on the honor system here.)

4. Everyone else scatters while the it person counts to twenty. Then the it person starts calling out "Marco." After she calls out, everyone else must answer back "Polo." The it person walks and swims around, trying to tag someone, keeping her eyes closed the whole time.

5. This game is actually a lot more challenging than it might sound. If you have boundaries set and several people playing, there are only so many places they can go to hide. And it's hard to move fast in water, so eventually the it person usually tags someone.

6. The person eventually tagged becomes the new "it," and the game continues.

If you happen to be in an area where everyone can't touch the bottom or you're playing with younger kids, it's a good idea to have weaker swimmers wear life jackets. You want everyone to feel safe and secure with this game.

Instead of saying "Marco" and "Polo," how about saying something related to animals instead? You could try to theme it around a certain genre of animals. For instance, if you choose birds, you could say "bluebird" and "cardinal."

GAME: Outdoor Scavenger Hunt

Ages: 5 and up
Materials: Paper, pen, prize
Length: 15 minutes
Number of players: 2 or more
How to:

It's a blast to create your own scavenger hunt. Whether you're creating the clues for someone else or going on the hunt yourself, it's a fun way to get outside. Be sure to mix the clues up, and don't make them too easy. Remember, make 'em work for it.

1. Create your own fun by putting together an outdoor scavenger hunt for your brother, sister, friends, or even parents. First, every good scavenger hunt needs a good prize to find at the end. It doesn't have to cost a lot of money. It can be something small like a drawing, a poem, or even a little piece of candy. But it's definitely more fun to have something at the end to reward you.

2. To get ready for the hunt, you need to write good clues. Make sure every clue points players to something specific outside. For example, a clue like "look under a tree" isn't as effective as "look under the tree where the red birdhouse hangs." Place the next clue under this tree, and so on and so forth.

3. Create at least ten to twenty clues total. The hunt part will go fast, so even if it feels like you have a lot done, do a few more.

4. Number them as you go so when you're setting out the clues, you won't get mixed up from one to the next (make sure no one is looking). Don't

forget to set aside the first clue for the players. They need something to get started.

5. Place your prize at the end, after the very last clue. You can put something on the last clue pointing the players to the treasure.

6. Once all your clues are in place, you're all ready. Give your players the first clue, and then let them be off.

Adjust your clues to your audience. If you have younger kids doing the hunt, you'll want to make them easier. If you have older kids, make it harder. If you really want a challenge, try to write your clues so they all rhyme.

Work in as many animal clues and locations as possible. Where do birds build a nest? Where do worms crawl? Where do squirrels climb?

PROJECT: Handprint Mosaics

Handprint art is one of the most classic, beloved gifts of all time. Every mother, father, and grandparent will love it. Best of all, you don't have to spend a lot of money. Since you already have the most important part of making this gift—a hand—it's going to be a cinch. Plus, it'll make the perfect present for the holidays!

Supplies: Plate or tray, pencil, glue, beans

Ages: 3 and up

Time: 20 minutes

How-To:

1. Look for the perfect plate or tray to make your handprint on. You can use an old one you have or look at a thrift store or garage sale to see if you can pick one up for less than $1. You don't have to stick to plates or trays either. You might also use the bottom of a terra-cotta pot or a large picture frame.

2. Once you choose what your handprint will go on, trace your hand with a pencil, pressing lightly.

3. Using a strong glue that will dry clear, apply it on your handprint in small sections. You'll want to do it a little bit at a time so it doesn't dry before you're ready to apply your mosaic.

4. Now it's time to apply your beans. Place them one at a time onto the glue. Press gently. Work in small sections, filling each one out completely before moving to the next. This is where you can have a little bit of fun with color and what you place where. Look at the mosaic overall. If you make a mistake or want to move something around, now is the time.

5. If you want to add on a message or date with mosaics, use your finger to write it out in glue first. Then line each letter with your beans, spelling out your message.

6. Once you have your handprint filled up, let it dry for at least 24 hours.

7. After it's dry check to make sure everything is stuck down. If needed, glue down some of the loose items. You can make several of these for very little money. It's also a great project to do with a small group or class.

MORE MOSAIC NATURE IDEAS

Small pieces of bark
Pebbles
Dried flower petals
Twigs
Seeds

TIPS AND TRICKS

Look for a tray or something large where you can make mosaics with several hand-prints. Or try making mosaic handprints on a terra-cotta pot or other garden item that will make a good gift.

ANIMAL TWIST

Try making an animal mosaic too. You can find animal shapes or shadows online, and then you fill in with the same types of mosaics listed above.

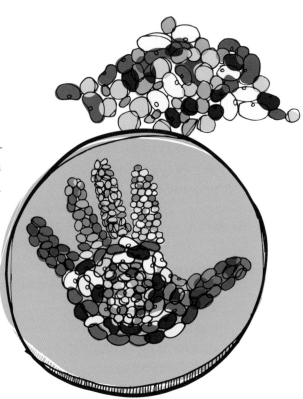

PROJECT: Four-Season Garden

Plant a garden in spring that will still look good in winter. Yes, it really is possible. It just takes a little research and planning. Here's how to get a garden that you can enjoy in all four seasons.

Supplies: Seeds, plants, soil (if needed)

Ages: Any age

Time: 1 hour

How-To:

1. To kick things off, you need a spot for your garden. If you don't already have a space cleared and ready for planting, get to work. You can till up a fresh area, put in a raised bed, or even create an area with several containers. You don't need a huge space—it can be as big or small as you want.

2. If needed, fill your new planting area with soil. Try mixing in a little organic matter on top to get your garden started off on the right foot.

3. Now for the planning—it's best to create a plan now for the whole season so you can be sure to have something blooming (or to eat) at all times. You can also make a calendar. Then you'll know exactly when to plant your next round.

4. Once you know which plants you're going to plant, dig in as early as possible in spring. While you're planting keep in mind that you'll be adding along the way. You might even want to make a little diagram so you'll know what should go where.

5. Take good care of your plants. Keep them watered, and make sure the weeds stay out. This will help ensure they live a long life.

6. Keep an eye on your calendar, and when it's time to plant new seeds or add a new season of plants, get them in the ground as soon as you can.

Here's a good planting plan to get you a four-season garden:

Spring: Plant pansies along the front edge, ornamental grasses in the back, and carrots in the middle. You'll enjoy the pretty colors all spring. Then in early summer you'll start to get carrots.

Summer: In early summer add in some native perennials like coneflowers or blanket flower just in front of the grasses. After you've pulled up all your carrots, replace the space with a couple of pumpkin seeds. Remember, pumpkins are vines and need room to grow, but if you get these in by midsummer, you'll have your own jack-o'-lantern in October.

Fall: The perennials might not have flowers their first year, but now they're good and established for next year. After you pick your pumpkins, it's time to plant your garlic. It will stay in the garden over winter and come up in spring. If you don't want to plant garlic, plant tulip bulbs instead.

Winter: Now is the time to admire the beauty of your frozen garden. The ornamental grasses and perennials look great in the garden, and they can still be a food source for birds. Even though it's cold out, your garden can still look good.

TIPS AND TRICKS

When planning your garden, ask yourself certain questions. Do you want to have things you can eat? Do you mostly like flowers? How big of a space do the plants require? When do these plants bloom? Do they need sun or shade? These are all factors you should consider.

BE A SCIENTIST: Make a Mini–Compost Bin with Worms

It's pretty cool when you can turn apple cores, banana peels, eggshells, and coffee grounds into soil through composting. It's not just regular soil either. It's gorgeous, rich, dark soil that is perfect for growing plants. Now add worms into the mix—they make the process even faster—and it's even more fun!

Supplies: Recycled ice-cream bucket, soil, newspaper, red wiggler worms

Time: 20 minutes

Observe and learn: Don't overdo it. Your worms are pretty amazing, but they aren't miracle workers. Start off small and see what they can handle. Watch them closely and increase what you give them a little at a time.

How-To:

1. An old ice-cream bucket makes the perfect vessel for a mini–composting bin. You'll want to make sure to add holes to the top of it, but don't make those holes too big. Red wiggler worms are small and could easily escape!

2. Fill your ice-cream bucket with about 50 percent soil and 50 percent "brown" matter like shredded newspaper or even little pieces of cardboard. You don't want the bucket to get too damp.

3. Add your worms to the mixture and give them a couple of days to make themselves at home. It's really important that you use red wiggler worms, not just worms you dig up in your backyard. (The worms in your backyard are much bigger than red wigglers.) Not all worms can eat and digest scraps.

4. Add a few kitchen scraps to your mixture and give your worms time to eat the items. As they eat, they will turn the scraps into soil and mix it in with the other soil and newspaper.

5. If you're successful on a small level, move your worm compost into a bigger container and add more worms.

Worm composting is called vermicomposting. It's where you use worms to speed up the process of composting. The worms eat the scraps and poop it out to make great garden soil.

ANIMAL TWIST

Use this project as an excuse to do some research on worms. How many different types of worms are there in the world? What category are these part of?

GAME: Kick the Can

Ages: 5 and up
Materials: An old can
Length: 10 to 20 minutes per game
Number of players: 4 or more
How-To:
Kick the Can is one of the oldest and simplest games around. It's like hide-and-seek with a twist. It breaks down into three main parts.

Part 1: To get things started, choose someone to be the seeker. Try drawing sticks to decide; the shortest one is the seeker. Keep in mind that it helps when the seeker can run pretty well, so you might not want a younger player to be the seeker or it will be a really short game. Next, the seeker puts a can upside down in a nice big, open area. Then he puts his foot on the can and starts counting to fifty (keep those eyes closed) while everyone runs to hide.

Part 2: After the seeker has counted to fifty, he starts to look for all the other players hiding. When he finds someone the seeker calls the person out by name and then it's a race. If the seeker can get back to the can before the person he found gets there and kicks it, then that person is captured. (The captured players must stay in a designated area near the can. Figure this area out before the start of the game.) If the person beats the seeker, he kicks the can and the seeker has to retrieve it and start counting again.

Part 3: Once the seeker has captured a player, he continues on, searching for more. Meanwhile, the other players try to free the captured players. They do this by trying to sneak up and kick the can without the seeker spotting them. This will free any captured players and will force the seeker to start all over again. Also, if someone kicks the can while being chased by the seeker, this too would release the captured. Once all the players are captured, it's time to pick a new seeker and start a new game.

TIPS AND TRICKS

To make it easier, you can play Kick the Can where the seeker simply has to see a player and call out his name to be captured. It's especially fun and/or challenging to play this game at dusk when it's harder to spot people hiding.

ANIMAL TWIST

Every time there's a new seeker, they get to change the animal theme. Maybe they are an owl, and all the other players are birds. Or maybe they are a snake

PROJECT: Marble Checkers

Here's a simple project to turn some of your best nature photos into pieces for a checkerboard. Flowers and leaves make great art and are easy subjects to take photos of because they barely move. They'll make great checkers pieces—the leaves versus the flowers. After you have your photos selected, it's time to make the pieces. Here's how

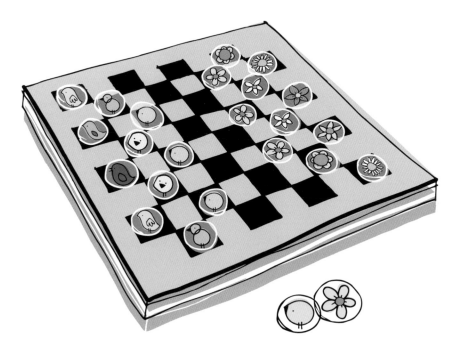

Supplies: Large, clear marbles with flat sides, round hole punch, clear glue, construction paper

Ages: Kids 8 and up can do this project all by themselves; kids 3–7 might need a little help from adults.

Time: The project itself only takes 15 to 20 minutes, but the marbles will need to dry overnight.

How-To:

1. First off, decide which photos to use for the checkers. If you don't have photos, use this as an excuse to get out in nature and take some. Have them printed at your local photo shop as wallet sizes. This will get them small enough to make a nice-size checker.

2. Use a round hole punch (about 3/4 inch or 1 inch) to punch your hole into the photo (and to punch out the photo in the round shape). When shopping at the craft store, look for your clear marbles and hole punch at the same time to make sure they will line up.

3. Place your photo face down on the flat side of the marble. (These marbles are available at local craft stores.) Then apply glue that dries clear to the back of the photo. Press down hard to make sure you don't have any air bubbles. Repeat with your other marbles and photos.

4. Let the marbles dry overnight. To get a secure hold, you might even consider stacking a few heavy books on top.

5. The next day clean off the front of the marbles and the excess dried glue. Then cover with a piece of construction paper so that the marbles have a smooth and colorful back.

6. They're ready to use. Get out a checkerboard and start a game. If you don't have a checkerboard, consider making your own out of a large piece of cardboard. This is a fun side project, and then you can decorate it any way you want. This would make a nice gift too.

TIPS AND TRICKS

What are the best photos to use for the marbles? Close-ups work great. Or at least try to find a portion of the photo that you can easily crop so that people can still tell what it is. Remember to have fun thinking what else you could take pictures of next. It would be great to make nature marbles that you could change out each season.

ANIMAL TWIST

Put animal pictures on the marbles! You can do all one image or try different themes like fish, snakes, birds, or small mammals.

GAME: Capture the Flag

Capture the Flag is a game of team pride. You need at least four people on each team and at least three teams to really make it a good game. It also really helps if you have a good amount of space for people to play. Keep in mind that this game could go really fast or it could take a lot of time. Don't rush through it though. Strategize and put a plan together.

Ages: 6 and up
Materials: 2 flags, markers to decorate
Length: 1 hour or more
Number of players: 12 or more
How-To:

1. When you play Capture the Flag, you first have to create a flag. Each team makes their own (teams can be made up of two to six players each). As you create your team name and flag, take a lot of pride in it. This is what you'll be protecting, so take a little extra time with it.

2. Once all the flags are created, the teams find a spot to place them. It has to be out in the open, but think about placement a little bit first. Where you put your flag could have a big impact on how you do in the game.

3. Now it's time for the game to begin. The point of the game is to capture other team flags while protecting your own. Again, this is where strategy comes into play. Will you send two people to go look for other flags while another couple stay back to guard your flag? If you're protecting your own flag, you must stay at least 20 feet away at all times. You can't sit next to it.

4. If someone steals your flag and then you tag her, she has to give it back.

5. Whichever team still has its flag at the end and has the most flags of other teams is the winner.

TIPS AND TRICKS

You can decide as a group how long you want the game to go on and how many points you get for keeping your flag protected versus capturing others. Once the flags are out, a good rule is to set a timer for 30 minutes or an hour.

ANIMAL TWIST

Have your entire team theme be centered around an animal. Then really take pride in that. This means you can make your flag to reflect your animal and even give teammates animal names.

BE A SCIENTIST: Create Homes for Backyard Animals

Supplies: Sticks, flowerpot, old bricks, dirt, wood (depending on the type of animal)

Time: 20 minutes

Observe and learn: Talk about what makes a good home for an animal. All animals want to feel safe and secure, right? Think about this and how you can help as you're creating homes for animals in your backyard.

How-To:

1. Before you start creating animal homes, you need to do a little research. What types of homes do animals use? Go on a hike and do a little research to figure out what types of animals you can create homes for.

2. For this project, let's build a home for a toad and the bugs in your backyard. You want these animals to feel safe, so you want to offer them lots of cover. For the toad, you can turn a flowerpot on its side to immediately create a little haven. For bugs, you'll want to stack up sticks, bricks, wood, and other items to give them little places to crawl.

3. After you create the homes, you need to leave them alone! Animals don't like it if you go in and mess around in places they live. It won't feel safe to them. So you can observe, but don't move things around too much.

4. If you don't see any animals moving in right away, don't give up. You can try building something in a different location to see if it makes a difference. For the best results, you'll want to put something not in the open—tucked away in a cool, slightly dark location.

Of course, you can always create an animal home by putting out a birdhouse too. But did you know that most birds don't even use birdhouses? Look for nesting birds on tree branches and in tree cavities.

ANIMAL TWIST

For an extra animal tie-in, do an outdoor hike and try to identify places, brush piles, and tree holes that could be home to different animals.

PROJECT: Nature Candles

Half the fun of this project is finding the objects to go in it. Seashells are one of the best and easiest things to put down into candles—what a great way to remember that vacation to the beach. You don't need a lot. Just a few items will go a long way. Take a look at how to make these beach-themed nature candles

Supplies: Jar, candle gel, wick, sand, seashells, candle scent

Ages: 6 and up

Time: 20 minutes

How-To:

1. Get all your supplies. Things you want to think about: Make sure the wick you buy is long enough for your jar. You want to have at least an inch of wick beyond the top of the jar. You also want to make sure to get a clear gel so you can see your objects in the candle.

2. Pour about an inch or two of sand in the bottom of the jar. Place your seashells in the bottom, leaving a place for the wick in the center.

3. Heat up your gel, following the directions on the container. Don't overheat!

4. Whatever candle scent you chose, stir a few drops in with a spoon. Take a little sniff, and if you don't smell it, add a few more drops.

5. Place your wick in the center of the jar and have someone hold it in place.

6. This is where you have to be careful. The person who is holding the wick needs to be still. Then have an adult pour the hot gel gently into the jar, making sure she steers clear of the helper.

7. Don't touch the jar! But you do want to hold up the wick while the gel starts to set. This is a boring job, but you'll want to hold it for about 10 minutes. By this time the gel will start to solidify.

8. Wrap the top of the wick around a pencil and let it rest across the top of the

jar. Let it sit there for a couple of hours, making sure the wick doesn't try to bend too much.

9. After the gel has completely settled, trim the wick so that you only have a small piece left.

10. Light your candle and enjoy your new creation.

TIPS AND TRICKS

Try a few other nature-related objects in the bottom of your candle. For instance, pinecones or rocks look nice. Go on a hike or collect things over the various seasons, and then when it's time to make your candles, go to your nature stash to see what's available. These candles also make a nice gift. If you're buying supplies to do one or two, you might as well buy a few extra supplies to make five or six. Then give them away to family and friends for the holidays.

ANIMAL TWIST

You know those marbles you made earlier for a checkerboard? Create animal marbles, and then put them down into the candles. They'll look so cool!

GAME: Ultimate Frisbee

Fall is football season, which means it's also the perfect time to play Ultimate Frisbee. This game is like of mix of soccer (lots of running) and football (kickoffs and passing). But luckily, you can still use your hands, and there's no tackling involved.

Ages: 7 and up

Materials: Frisbee

Length: 45 minutes (2 20-minute halves and a 5-minute halftime)

Number of players: 6–14

How-To:

1. To start things off, you need a good field. If you have access to a football field or a soccer field, this is perfect. But if you're just in the backyard, make your own with a designated "goal" area on each end. Keep in mind that you're going to be doing a lot of running, so a bigger field is good. Also, the bigger the field, the more challenging it will be, so if you want to take on a football field, make sure you have older players.

2. Next, you flip a coin or play a quick game of Rock, Paper, Scissors to

figure out who kicks off first. Once you decide, each team lines up at opposite end zones for kickoff.

3.   One person flings the Frisbee as far as he can toward the other team. Everyone runs together, and the other team takes control of the Frisbee first. (The kickoff team cannot run and get the Frisbee. They have to wait for someone on the opposite team to take it first.)

4.   In Ultimate Frisbee you can't actually run with the Frisbee. If you do, that's a penalty. You have to constantly pass it from one player to the next. And one player can't hold it for more than 15 seconds or they'll get a penalty.

5.   You also can't tackle players or even touch them for that matter. You can do everything you can to get in front of them and steal the Frisbee away for your team, but no contact. This would be a foul.

6.   If a player does hold onto the Frisbee for more than 15 seconds or he runs with it, it goes to the opposite team. If someone commits a foul, the Frisbee either goes to the opposite team or the person who the foul was committed on gets a free pass to an open player.

7.   The object of the game is to get the Frisbee down the field and score in your goal. Every time a team scores, there's a new kickoff as well. Keep track of the points, and whoever has the most at the end is deemed the winner.

8.   Ultimate Frisbee is usually limited to no more than seven players per side, fourteen total. If you have more than fourteen people who want to participate, you can substitute throughout the game without stopping play.

9.   You can have a ref if you'd like. Otherwise, everyone is on the honor system, and you can all call it as a team (and vote if there are arguments).

ANIMAL TWIST

Whichever team has control of the Frisbee gets to call out an animal. Then everyone has to communicate and call for the Frisbee using that sound!

PROJECT: Fall Bird Feeders

Ready to get crafty? Fall is a great time of year to make
your own bird feeder. You don't have to go to the lumber
or hardware store either. You can make both of these bird
feeders from recycled items that you already have in your
house or outside. Make them and then hang 'em out for
your feathered friends or give a couple to a friend.

LOG SUET FEEDER

Supplies: Log, suet, drill, drill bit, wire, eyehook

Ages: 5 and up

Time: 15 minutes

How-To:

You'll definitely need help from an adult with this one.
First find a good-size log that won't be too heavy when
you hang it from a wire. Next, get a drill and a large drill bit.
You'll want a big bit, perhaps an inch wide or more, because
you're going to put suet in these holes. Mark on your log
where you want your holes to be. It works nicely to stagger them. Finally, it's
time to drill the holes. Wear protective goggles as an extra precaution. You can
either have the hole go all the way through or drill at least half an inch into the
log for each hole. Fill with suet and hang with wire and an eyehook.

PLATE FEEDER

Supplies: Plastic plate, drill, wire, silverware, hot-glue gun and glue sticks,
bird seed

Ages: 6 and up

Time: 20 minutes

How-To:

This is a fun feeder. If you don't have an old plastic plate or silverware around
the house, hit up your local thrift shop. You can pick some up for just a few
bucks. First off, drill small holes in four different areas of your plate. Think
of it like a clock, and mark and drill at the 12, 3, 6, and 9 o'clock positions.
Next, thread your wire through, one hole at a time, and secure. Leave about
18 inches of wire loose on each section. Then pull those wires together in the
center, making sure the plate stays nice and even. Using hot glue, secure a fork
and spoon onto the outer rim of the plate. This is just for looks—the birds

aren't really going to use them. Then hang it in a tree and fill with seed.

What else can you recycle to turn into a feeder? Walk around your garage, basement, or a thrift store for a little inspiration. Old baskets, milk jugs, and coffee cans turned on their sides are all viable options. Also grow your own gourds or buy one at the farmers' market to turn into a birdhouse.

Challenge yourself to learn more about what birds eat and which birds will come to different feeders.

GAME: Flashlight Tag

You can do a lot with a flashlight, and it's especially fun when you can turn it into a game. This takes the classic game of tag and mixes in a little bit of hide-and-seek. Make sure everyone has a good working flashlight before you get started. Then let the fun begin!

Ages: 3 and up
Materials: Flashlights
Length: 15 minutes per game
Number of players: 2 or more
How-To:

1. With every good game of tag, you need a home base. This is where the "it" person counts at the beginning. And it's also a safe haven if some players need a rest. (Of course, you might have to make a rule that you can't stay at home base more than a minute.)

2. To get started, everyone except the person who is it runs to hide, carrying their flashlights with them.

3. Once the person who is it counts to thirty, he sets out to hunt the hidden players. Here's where the game is like tag. In order to find someone, you have to "tag" the person with your flashlight beam, right on the chest.

4. If you spot someone, you absolutely have to tag him on his chest to actually make it count. If you flash your beam on his leg but then he runs to home base before you can get him on the chest, then he's safe.

5. Once you find someone, he then helps you find the other hidden players with his flashlight. This game is especially fun with a large group, especially when you have five or six players, all searching for the last couple of hidden players with their flashlights.

This game is perfect for cool autumn temperatures. Put on a jacket and head outside right at dusk. If you want to make it easier to know when people tag you, use masking tape to make the X on everyone in the same spot. Then when the flashlight hits it, you'll know for sure that you've been hit!

ANIMAL TWIST

After you're done with the game, take those flashlights and see if you can make different animal shapes on the wall.

BE A SCIENTIST: Put Together Your Own Field Guide

Field guides have been around for decades. They are picture books highlighting different species. In addition to photos or sketches, they often include tons of information about the plants or animals. Most will include the range, which is where they live, and in what seasons you can find them. Field guides can include species throughout the country or regional species. You may or may not have them in your area . . . until now. It's time to make your own neighborhood field guide.

Supplies: A notebook, glue stick, scissors, access to a printer or copier

Time: 30 minutes

Observe and learn: As you go through field guides at the library, make little notes about interesting facts and tidbits. You'll want to keep these notes in your book too.

How-To:

1. First of all, you have to do your research. This is a perfect activity to do at the library. Go to check out the animal, bird, butterfly, and reptile books.

Look for field guides or books about the animals in your state. You can pick as few or as many as you want, but it would be a good start to choose ten birds, ten bugs, ten butterflies, and ten mammals to include in your field guide.

2. Go through and either print pictures from the Internet or make copies of the animals you want in your field guide. Write down everything you think is important to know.

3. Use the books you find as a good guide, but don't follow them exactly. Feel free to add notes about these animals that you know or find. Also make note of whether you've seen them in your backyard.

4. Once you have your field guide made, make a goal to see these animals in the next year. You can turn your guide into a journal of sorts and write down the date you saw each animal.

This would make a great gift too. Do some research for a family or friend and make them a field guide for their area.

ANIMAL TWIST

Every time you see an animal in your field guide, challenge yourself to write something about it. This is a great way to push yourself with creative writing.

PROJECT: Container Gardening

Container gardening is a quick and easy way to get growing. Anyone can have containers; whether you live in a house, apartment, or condo, you can always find a spot to tuck a container with a few plants. Here are the top things to remember when growing in containers.

How-To:

1. Get a good soil mix. You can't just use the soil in your backyard. Invest in a good potting mix that's specifically designed for containers. It'll pay off.

2. Don't forget to water. Many container plants don't make it because they don't get enough water. Plants in containers need more water than usual. Let your sense of touch be your guide—if the soil feels dry, it's time to water.

3. Less is more. Don't overfill the container. A few plants can go a long way. It might look bare in the beginning, but it won't take long to fill in.

4. Mix it up. At the least you'll want more of a tall plant with a trailing one. Read the plant labels first. Plant second.

5. Plan your plants ahead of time. Some plants need sun. Some like shade. Do a little research first, and then go in with a plan so you know which plants to pair together.

6. Get inspiration from your garden center. They have containers there, ready to buy as is. Buy one of these or at least look at what's in them. They'll provide a good guide for what you should be buying.

7. Learn the magic of succulents. Succulents do great in containers—they don't require as much water, and they'll grow almost anywhere. Hens and chicks is one option, but there are several others too. Succulents are especially great if you have a shallow container because they don't need a huge space for the roots.

8. Save money. If you're looking to save money on your containers, consider growing some plants from seed. For example, zinnias are good ones to grow that will do great in containers. Start the seeds inside first and then plant the seedlings directly into the containers.

When It Comes to Containers, Here Are Three Different Directions to Try

1. The traditional route. Find a pot. There are hundreds to choose from. Place your container where you want it first (in case it gets too heavy to move), then fill with soil and your plants.

2. Hanging baskets. Again, there are many options on the market. If you have the space, try a design. For instance, alternating pinks and purples along the eaves of a house would look gorgeous.

3. Unique containers. Here anything goes. Look for baskets, old pans, or anything else you can find to turn into a container. Remember to give your plants space, so if you have a small item, only put in a few plants. And if you use a shallow item, like a shoe, use succulents.

Most people grow annuals in containers and get new plants each year, but you can use perennials too. If you want your perennials to survive from one year to the next, be sure to protect them over winter, either by bringing them inside or covering them.

Try planting a container with flowers that will attract birds, bees, or humming-birds. You'll want to look for good nectar plants. Petunias are always a good go-to flower for this.

PROJECT: Fun in the Snow

Whether you live in a place that gets snow regularly or a place that rarely sees it, it's good to be prepared when this fluffy white stuff starts to fall. It's a blast to play with! Here are a couple of snow activities to try—one where you can be artistic and another you can eat. Don't forget to bundle up with snow pants and warm gloves. You'll be glad you did.

HOUSEHOLD SNOW PEOPLE

Supplies: Wooden spoons, pipe cleaners, yarn, and anything else you can think of

Ages: 3 and up

Time: 20 minutes

How-To:

1. Go beyond the ordinary carrot nose and twig hands. Use your imagination to create a unique snow boy or snow girl with items from your own house. So after you have your three balls rolled and stacked up, start peeking around in drawers and cabinets for things to decorate your snow person with.

2. Start by looking for arms—pipe cleaners, wooden spoons, or anything else that is sturdy and will stick out should work.

3. Next, look for things that will work as eyes and buttons. If you decide to use something flat like real buttons, remember you'll need a good way to attach them. You might be able to use an unrolled paper clip or something similar.

4. The mouth might be the trickiest. If you can't find anything good to use and shape, then think about using snow paint.

5. Finally, don't forget to decorate the top of the head. Add on yarn for hair or borrow one of your hats to place on top. Remember, the most important thing is to have fun. There's no right or wrong way to make your snow person.

TIPS AND TRICKS

You can use a washable paint and paintbrushes for snow paint. Or make your own using a spray bottle, water, and food color. Once you have your snow paint ready, have fun with it. Try playing tic-tac-toe in the snow with paint. You can also create cool art pieces with your paint.

SNOW ICE CREAM

Supplies: Milk, snow, sugar, vanilla, food coloring

Ages: 3 and up

Time: 5 minutes

How-To:

1. Snow ice cream is easy to make, but exact measurements are a bit hard to give. Start off by mixing roughly 10 cups of snow along with 1/2 cup of sugar, 1/2 teaspoon of vanilla, and 1 cup of milk. Stir. Check the consistency and taste. You might want to add more sugar or milk right away.

2. After you have a good consistency, you can add color. Put in a few drops of food coloring and mix. Remember, you only need a few drops.

3. If you want to add in any other flavors, experiment by slicing up fresh fruit to go with your snow ice cream. Fresh bananas, strawberries, or blueberries are all great options. If your ice cream starts to melt, just add some more snow on top. Freshly fallen snow is the best.

TIPS AND TRICKS

You'll want to use fresh clean snow. Try collecting snow off your porch rail or your patio furniture. You can also scrape off the top layer of snow and use the purest snow from the middle of a snowdrift.

ANIMAL TWIST

Let's see those snow animals and sculptures. It's not as hard as you think. You just need to take the time to add details.

PROJECT: Vintage Birdhouses

Want to create a unique, interesting birdhouse for the birds in your backyard? Now you can, using an album cover from an old vinyl record. The whole project shouldn't cost more than $5 to $10 and maybe even less if you already have some of the supplies at home. It's a great gift, especially for someone who likes music and birds.

Supplies: Birdhouse, vinyl album covers, paper, scissors, glue, string, 2 screws, outdoor sealer

Ages: Any age, though younger kids might need a little help

Time: 20 minutes

How-To:

1. First things first—you need a birdhouse. If you already have one at home that you want to redo, just clean it up a bit and it should be fine to use. If you don't have a birdhouse at home, check out your local nature

store or even craft store. You just need a basic design. Don't spend extra money on anything fancy. Most craft stores have a wood section, and you can pick up a pre-built birdhouse for less than $5.

2. This is the fun part. Go to a local rummage sale or thrift store to look for old vinyl albums. You can usually pick them up for less than $1. There might even be some old albums in your attic. Look for colorful ones that have fun designs. Also, look for ones that you can cut in many different ways so they'll still look unique.

3. Once you have your birdhouse and vinyl albums, use a piece of paper to trace all the sides (and roof) of the birdhouse. These will be your patterns for cutting out the album cover, so try to make them as exact as possible. You'll need to make as many patterns as you have different shapes.

4. Use your new patterns to then trace the cardboard album covers you have. Be sure to position the patterns so you're cutting out interesting and/or colorful sections of the album.

5. Cut out the shapes.

6. Glue the shapes onto the birdhouse using a strong glue like Mod Podge from a craft store.

7. After letting it dry, add screws to the top in the front and back of the birdhouse. Tie a string to the screws so the birdhouse has something to hang from.

8. Spray with a sealer especially made to withstand the outdoors. Hang up your newly decorated birdhouse and wait for the birds to come make it home.

ANIMAL TWIST

Now that you've made a birdhouse, do some research on which types of birds might use it.

GAME: 20 Questions

The game 20 Questions is a great game because you can play it almost anywhere. You can play it while you're out looking for birds. You can play it on the road while on the way to the lake. You can play it while you're out on the canoe. It's really one of the most versatile games out there. Best of all, anyone can play.

Ages: 3 and up
Materials: None
Length: 5–10 minutes for each game
Number of players: 2 or more
How-To:

1.   Pick someone to go first. Then think of something in nature. It can be anything—an animal, an object, etc. Try to pick something that will take players lots of questions to figure out. So just picking a bear is okay, but challenge yourself to think of something a bit harder.

2.   The other players in the game start to ask questions about what the item is. (For example: Is it an animal? Does it live in the wild? Does it have fur?) Everyone should take turns asking questions so it's not the same person asking the questions.

3.   The person who is "it" must answer the questions truthfully and keep count of how many questions are asked.

4.   Choose your questions carefully! You only get twenty. After you hit twenty the it person can either reveal what her item is or she can give some good clues so the guessing can continue. Whoever guesses the item correctly gets to be the person to go next.

TIPS AND TRICKS

If you're trying to guess what the item is, work together as a team. You all have to share the questions, so you might as well share ideas. Make sure you agree on the specific questions to ask to give you the best chance for guessing the item. If younger players need help, have them team up with an older child or adult.

ANIMAL TWIST

This is so much fun to play as just an animal theme. Make sure to pick something hard!

GAME: Simon Says

Simon Says is a pretty simple game if you think about it. All you have to do is follow along and do exactly what you're told. Don't get too confident though—it really is a lot harder than it sounds. Play this game with just a couple of people or play it with a group of twenty.

Ages: 3 and up
Materials: Plate or tray, pencil, glue, beans
Length: 15 minutes
Number of players: 2 or more
How-To:

1.   Simon Says is basically a game of copycat, so if you can just copy someone, you should be able to do pretty well. You have to do whatever Simon tells you to do. To get the game started, pick someone to be Simon. It's best if this person has played before and knows how the game works. 2. Simon must start every command with the words "Simon says." (Example: Simon says to touch your toes. Simon says to hop on one foot. Simon says to do five jumping jacks.) Everyone must follow along to whatever Simon demands, and they must do the task until Simon tells them to stop. (Example: Simon says you can stop hopping on one foot.) Of course, if Simon tells you to do five jumping jacks, you can stop after five. But if Simon tells you to pat your head, you better not stop patting until Simon says.

3.   Here's the thing, though. Simon can be very tricky. He will try to give you a command without first saying "Simon says." So if he does, and you follow along, you've been tricked and you're out of the game.

4.   Remember, this is a listening game more than anything. Listen very carefully and only pay attention to commands that start with "Simon says." Everything else is probably a trick, so just ignore it. If you can follow along exactly and be the last person standing at the end, you could be the winner.

TIPS AND TRICKS

When you are Simon, here's a good way to trick people—do the actions with them. Most people get used to following along, so if you are doing the commands with the other players, give a command that doesn't say "Simon says" first—they'll be less likely to notice if you're doing it with them.

ANIMAL TWIST

Animal Simon Says is centered around animal actions, movements, sounds, and more.

ANIMALS BY STATE AND PROVINCE

It's common for states to designate an official state bird, but it doesn't end there. Many states and Canadian provinces have official mammals, reptiles, butterflies, and even fish. Here's a look at each state and province, highlighting the official animals for each one.

United States

ALASKA
Bird: Willow ptarmigan
Fish: King salmon
Insect: Four-spot skimmer dragonfly
Land mammal: Moose
Marine mammal: Bowhead whale

HAWAII
Bird: Nene (Hawaiian goose)
Fish: Humuhumunukumukuapua'a
Insect: Kamehameha butterfly
Mammal: Hawaiian monk seal
Marine mammal: Humpback whale

WASHINGTON
Amphibian: Pacific chorus frog
Bird: American goldfinch
Fish: Steelhead trout
Insect: Green darner dragonfly
Mammal: Olympic marmot
Marine mammal: Orca whale

OREGON
Animal: American Beaver
Bird: Western meadowlark
Fish: Chinook salmon
Insect: Oregon swallowtail butterfly

CALIFORNIA
Animal: California grizzly bear
Bird: California quail

Fish: California golden trout
Insect: California dogface butterfly
Marine fish: Garibaldi
Marine mammal: California gray whale
Reptile: Desert tortoise

MONTANA
Animal: Grizzly bear
Bird: Western meadowlark
Butterfly: Mourning cloak
Fish: Blackspotted cutthroat trout

IDAHO
Bird: Mountain bluebird
Fish: Cutthroat trout
Insect: Monarch butterfly
Raptor: Peregrine falcon

WYOMING
Bird: Western meadowlark
Fish: Cutthroat trout
Mammal: Buffalo (Bison)
Reptile: Horned lizard

NORTH DAKOTA
Bird: Western meadowlark
Fish: Northern pike

SOUTH DAKOTA
Animal: Coyote
Bird: Ring-necked pheasant
Fish: Walleye
Insect: Honeybee

montana

idaho

wyoming

north dakota

south dakota

NEVADA
Animal: Desert bighorn sheep
Bird: Mountain bluebird
Fish: Lahontan cutthroat trout
Reptile: Desert tortoise

UTAH
Animal: Rocky Mountain elk
Bird: California gull
Fish: Bonneville cutthroat trout
Insect: Honeybee

COLORADO
Animal: Rocky Mountain
bighorn sheep
Bird: Lark bunting
Fish: Greenback cutthroat trout
Insect: Colorado hairstreak butterfly
Reptile: Western painted turtle

ARIZONA
Amphibian: Arizona tree frog
Bird: Cactus wren
Butterfly: Two-tailed swallowtail
Fish: Apache trout
Mammal: Ringtail
Reptile: Arizona ridge-nosed
rattlesnake

NEW MEXICO
Amphibian: New Mexico
spadefoot toad
Animal: Black bear
Bird: Greater roadrunner
Butterfly: Sandia hairstreak butterfly
Fish: New Mexico cutthroat trout
Insect: Tarantula hawk wasp
Reptile: New Mexico whiptail lizard

NEBRASKA

Bird: Western meadowlark
Fish: Channel catfish
Insect: Honeybee
Mammal: White-tailed deer

KANSAS

Amphibian: Barred tiger salamander
Animal: Buffalo (Bison)
Bird: Western meadowlark
Insect: Honeybee
Reptile: Ornate box turtle

MISSOURI

Amphibian: North
American bullfrog
Animal:

Missouri mule
Aquatic animal: Paddlefish
Bird: Eastern bluebird
Fish: Channel catfish
Insect: Honeybee
Invertebrate: Crayfish
Reptile: Three-toed box turtle

OKLAHOMA

Amphibian: Bullfrog
Animal: Buffalo
Bird: Scissor-tailed flycatcher
Butterfly: Black swallowtail
Fish: White bass
Flying mammal: Mexican
free-tailed bat
Fur-bearing animal: Raccoon
Insect: Honeybee
Reptile: Collared lizard

ARKANSAS
Bird: Northern mockingbird
Butterfly: Diana fritillary
Insect: Honeybee
Mammal: White-tailed deer

TEXAS
Bird: Northern mockingbird
Fish: Guadalupe bass
Flying mammal: Mexican free-tailed
  bat
Insect: Monarch butterfly
Large mammal: Texas longhorn
Reptile: Texas horned lizard
Small mammal: Nine-banded
armadillo

MINNESOTA
Bird: Common loon
Butterfly: Monarch
Fish: Walleye
Reptile: Blanding's turtle

IOWA
Bird: American
goldfinch

WISCONSIN
Animal: Badger
Bird: American robin
Fish: Muskie
Insect: Honeybee
Wildlife animal: White-tailed deer

ILLINOIS
Amphibian: Eastern tiger salamander
Animal: White-tailed deer
Bird: Northern cardinal
Fish: Bluegill
Insect: Monarch butterfly
Reptile: Painted turtle

INDIANA
Bird: Northern cardinal

MICHIGAN
Bird: American robin
Fish: Brook trout
Mammal: White-tailed deer
Reptile: Painted turtle

OHIO
Animal: White-tailed deer
Bird: Northern cardinal
Insect: Ladybug
Reptile: Black racer snake

PENNSYLVANIA
Animal: White-tailed deer
Bird: Ruffed grouse
Fish: Brook trout
Insect: Firefly

MARYLAND
Bird: Baltimore oriole
Crustacean: Blue crab
Fish: Striped bass
Insect: Baltimore checkerspot
butterfly
Reptile: Diamondback terrapin turtle

DELAWARE
Animal: Horseshoe crab
Bird: Blue hen chicken
Bug: Ladybug
Butterfly: Tiger swallowtail
Fish: Weakfish
Macro-invertebrate: Stonefly
Wildlife animal: Gray fox

NEW JERSEY
Animal: Horse
Bird: American goldfinch
Bug: Honeybee

NEW YORK
Animal: American Beaver
Bird: Eastern bluebird
Freshwater fish: Brook trout
Insect: Nine-spotted ladybug
Reptile: Snapping turtle
Saltwater fish: Striped bass

MAINE

Animal: Moose
Bird: Black-capped chickadee
Fish: Landlocked salmon
Insect: Honeybee

VERMONT

Amphibian: Northern leopard frog
Bird: Hermit thrush
Butterfly: Monarch
Cold-water fish: Brook trout
Insect: Honeybee
Reptile: Painted turtle
Warm-water fish: Walleye

NEW HAMPSHIRE

Amphibian: Spotted newt
Animal: White-tailed deer
Bird: Purple finch
Butterfly: Karner blue
Freshwater fish: Brook trout
Game fish: Striped bass
Insect: Ladybug

MASSACHUSETTS

Bird: Black-capped chickadee
Fish: Cod
Insect: Ladybug
Mammal: Right whale
Reptile: Garter snake

CONNECTICUT

Animal: Sperm whale
Bird: American robin

Insect: European praying mantis
Fish: American shad
Shellfish: Eastern oyster

RHODE ISLAND

Bird: Rhode Island red (chicken)
Fish: Striped bass

VIRGINIA

Bat: Virginia big-eared bat
Bird: Northern cardinal
Fish: Brook trout
Insect: Tiger swallowtail

WEST VIRGINIA

Animal: Black bear
Bird: Northern cardinal
Butterfly: Monarch
Fish: Brook trout
Insect: Honeybee
Reptile: Timber rattlesnake

KENTUCKY

Animal: Gray squirrel
Bird: Northern cardinal
Butterfly: Viceroy
Insect: Honeybee

TENNESSEE

Amphibian: Tennessee
cave salamander
Bird: Northern
mockingbird
Butterfly: Zebra
swallowtail
Commercial fish:
Channel catfish
Insect: Firefly, lady-
bug, and honeybee
Reptile: Eastern box
turtle
Sport fish:
Smallmouth bass
Wild animal: Raccoon

NORTH CAROLINA

Bird: Northern cardinal
Fish: Channel bass
Freshwater fish: Southern
    Appalachian brook trout
Insect: Honeybee
Mammal: Gray squirrel
Reptile: Eastern box turtle

SOUTH CAROLINA

Amphibian: Spotted salamander
Animal: White-tailed deer
Bird: Carolina wren
Butterfly: Tiger swallowtail
Fish: Striped bass
Insect: Carolina mantid
Reptile: Loggerhead sea turtle
Spider: Carolina wolf spider

LOUISIANA

Amphibian: Green tree frog
Bird: Brown pelican
Crustacean: Crawfish (Crayfish)
Freshwater fish: White perch
Insect: Honeybee
Mammal: Louisiana
black bear
Reptile: American
alligator
Saltwater fish: Spotted
seatrout

MISSISSIPPI

Bird: Northern mockingbird
Butterfly: Spicebush swallowtail
Fish: Largemouth bass
Insect: Honeybee
Land mammal: Red fox and
    white-tailed deer
Marine mammal: Bottlenose dolphin
Reptile: American alligator
Waterfowl: Wood duck

GEORGIA

Amphibian: Green tree
frog
Bird: Brown thrasher
Butterfly: Tiger swallowtail
Fish: Largemouth bass
Insect: Honeybee
Mammal: Right whale
Reptile: Gopher tortoise

ALABAMA

Amphibian: Red hills salamander
Bird: Northern flicker
Butterfly: Eastern tiger swallowtail
Freshwater fish: Largemouth bass
Insect: Monarch butterfly
Mammal: Black bear
Marine mammal: West
Indian manatee
Reptile: Alabama red-bellied turtle
Saltwater fish: Fighting tarpon

FLORIDA

Animal: Florida panther
Bird: Northern mockingbird
Butterfly: Zebra longwing
Fish: Largemouth bass
Marine mammal: Manatee
Reptile: American alligator
Saltwater mammal: Dolphin
Saltwater reptile: Loggerhead sea
    turtle
Tortoise: Gopher tortoise

yukon

nunavut

north west territories

british columbia

alberta

saskatchewan

manitoba

Canada

YUKON
Bird: Common raven

NORTHWEST TERRITORIES
Bird: Gyrfalcon

NUNAVUT
Bird: Rock ptarmigan

BRITISH COLUMBIA
Animal: Spirit bear
Bird: Steller's jay
Fish: Pacific salmon

ALBERTA
Animal: Bighorn sheep
Bird: Great horned owl
Fish: Bull trout

SASKATCHEWAN
Animal: White-tailed deer
Bird: Sharp-tailed grouse
Fish: Walleye

MANITOBA
Animal: Plains bison
Bird: Great gray owl
Fish: Walleye

ONTARIO
Bird: Common loon

QUEBEC
Bird: Snowy owl

LABRADOR
Bird: Atlantic puffin

NEWFOUNDLAND
Animal: Caribou
Bird: Atlantic puffin

NEW BRUNSWICK
Bird: Black-capped chickadee

NOVA SCOTIA
Bird: Osprey

PRINCE EDWARD ISLAND
Bird: Blue jay

ABOUT THE AUTHORS

Stacy Tornio is a master gardener, master naturalist, and the author of six books, all dedicated to getting kids and families outside. Though she's a native Oklahoman, she now resides in Milwaukee, where she enjoys watching her two children explore nature in their own backyard and beyond. Stacy loves gardening and even had her own veggie stand at the farmer's market when she was a kid. Today, she's still growing veggies, along with lots of other plants and flowers. She enjoys trying unique varieties like purple carrots, orange coneflowers, and any type of daisy. Stacy also worked on the national birding and gardening magazine, *Birds & Blooms*, for ten years.

Ken Keffer was born and raised in Wyoming. A naturalist and environmental educator, he has worked in Alaska, Maryland, New Mexico, Ohio, Wisconsin, and the Gobi Desert of Mongolia. During this time, he's studied flying squirrels, camels, prairie dogs, and lots and lots of birds. Ken is a freelance writer—you can see his articles regularly in *Birds & Blooms*, *Outdoors Unlimited*, and *Parks and Recreation* magazines. When he's not traveling or educating others about nature, he enjoys birding, snowshoeing, fly fishing, and walking his dog, Willow the Wonder Mutt. Visit Stacy and Ken's website, destinationnature.net, to learn more about them and their books.

ken and stacy